HABLANDO DE TURISMO

Spanish for the Tourism Industry

Coursebook

UNIVERSITY COLLEGE CHESTER
LANGUAGES DEPARTMENT

Author:

Dolores Ponte Miramontes

Editors:

Gabrielle Carty

Cathy Power

Series editor:

Frédérique Rantz

CERT

THE STATE TOURISM TRAINING AGENCY
IN IRELAND

Hablando de Turismo is a complete audio language course which consists of:

— one coursebook (ISBN 1 870387 40 6)

— two cassettes (2 x 90min) available with scripts and translations booklet   (ISBN 1 870387 41 4)

Published in Ireland by: CERT Publications, CERT House, Amiens Street, Dublin 1.
Tel: +353-1-874 2555. Fax: +353-1-874 2821

CERT is the Irish state agency responsible for the recruitment, education and training of personnel for the tourism industry in Ireland.

CERT was established in 1963 to develop a highly skilled tourism workforce and to ensure high operational standards in the industry.

The services offered by CERT to the industry include:
- Identification of manpower and training needs and development of national training structures and programmes
- Recruitment, training and formal education of young school leavers preparing for careers in the industry
- Provision of on-the-job and specialist training services to existing industry personnel and proprietors
- Provision of advisory and business development services to the industry
- Training for unemployed people to enhance their prospects of finding jobs in the hotel, catering and tourism industry

Other audio language courses in the Languages for Tourism series:

Available from bookshops:
Parlez Tourisme! — French for the Tourism Industry, Gill & Macmillan, Dublin, 1995

Available from CERT:
Benvenuti! — Italian for the Tourism Industry, CERT, Dublin, 1995
Tourismus auf Deutsch — German for the Tourism Industry, CERT, Dublin, 1995

Still available from CERT:
(cassettes and workbook)
Bon Séjour! — French for the Hotel and Catering Industry, CERT, Dublin, 1992
Schöne Tage! — German for the Hotel and Catering Industry, CERT, Dublin, 1993

ACKNOWLEDGMENTS

CERT would like to thank the many people involved in the preparation of this book.
In particular, CERT acknowledges:

- the support of the LINGUA programme of the European Union which partly funded the development of CERT *Languages for Tourism* series.
- CERT's partners in the LINGUA project within which the *Languages for Tourism* series has been developed: AFPA in France, SEID in Spain, Horizonte in Germany, Study Centre in Italy and HAU in Greece. All partners were associated with the language needs analysis and syllabus design which took place in preparation for the development of the audio language courses.
- The many tourism operators and language trainers who took part in the language needs analysis carried out as part of the project.

Colm Maguire for the cultural sections, *'La Hora del Café'*

Gabrielle Carty for the translations of the tapescripts

Noreen O'Shea and **Dorothy Kenny** for the first draft of the glossary

Antonio López Mariño and **Reinhard Schaeler** for use of their photographs

Regis López and his team in SEID, Valencia who supplied authentic materials for
Hablando de Turismo and authenticated the Spanish language as used in the tourism sector
The cast for the tapes: **Ignacio Hernández Lasa, Antonio López Mariño,
Begoña Álvarez O'Neill** and **Monica Vásquez O'Reilly**

The following for permission to reproduce material in this volume:
El Semanal, Madrid; Club Tiempo Libre, Madrid; Mar Sol, Burgos; Little Killary Adventure Centre, Renvyle,
Co. Galway; Dublin City University; Ayuntamiento de Cangas de Onis, Oviedo, Asturias;
Dublin Tourism; Patronato Provincial de Turismo de Soria; Lough Muckno Leisure Park, Castleblaney,
Co. Monaghan; Bus Éireann, Dublin; Organització Fira de Barcelona;
The Catering Equipment Association, Dublin.

*Please note that the prices, times and lists of activities given in this book are mainly from 1994
and are subject to change.*

*Every effort has been made to contact copyright holders of material reproduced in this volume.
Any omissions will be rectified in subsequent printings if notice is given to the publishers.*

Design and typesetting **Des Kiely & Associates,** Donnybrook, Dublin 4
Cover design **Niamh Lehane,** Design Consultant
Cover illustration **Mary Murphy**
Printed and bound in Ireland at **Blacks Printers,** Cavan

TABLE OF CONTENTS

Introduction

Hablando de Turismo is a new audio language learning package for students of tourism or professionals working within the tourism industry in the following areas:

- Tourist information
- Travel information
- Sports and leisure
- Tours and excursions
- Conference centres and trade fairs

It has been designed for people with little or no Spanish who want to communicate effectively with Spanish-speaking visitors and upgrade their overall standard of service.

All of the activities have been designed from the point of view of people who work in the tourism industry and aim to meet their on-the-job needs. Considerable emphasis is placed on active learning with a balance between listening and speaking skills throughout.

The course is divided into two main parts and consists of nine units.
Units 1 to 4 cover all the basic general language a professional in tourism needs. Units 5 to 9 look at specific areas of the tourism industry and introduce specialised vocabulary and functional language related to specific work situations.

Learners can monitor their progress in the **Test your Competence** sections included at the end of the first and second parts of the course book.

The course book is designed to be used in conjunction with the audio cassettes. A complementary booklet containing the tapescripts and their English translations is supplied with the cassettes.

Users' guide

Purpose

Hablando de Turismo is an audio language learning package designed to meet the needs of students of tourism and of professionals already employed in the tourism industry, whether studying alone or in a group.

Level

Hablando de Turismo aims at providing students with a foundation level in Spanish for tourism. It is aimed at both beginners and lower intermediate students. It can also be used as a refresher course by people who have studied Spanish at school but need a more practical and professional knowledge of the language. Units 1 to 4 can be used in a self-study mode by complete beginners; Units 5 to 9 would, however, perhaps need the help of a teacher as the language presented is more complex in nature. Lower intermediate students should be able to cope with the material on their own.

Materials

The package consists of
- a course book with learning units, a key to the exercises, a grammar summary and a glossary;
- two 90 minute audio cassettes and a complementary booklet with tapescripts and their English translation.

Components

Hablando de Turismo consists of nine units. The first four units include most of the general language you will need as a professional working in tourism. At the end of Unit 4, you will be able to review your progress before you move on to the next five units which look at specific areas of the tourism industry: tourist information, travel information, sports and leisure, excursions and tours, conferences and fairs. Once you have studied the first four units, you can use *Hablando de Turismo* as you wish. Depending on your area of work or study, your time and your preferences, you can tailor *Hablando de Turismo* to fit your own specific needs.

How to Use the Course

Listening passages

All the interactions are situational and take place in various working environments with which you are probably already familiar.

To start with we recommend that you read the questions that accompany each listening passage before you listen to the tape. This will focus your listening and help you to concentrate on the key words and expressions necessary to understand the passage. You can then listen to the tape as many times as you need as this will help you build up your listening skills.

> *When you are doing exercises that require your participation, remember to* ***stop the tape*** *each time before you answer.*

How to say it

This section includes a selection of key structures and phrases related to the given situation. Study them and see how the Spanish language works. Many of these structures and phrases are used in the **Language Practice** exercises, in both listening and speaking activities, so do look back at the **How to say it** section if you get stuck for a word or an expression.

Help!

This section provides you with a list of useful vocabulary to help you understand the exercises. It is advisable to check to see if there is a *Help!* section and study it before doing any of the listening activities.

Test your Competence

After units 4 andt 9 you will find a **Test your Competence** section which you can use to check your progress. Do not attempt to move on if you find you are having difficulty doing the exercises in Test you Competence 1. The exercises combine the language skills most necessary in your industry, particularly listening and speaking skills. Some of the exercises also aim at developing your reading and writing skills. You will find the answers near the back of the book.

La hora del café

A series of short articles, in English, give you practical information to help you to reach a better understanding of the Spanish people you will meet in your workplace, in your own country or when on holiday in Spain. They are written in a humorous vein and should provide you with a well-deserved excuse for a coffee break. They appear at the end of each learning unit.

At the back of the workbook you will find:

Answer Keys

The answer keys have been provided for students who are working on their own in a self-study mode.

Grammar Summary

Some of the key aspects of Spanish grammar have been provided for you for easy reference. For more detailed explanations you should consult your Spanish grammar.

Glossary

Here you can check the meaning of words you don't know. In this glossary the combinations **ch** and **ll** are alphabetised under the letters **c** and **l**. However, these combinations were traditionally regarded as separate letters, so that in some dictionaries you can still find that words beginning with **ch** or **ll** follow words beginning with **c** or **l** — for example, you might find *chaqueta* comes after a word like *cueva* and *llamar* could come after *luz.*

In the complementary booklet you will find:

Tapescripts and translations

When you are using the book and the audio cassettes on your own, if you need to do so, you can refer to the complementary booklet containing the tapescripts and their English translation.

Working on your own

There are a few things worth remembering when working on your own.

- **Motivation:** To maintain a high level of motivation, you will need to define your needs and set yourself workable, realistic goals. Think about what you need Spanish for and make a list of the situations and types of exchanges in which you are involved through your work. Try to concentrate on these when you are studying with *Hablando de Turismo.*

- **Little and often:** People learn in different ways and at different speeds but remember that it is better to do a little every day than a lot once a month. Decide how much time you can set aside for Spanish. Organise a regular time for practice and try to stick to it.

- **Practice:** You will need plenty of time and practice before you feel confident in the language, but remember that Spanish visitors will really appreciate your efforts and that you don't have to be fluent to communicate. You are lucky to work in an industry where you don't need to travel to the country to practise, so do not hesitate to start using Spanish from the very beginning.

- **Pronunciation:** Compared with English, attempting Spanish pronunciation is quite easy since the Spanish written language is a faithful representation of the sounds of the spoken language. But there are two things regarding Spanish pronunciation that you must bear in mind:

  Word groups. Words linked closely within a given sentence run together in pronunciation, e.g. Me llamo Ana (mellamoana).

  Stress. In all words with more than one syllable there is a **stress** (one syllable pronounced more vigorously than the rest). This **stress** generally falls on the syllable next to the last (the penultimate) or on the last one. The penultimate syllable bears the **stress** in words ending in a vowel, -n or -s, e.g. española, llaman, lunes; otherwise the last syllable bears the **stress,** e.g. hotel, ciudad. When the **stress** does not conform to this rule, this is indicated by means of a written **accent,** e.g. café, magnífico. So remember that when a word bears a written **accent** you must place an emphasis on the syllable marked.

Communication strategies

This course cannot possibly include all the vocabulary you may meet or need in performing tasks in Spanish in your section of the industry. This leads to the need to develop communication strategies which can be used to cope with unknown words.

Strategies for understanding:

Ignoring words which are not vital for comprehension, concentrating instead on the key words; positively focussing on what you do understand rather than on what you don't; using the context, the speakers, visual clues, etc. to help listening comprehension; studying the layout, captions and visuals to aid reading comprehension; using the skill of prediction in trying to work out what is being said or is written down; asking the Spanish native speaker to speak more slowly or to repeat what they have just said; checking understanding by paraphrasing or repeating the information to the speaker.

Strategies for speaking:

Making use of gestures and mime to help convey message; using 'approximate' words which share a similar meaning to the word you are looking for: e.g. *escalada/montañismo, monumento/castello, conferencia/congreso;* checking that the information you have given has been understood by paraphrasing or repeating it; using verbal fillers to create a space to think of what or how to say something next, e.g. *'Un momento, por favor'* or *'Momentito';* describing the qualities of something, e.g. size, shape, colour, if you don't know the word in Spanish.

x

THROUGHOUT THIS BOOK THESE SYMBOLS ARE USED TO GUIDE YOUR STUDY:

Listen to the tape

Stop the tape at the signal
Remember to stop the tape at the signal. Once you have replied, switch it on again to hear a model answer and the next question or item.

Speak your answers

Write your answers in Spanish

Read material for an exercise

How to say it — key structures and phrases

Special Help! — key vocabulary section

La hora del café — cultural section

Objectives

At the end of this unit you will be able to:

- Greet and respond to greetings

- Say who you are and what you do

- Ask somebody's name, address, telephone number and nationality

- Give this information about yourself

- Spell names

- Say good-bye

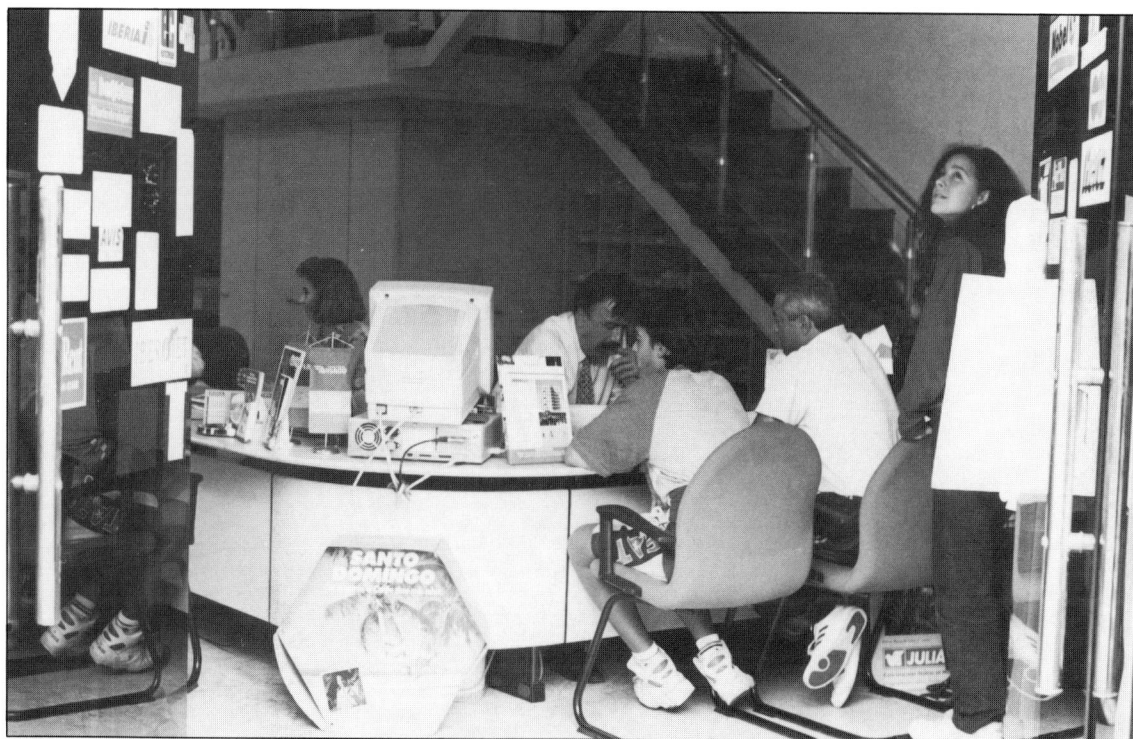

(A.L.M.)

GREETING

Listening 1 - At the airport/En el aeropuerto.

a. Listen to the guide greeting the members of the "Colegio de Arquitectos", who are travelling to Dublin.

Number the names of the participants on the list below in the order they are met by the guide:

COLEGIO DE ARQUITECTOS
Viaje Barcelona-Dublín
Lista de participantes

Antonio GARCÍA	☐	Pablo PÉREZ	☐
Luisa RAMA	☐	Fernando LÓPEZ	☐
Carmen OTERO	☐	Juan ROMERO	☐
Alberto BLANCO	☐	Jorge GONZÁLEZ	☐
Mercedes IGLESIAS	☐	Concha MONTES	☐

b. Listen to the tape as many times as necessary and tick the following words/expressions each time you hear them:

	1	2	3	4	5	6	7	8	9	10
Hola										
Buenos días										
Bienvenido/Bienvenida										
¿Cómo se llama (usted)?										
¿Cuál es su nombre?										
Por favor										

H O W   T O   S A Y   I T

Hola **, señor/señora.**	Hello.
Buenos días	Good morning/afternoon.
Buenas tardes	Good afternoon/evening.
Buenas noches	Good night.
Bienvenido/bienvenida	Welcome.

¿Cuál es su | nombre | , por favor? **apellido**	What is your | name | , please? surname
¿Su | nombre | , por favor? **apellido**	Your | name | , please? surname
¿Cómo se llama (usted)?	What is your name?
¿Es usted | el señor López? **la señora Blanco?**	Are you | Mr López? Mrs Blanco?
Yo soy Antonio Rama.	I am Antonio Rama.
Me llamo Carmen Otero.	My name is Carmen Otero.

S P E L L I N G

Listening 2

Listen to the Spanish alphabet and repeat each letter as you hear it.

A - B - C - D - E - F - G - H - I - J - K - L - M - N -
Ñ - O - P - Q - R - S - T - U - V - W - X - Y - Z

Listening 3 - At the Conference Centre/En el Centro de Congresos

a. Listen to the conference assistant at the computer trade fair giving badges to the
participants. Complete the names of the participants by filling in the missing letters.

1. P __ __ S __ A   2. __ I __ __ N E __   3. F E __ E __ I __ O

4. S __ A __   5. __ E S __ __ __ S

3

b. Listen to the tape again. Then circle the countries and cities you hear on the table or on the map below:

España	Luxemburgo	Irlanda	Alemania
Francia	Grecia	Portugal	Dinamarca
Italia	Austria	Inglaterra	Suecia
Bélgica	Finlandia	Holanda	Noruega

? HELP!

Nacionalidades	
español/española	irlandés/irlandesa
francés/francesa	portugués/portuguesa
italiano/italiana	inglés/inglesa
belga	holandés/holandesa
luxemburgués/luxemburguesa	alemán/alemana
griego/griega	danés/danesa
austríaco/austríaca	sueco/sueca
finlandés/finlandesa	noruego/noruega

HOW TO SAY IT

¿De dónde es (usted), por favor?	Where are you from, please?
Soy de Sevilla.	I am from Seville.
¿Cuál es su | nacionalidad?	What is your | nationality?
| dirección?	| address?
| número de teléfono?	| telephone number?
¿Su | nacionalidad |	Your | nationality |
| dirección | , por favor?	| address | , please?
Mi | nacionalidad | es ...	My | nationality | is ...
| número de teléfono |	| telephone number |
¿Cómo se escribe, por favor?	How do you write it, please?
¿Puede deletrearlo, por favor?	Can you spell it, please?
Aquí tiene | su acreditación.	Here is your badge.
Tome |	
Muchas gracias.	Thank you (very much).
Adiós.	Good-bye.

DEALING WITH NUMBERS

Listening 4

Listen to the tape and repeat the following numbers from one to fifty:

0	cero	13	trece	26	veintiséis	39	treinta y nueve
1	uno/a	14	catorce	27	veintisiete	40	cuarenta
2	dos	15	quince	28	veintiocho	41	cuarenta y uno/a
3	tres	16	dieciséis	29	veintinueve	42	cuarenta y dos
4	cuatro	17	diecisiete	30	treinta	43	cuarenta y tres
5	cinco	18	dieciocho	31	treinta y uno/a	44	cuarenta y cuatro
6	seis	19	diecinueve	32	treinta y dos	45	cuarenta y cinco
7	siete	20	veinte	33	treinta y tres	46	cuarenta y seis
8	ocho	21	veintiuno/a	34	treinta y cuatro	47	cuarenta y siete
9	nueve	22	veintidós	35	treinta y cinco	48	cuarenta y ocho
10	diez	23	veintitrés	36	treinta y seis	49	cuarenta y nueve
11	once	24	veinticuatro	37	treinta y siete	50	cincuenta
12	doce	25	veinticinco	38	treinta y ocho		

Listening 5

Listen to the tape. As you hear the numbers circle them on the card below.

0	10	20	30	40
1	11	21	31	41
2	12	22	32	42
3	13	23	33	43
4	14	24	34	44
5	15	25	35	45
6	16	26	36	46
7	17	27	37	47
8	18	28	38	48
9	19	29	39	49

Listening 6 - At the tourist information office/En la oficina de turismo

A tourist wants some telephone numbers. Listen to the tape and match the list of places with the corresponding telephone numbers.

1. Comisaría de Policía   ☐   A. 257 43 25

2. Aeropuerto   ☐   B. 239 45 76

3. Ayuntamiento   ☐   C. 231 56 84

4. Hospital Provincial   ☐   D. 287 43 19

5. Estación del tren   ☐   E. 221 79 43

Listening 7

Listen to the Listening 3 passage again and circle the correct answers below:

1. La dirección del señor Pessoa es: Rúa dos Santos, 16
                                                            26
                                                             6

2. La dirección del señor Jiménez es: Paseo del Mar,   12
                                                            32
                                                            10

3. La dirección del señor Federico es: Piazza da Vinci, 44
                                                            14
                                                            40

4. La dirección del señor Shaw es: 9,   Pembroke Road
                                          49
                                          16

5. La dirección de la señora Resnais es: 3,   Rue du Soleil
                                           6
                                           7

Saying who you are and what you do

Listening 8

Look at the pictures below. They show people who work in various areas of the tourism industry. Now listen to these people introduce themselves and say what they do. Number the pictures in the same order as you hear the people introduce themselves.

Example: 1.   A

            2. ☐   4. ☐

            3. ☐   5. ☐

? HELP!

Profesiones	Professions
Guía	Tour Guide
Azafata de congresos	Conference Assistant
Recepcionista	Receptionist
Informador de turismo	Tourist Information Officer
Operador turístico	Tour Operator

LANGUAGE PRACTICE

Exercise 1 - At the campsite/En el camping

Campers are arriving and want to book in. Take down their surnames **(apellidos)** as you hear them spelt out on the tape:

CAMPING LA MONTAÑA	
1.	4. ....
2.	5. ....
3.	6. ....

Exercise 2

Match a word or phrase in A with the corresponding word or phrase in B.

A. **Gracias.**
Adiós.
Buenos días.
¿Cuál es su dirección?
¿Cómo se llama?
Buenas tardes.
¿Cómo se escribe?
¿Cuál es su nacionalidad?
¿Es usted azafata?
Aquí tiene su acreditación.

B. Buenos días.
Muchas gracias.
De nada.
Mercedes López.
No, soy guía.
M-E-R-C-E-D-E-S
Soy mejicana.
Calle Alameda, 54.
Adiós.
Buenas tardes.

Note: If you are uncertain of a word, you can check it in the glossary at the back of the book.

Exercise 3

a. Give information about yourself answering the questions on the tape.

b. Now look at the identity cards below and introduce yourself as if you were Ana Pérez and Juana Otero. You can find model answers in the Answer Key Section.

1. NOMBRE:	Ana
APELLIDO:	Pérez
DIRECCIÓN:	Paseo de la Habana, 34
	Sevilla. España
TELÉFONO:	452 32 43
PROFESIÓN:	Guía turística

2. NOMBRE:	Juana
APELLIDO:	Otero
DIRECCIÓN:	Calle de León, 16
	Buenos Aires. Argentina
TELÉFONO:	356 42 19
PROFESIÓN:	Azafata de congresos

Exercise 4 - At the Conference Centre/En el Centro de Congresos

The conference assistant is greeting participants and giving them badges.

Complete the dialogue below by filling in the missing words. Then practice it aloud.

- Hola. Buenos .... ¿ .... usted Ramón Gómez?

- Sí. Yo .... Ramón Gómez.

- Aquí .... su ....

- Gracias.

- De .... Adiós.

Now listen to the dialogue on the tape and check your answers.

Exercise 5 - At the hotel reception/En la recepción del hotel

You are greeting guests at the reception of a hotel. A guest, who has booked a room in advance, arrives. You need further information to fill out his registration form. You play the part of the receptionist according to the instructions given below.

Receptionist:	*Say good morning.*
Guest:	Hola. Buenos días.
Receptionist:	*Ask his name.*
Guest:	Jaime García.
Receptionist:	*Ask him to spell it.*
Guest:	J-A-I-M-E, G-A-R-C-I-A.
Receptionist:	*Ask him his address.*
Guest:	Plaza de España, 54. 28005 Madrid.
Receptionist:	*Ask him his nationality.*
Guest:	Soy español.
Receptionist:	*Thank him.*

Note: Check the answers on the tape but remember that they are model answers only.

GREETINGS AND GOOD-BYES

The Spanish are a warm and welcoming people, and this is reflected in their greetings and good-byes. Handshakes, hugs, kisses ... you could get them all!

The Handshake
The handshake is the formal way of greeting someone in Spain. For example, businessmen meeting for the first time would exchange handshakes accompanied by a polite *Encantado.*

Besos
Besos (kisses) are usually used as a greeting between young people, between adults and children and between adult men and women who are on friendly terms. Usually two *besos* are given, one on each cheek. In fact, the kiss doesn't always "land" — often the two cheeks touch and the air, rather than the other person, gets kissed! *Besos* can be exchanged both on meeting and on saying good-bye.

Abrazos
Abrazos (pronounced "abrathos") means hugs, and they are often exchanged by good friends on meeting or saying farewell. They are a typical representation of the outgoing Spanish nature: warm and embracing.

That noise!
Many people encountering a group of Spaniards are amazed at the amount of noise they can create, and it's true — the Spanish are a noisy people! They enjoy animated conversation and often accompany their words with gesticulation and a touch of drama. So, next time you see a group of Spanish people having a row, don't worry — they're probably just talking about the weather!

Objectives

At the end of this unit you will be able to:

● Give information about the time of day

● Give information about dates

● Give information about times of services

● Give information about prices and accept payments

● Thank and respond to thanks

(A.L.M.)

GIVING INFORMATION ABOUT THE TIME

Listening 1 - At the hotel reception/En la recepción del hotel

a. The hotel receptionist is telling tourists the time. Listen and check the times on the clocks.

A.   1.30

B.   3.00

C.   10.50

D.   2.20

E.   12.45

F.   5.10

b. Listen to the receptionist again and repeat each time as it is given on the tape.

Listening 2 - At the conference centre/En el centro de congresos

A conference assistant is giving the time to participants. Listen and write in the time on the clocks below.

A.

B.

C.

D.

E.

F.

GIVING INFORMATION ABOUT THE TIME

Listening 3

What is the correct time? Listen to the tape and tick the correct clock.

A.

2,00    11,00

B.

3,15    6,15

C.

12,45    1,45

D.

8,20    1,20

E.

6,10    8,10

F.

mediodía     medianoche

H O W   T O   S A Y   I T

¿Qué hora es	, por favor?	What time is it	, please?
¿Tiene hora		Do you have the right time	
Es la 1	y ...	It is	... past 1
Son las 2, 3	menos ...		... to 2, 3
Es	mediodía.	It is	midday.
	medianoche.		midnight.
Perdone.		Excuse me.	
Oiga.			
De nada.		You are welcome.	
No hay de qué.			

GIVING INFORMATION ABOUT THE TIME OF DAY, DATES AND TIMES OF SERVICES

Listening 4 - At the travel agency/En la agencia de viajes

a. Listen to the travel agent giving her itinerary to a client. Draw in the itinerary on the map below.

EXCURSIÓN A ANDALUCÍA

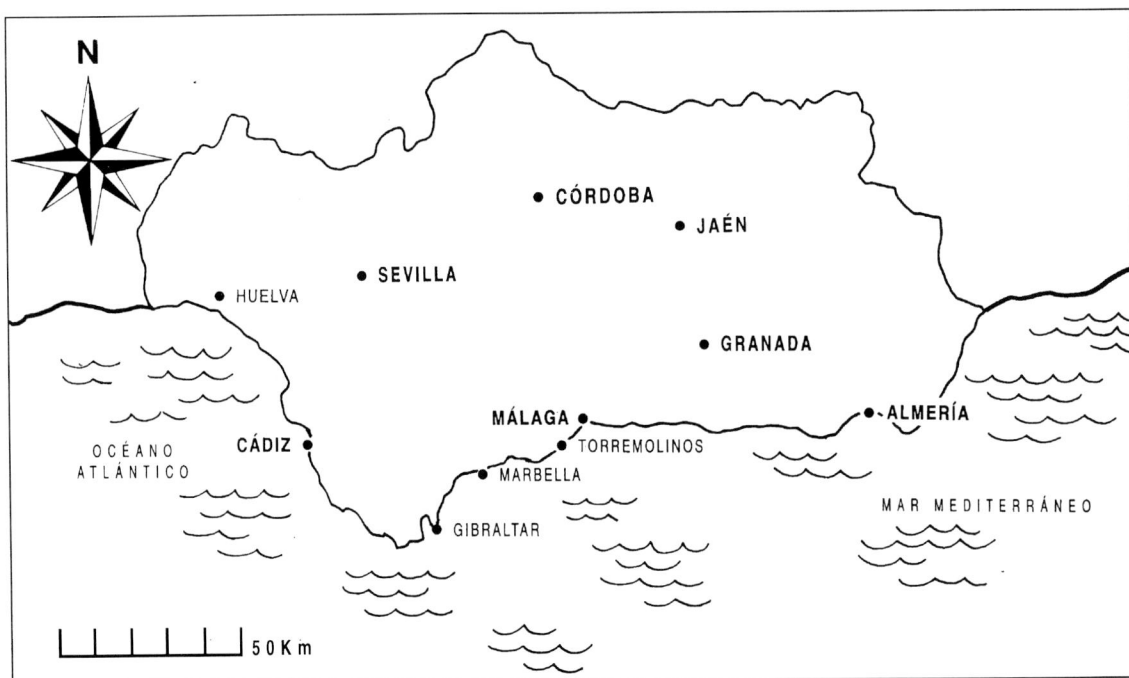

HELP!

DÍAS DE LA SEMANA	DAYS OF THE WEEK
lunes	Monday
martes	Tuesday
miércoles	Wednesday
jueves	Thursday
viernes	Friday
sábado	Saturday
domingo	Sunday

HELP!

mañana	morning and afternoon (until 2pm)
tarde	afternoon and evening (until 10pm)
noche	night

HELP!

ayer	yesterday
hoy	today
mañana	tomorrow
todos los días	every day

b. Listen again and indicate the towns visited on the table below.

	MAÑANA	TARDE	NOCHE
LUNES			
MARTES			
MIÉRCOLES			
JUEVES			
VIERNES			
SÁBADO			
DOMINGO			

Listening 5 - At the trade information centre/En la oficina de información de la institución ferial.

A businessman is checking the dates and locations of various trade fairs (**ferias de muestras**) in Spain. Listen to the secretary at the National Trade Information Centre giving him the information he needs and match the list of trade fairs below with the corresponding dates.

1.	Alicante	☐
2.	Madrid	☐
3.	Zaragoza	☐
4.	Valencia	☐
5.	Ferrol	☐
6.	Barcelona	☐
7.	Valladolid	☐
8.	Las Palmas	☐
9.	Sevilla	☐
10.	Gijón	☐
11.	Bilbao	☐
12.	Lleida	☐

a.   19-23 enero

b.   16-20 febrero

c.   4-7 marzo

d.   23-25 abril

e.   1-10 mayo

f.   19-27 junio

g.   16-25 julio

h.   7-22 agosto

i.   24-26 septiembre

j.   28-31 octubre

k.   9-12 noviembre

l.   15-27 diciembre

HELP!

MESES DEL AÑO	MONTHS OF THE YEAR
enero	January
febrero	February
marzo	March
abril	April
mayo	May
junio	June
julio	July
agosto	August
septiembre	September
octubre	October
noviembre	November
diciembre	December

Listening 6 - At the tourist office/En la oficina de turismo

The tourist information officer is giving information about opening times of tourist attractions and services. Listen to the dialogues and fill in the missing details.

1.
```
            BANCO

Abierto de ..... a .....
y de ..... a .....
Cerrado los ..................
```

2.
```
          EXPOSICIÓN

Abierta de ..... a .....
y de ..... a .....
Cerrada los ..................
```

3.
```
           PALACIO

Abierto de ..... a .....
Cerrado en ........................
```

4.
```
          CATEDRAL

Abierta de ..... a .....
```

HELP!

ESTACIONES DEL AÑO	SEASONS OF THE YEAR
primavera	Spring
verano	Summer
otoño	Autumn
invierno	Winter

24 HOUR CLOCK

Most timetables use the 24 hour clock.
Here is a table of equivalent times

1.00pm	= 13 horas
2.00pm	= 14 horas
3.00pm	= 15 horas
4.00pm	= 16 horas
5.00pm	= 17 horas
6.00pm	= 18 horas
7.00pm	= 19 horas
8.00pm	= 20 horas
9.00pm	= 21 horas
10.00pm	= 22 horas
11.00pm	= 23 horas
12.00pm	= 24 horas

How to say it

El banco abre a	la una.	The bank opens at	one o'clock.
	las dos.		two o'clock.
El castillo cierra a las ...		The castle closes at ...	
La exposición abre de ... a ...		The exhibition opens from ... to ...	
La catedral cierra de ... a ...		The cathedral closes from ... to ...	
Correos está abierto los domingos.		The post office is open on Sundays.	
El palacio está cerrado en invierno.		The palace is closed in winter.	
La feria abre mañana.		The fair opens tomorrow.	
todo el año		all year round	
¿Qué desea?		May I help you?	

GIVING INFORMATION ABOUT PRICES AND ACCEPTING PAYMENT

Listening 7

a. Listen to the tape and repeat the following numbers from fifty to ten thousand.

50 cincuenta	60 sesenta	70 setenta
51 cincuenta y uno/a	61 sesenta y uno/a	71 setenta y uno/a
52 cincuenta y dos	62 sesenta y dos	72 setenta y dos
53 cincuenta y tres	63 sesenta y tres	73 setenta y tres
54 cincuenta y cuatro	64 sesenta y cuatro	74 setenta y cuatro
55 cincuenta y cinco	65 sesenta y cinco	75 setenta y cinco
56 cincuenta y seis	66 sesenta y seis	76 setenta y seis
57 cincuenta y siete	67 sesenta y siete	77 setenta y siete
58 cincuenta y ocho	68 sesenta y ocho	78 setenta y ocho
59 cincuenta y nueve	69 sesenta y nueve	79 setenta y nueve

80 ochenta	90 noventa	100 cien	1.000 mil
81 ochenta y uno/a	91 noventa y uno/a	101 ciento uno/a	2.000 dos mil
82 ochenta y dos	92 noventa y dos	200 doscientos/as	10.000 diez mil
83 ochenta y tres	93 noventa y tres	300 trescientos/as	
84 ochenta y cuatro	94 noventa y cuatro	400 cuatrocientos/as	
85 ochenta y cinco	95 noventa y cinco	500 quinientos/as	
86 ochenta y seis	96 noventa y seis	600 seiscientos/as	
87 ochenta y siete	97 noventa y siete	700 setecientos/as	
88 ochenta y ocho	98 noventa y ocho	800 ochocientos/as	
89 ochenta y nueve	99 noventa y nueve	900 novecientos/as	

b, Now, try to say, and then listen to and repeat the large numbers below:

A) 1.854   B) 4.190   C) 2.513   D) 10.330

Listening 8 - At the bureau de change/En la oficina de cambio

How much money do these tourists want to change? Listen to the tape and write down the answers.

1. PTA = ... 2. US $ = ... 3. IR£ = ...

4. Peso = ... 5. DM = ... 6. Lira = ...

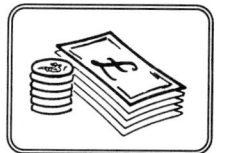

Listening 9 - At the duty-free shop/En la tienda libre de impuestos

a. Listen to tourists asking the price of goods in a duty-free shop and fill in the price of each object.

1. ....   2. ....   3. ....

4. ....   5. ....   6. ....

b. Listen to the tourists again and tick how they intend to pay.

	perfume/ perfume	bombones/ chocolates	vino/ wine	salmón/ salmon	cigarrillos/ cigarettes	té/ tea
en efectivo/in cash						
con talón/by cheque						
con tarjeta de crédito/ by credit card						

How to say it

¿Cuánto cuesta	este té?	How much does	this tea	cost?
¿Cuánto vale	esta mermelada?		this jam	

¿Cuánto es ?   How much is it?

Cuesta ... libras.   It costs ... pounds.

Son ... pesetas en total.   It is ... pesetas altogether.

¿Cómo quiere pagar?   How are you going to pay?
¿Cómo va a pagar?

Language Practice

Exercise 1 - Crossword/**Crucigrama**

ACROSS

1. After **martes**
5. The third month
6. Before **noviembre**
7. After **julio**
9. Between **jueves** and **sábado**
11. The eleventh month
13. Before **viernes**

DOWN

2. The first month
3. Before **domingo**
4. The second month
5. **marzo, abril**, ...
7. Between **marzo** and **mayo**
8. Before **julio**
10. After **lunes**
12. After **domingo**

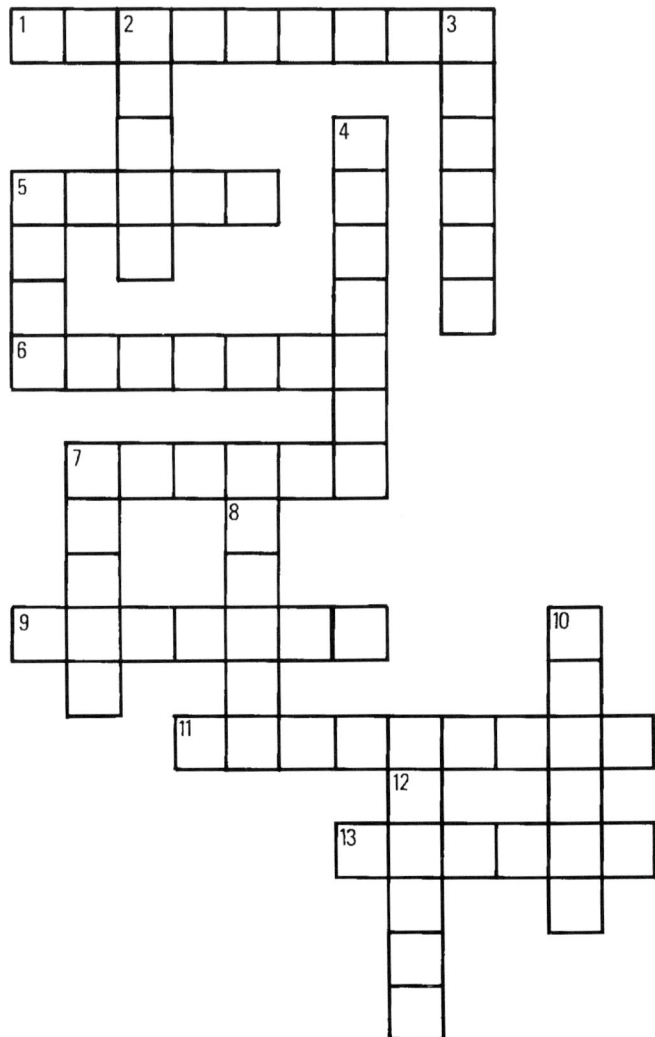

Exercise 2 - At the tourist office/En la oficina de turismo

You are working at the tourist information desk

a. Look at the signs below and practise giving information about the following places. You can check your answers in the Answer Key Section.

Example: 1. **La Galería Nacional está abierta de 9 a 6. Cierra los lunes.**

1.

NATIONAL GALLERY
Open 9.00am - 6.00pm
Closed on Mondays

2.

DUBLIN CASTLE
Open 10.00am - 12.30pm
1.30pm - 5.00pm
Closed on Sundays

3.

SWIMMIMG POOL
Open 8.00am - 10.00pm

4.

POST OFFICE
Open 9.30am - 5.15pm
Closed on Saturdays and Sundays

b. Listen to the questions on the tape and give the tourist the required information. You can check your answers in the Answer Key Section.

Example: **Q:**   **¿A qué hora cierra la Galería Nacional, por favor?**
　　　　　　A: **La Galería Nacional cierra a las seis de la tarde.**

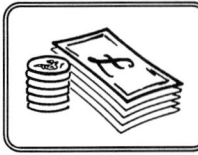

Exercise 3 - At the duty-free shop/En la tienda libre de impuestos.

You are working in a duty-free shop. Tell tourists how much these items cost.

Example: a. **Esto cuesta 255 (docientas cincuenta y cinco) ptas.**

a.   255 ptas

b.   160 ptas

c.   1.250 ptas

d.   585 ptas

e.   340 ptas

f.   2.530 ptas

g.   2.800 ptas

h.   5.900 ptas

Note: Check the answers on the tape, but remember they are model answers only.

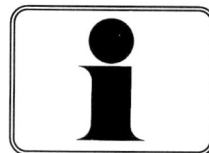

Exercise 4 - At the tourist office/En la oficina de turismo.

You are working in a tourist office. A visitor from Spain comes looking for information. Answer her questions according to the indications given below.

Visitor:	Buenos días.
Assistant:	*Greet the visitor and offer help.*
Visitor:	¿Abre el castillo hoy, por favor?
Assistant:	*Say yes, that the castle is open everyday.*
Visitor:	¿A qué hora abre?
Assistant:	*Say that it is open from 9.00am till 2.00pm.*
Visitor:	¿Está abierto por la tarde también?
Assistant:	*Say that you are very sorry, it is closed in the afternoon.*
Visitor:	¿Cuánto cuesta la entrada?
Assistant:	*Say it costs two pounds.*
Visitor:	Déme dos entradas, por favor.
Assistant:	*Give the visitor the tickets and thank her.*
Visitor:	Gracias. Adiós.
Assistant:	*Say good-bye to the visitor.*

Note: Check the answers on the tape but remember that they are model answers only.

THE RHYTHM OF LIFE

The working day in Spain was formed by the weather: the fierce heat in the middle of the day prevented the development of a 9am - 5pm regime. Instead, the day is in two halves: from the morning to 2pm and from 4.30 to 7.30 in the evening.

When people talk of the *mediodía* (midday) they really mean about 2 o'clock, the time when Spanish people have a good lunch and a little siesta. Just as lunch is taken late, so too is dinner, often at 9 or 10pm. Indeed when the heat is at its most oppressive in July and August, you will even smell the aroma of hot olive oil at 12.00 or 1.00 in the morning.

The Spanish call the hours between 12.00 midnight and 5.00am the *madrugada.* The different pub culture of Spain is perhaps at its most obvious during these hours. For a start, there is no fixed closing time - owners can close their premises when they like! Snack bars, where you can get something to eat with your drink, stay open until 1.30 or 2.00 in the morning — later in the big cities. Pubs don't close until 4 or 5am, and it's possible to get a full meal in a restaurant right into the early hours. People will often fix an appointment to meet at midnight, happy in the knowledge that the night is young!

Services
The banks are open from 9.00am to 2.00pm without a break, and then they close for the day. Many offices follow the same hours, so be careful if you're looking to do some afternoon business.

Shopping
The big stores stay open all day from 9.00am to 9.00pm. However, small shops often close from 2.00 to 4.30pm, and re-open from 4.30 to 7.30 in the evening.

Public Holidays
The Spanish are a hardworking people, which makes the arrival of the public holidays dotted throughout the calendar doubly welcome. An extra bonus is often in store if a company is going to *hacer puente* — make the bridge. This happens if a public holiday lands on a Tuesday or Thursday, in which case workers will usually take the Monday or Friday as a "bridge" to the weekend. And if the holiday is on a Wednesday, why, make an *acueducto,* of course!

Objectives

At the end of this unit you will be able to:

- Give directions

- Express distances

- Say how to get there

- Explain signs and notices

- Explain regulations

- Request people to comply with regulations

(A.L.P.)

GIVING DIRECTIONS INDOORS AND OUTDOORS

Listening 1: At the tourist office/En la oficina de turismo

a. The information officer at the tourist office information desk is giving directions to tourists. Listen to the first three dialogues and follow the directions and arrows on the maps below.

A.	La oficina de turismo		F.	El estadio
B.	Correos		G.	La piscina
C.	El banco		H.	El hotel
D.	La farmacia		I.	La agencia de viajes
E.	El museo			

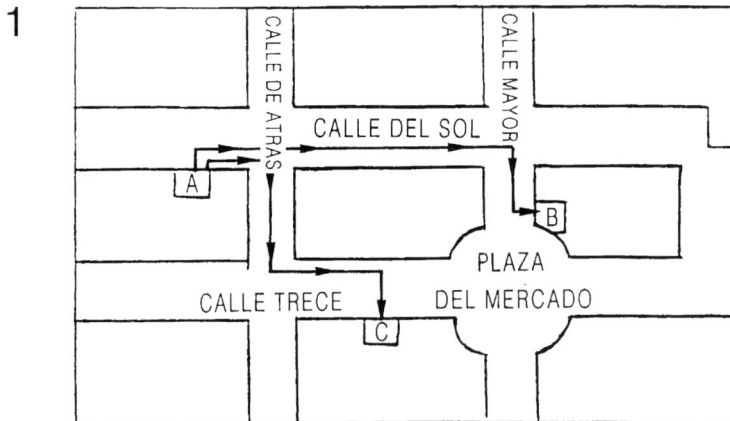

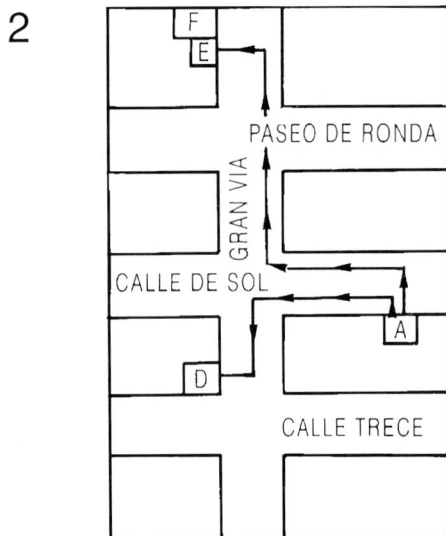

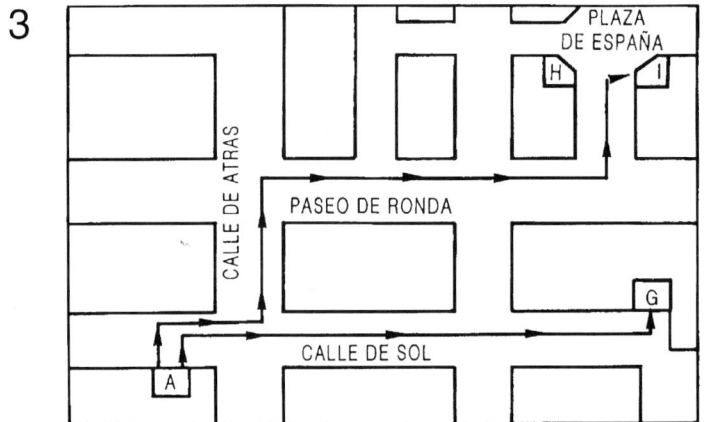

HELP!

primero/primera/primer	first
segundo/segunda	second
tercero/tercera/tercer	third
cuarto/cuarta	fourth
luego/después	then/after

b. Now listen to the next three dialogues, and indicate on the maps below the directions given and the letters corresponding to the buildings.

J. El cine   M. La cafetería

K. La iglesia   N El teatro

L. El restaurante   O. La librería

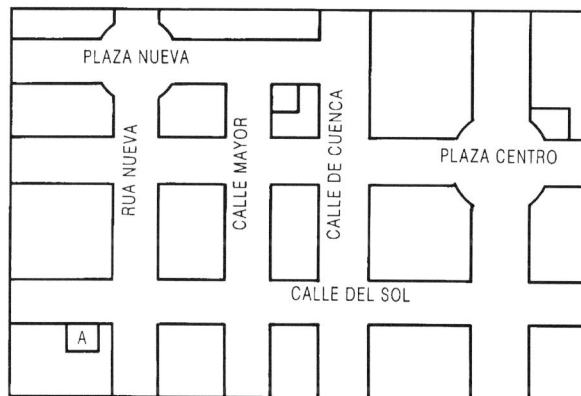

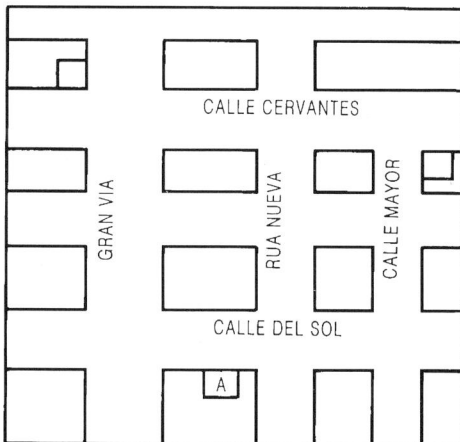

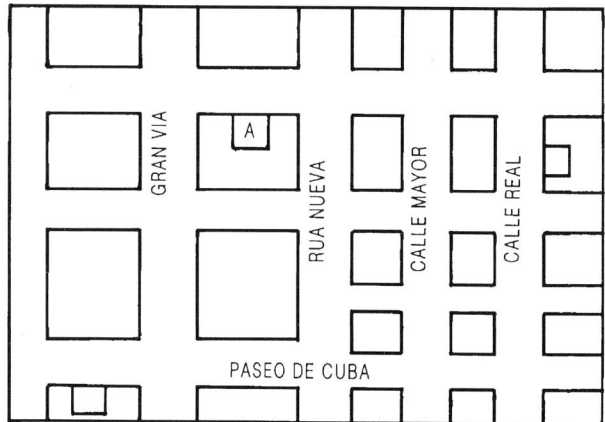

HELP!

a la izquierda	to the left	**enfrente**	opposite/in front of
a la derecha	to the right	**hasta**	as far as
todo recto	straight on	**hacia**	towards/to
entre	between	**la esquina**	the corner
al lado de	beside	**aquí mismo**	right here
al final/al fondo	at the end	**allí mismo**	right there

HOW TO SAY IT

¿Dónde está	**el museo?**		Where is the	museum?
	la cafetería?			coffee shop?
¿Dónde están	**los aseos/servicios?**		Where are the	toilets?
	las escaleras?			stairs?
¿Para ir	**a la librería?**		How do I get to the	bookshop?
	al teatro?			theatre?
¿Cómo se va	**al parque?**			park?
	a Correos?			post office?
Tome	**la primera calle**	**a la derecha.**	Take the first street	on the right.
	la cuarta	**a la izquierda.**	fourth	on the left.
Gire a la	**izquierda** **en el**	**semáforo.**	Turn left at the	traffic lights.
	derecha	**puente.**	right	bridge.
Continúe/siga	**todo recto.**		Continue straight on.	
Vaya			Go	
¿Hay	**una farmacia**	**por aquí?**	Is there a chemist	nearby?
	bares		Are there pubs	
Hay	**un cine.**		There is a cinema.	
	restaurantes.		are restaurants.	

Listening 2 - At the museum/En el museo

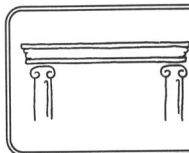

Listen to a guide telling a group of tourists how to find various facilities in the **Museo**. Locate the facilities and departments on the floor plans on the next page. Then indicate the order in which the facilities are mentioned by filling in the numbers in the boxes provided.

MUSEO

Planta principal

Planta baja

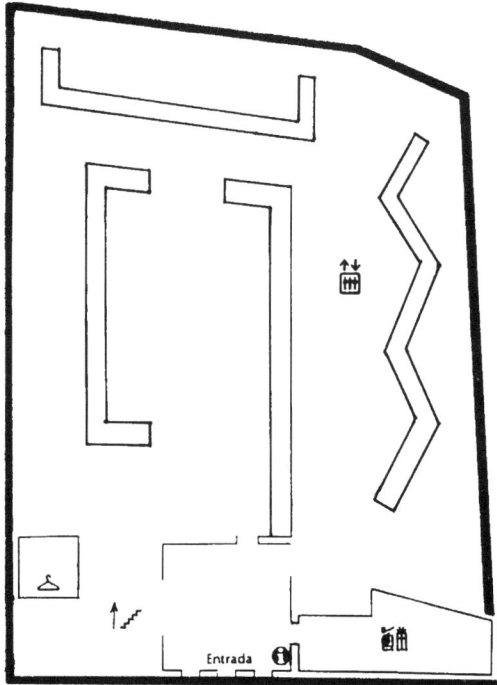
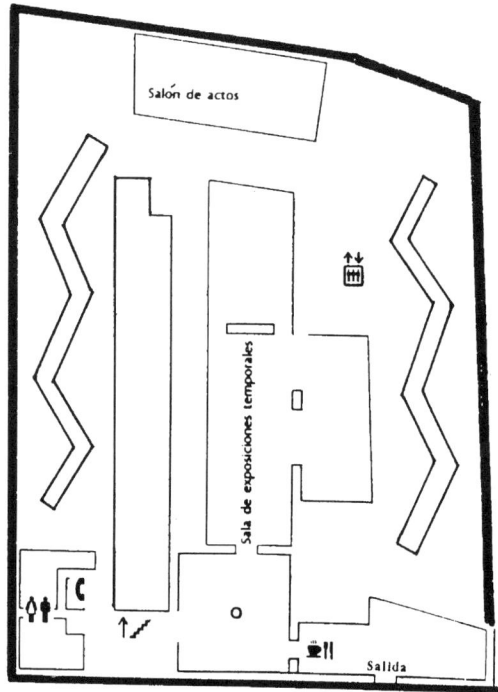

HELP!

	Escalera		Cafeteria-autoservicio
	Aseos		Guardarropa
	Ascensor		Información
	Teléfonos		Tienda-libreria

planta baja	ground floor
planta principal	main floor
entrada	entrance
salida	exit

los aseos	☐	los teléfonos	☐
los ascensores	☐	el autoservico	☐
la librería	☐	la cafetería	☐
el guardarropa	☐	las escaleras	☐

S AYING HOW TO GET SOMEWHERE, EXPRESSING DISTANCES

Listening 3 - At the museum/En el museo

The information oficer at the tourist information kiosk at the Prado Museum in Madrid is directing tourists to various places of interest. Listen and tick the appropriate mode(s) of transport to get to each destination.

Note: there may be more than one means of transport available.

Centro de Madrid

	a pie/ andando	taxi	metro	autobús	coche	tren
Parque del Retiro ③						
Ayuntamiento ①						
Hipódromo ⑦						
Estación de Atocha ②						
Ciudad Universitaria ⑥						
Parque de Atracciones ⑤						
Palacio Real ④						

Listening 4 - At the tourist office/En la oficina de turismo

The information officer at the tourist office in Alicante is giving information about some places in the area. Listen to her and fill in the distances and directions on the grid below.

Playas (beaches)	**Distancia km**	**Dirección**	**Pueblos** (towns)	**Distancia km**	**Dirección**
San Juan	4	norte	Benidorm		
Los Arenales			Santa Pola		
Castillos Castles)			Torrevieja		
La Mola			Elche		
Biar			Alcoy		

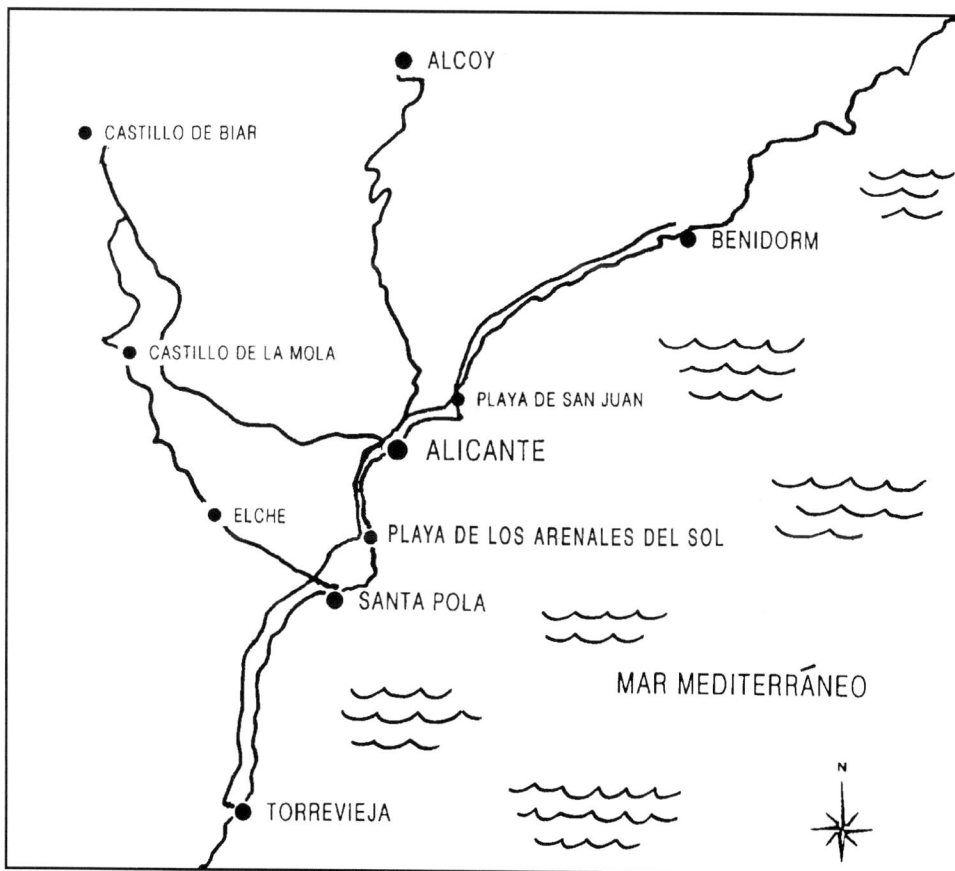

33

HOW TO SAY IT

Está	**lejos.**		
La playa está	**cerca.**		

It		is	far.
The beach			nearby.

Está	**a cinco**	**minutos.**	
El pueblo está		**kilómetros.**	

It		is	five	minutes	away.
The town				kilometres	

¿A qué distancia está? — How far is it?

¿A cuántos kilómetros está el hotel? — How many kilometres is the hotel from here?

REQUESTING PEOPLE TO COMPLY WITH REGULATIONS

Listening 5 - At the sports centre/En el centro de deportes

Listen to the leisure assistant explaining the meaning of the various signs below (left). Then match the English words with their Spanish equivalents. (The order of the Spanish words has been changed.)

1. Emergency exit
2. Private
3. Out of order
4. Gentleman
5. Cloakroom
6. No entry
7. Closed e

8. Entrance
9. Open
10. Exit
11. Engaged
12. Ladies
13. Cashier
14. Showers

a. **Abierto**
b. **Entrada**
c. **Guardarropa**
d. **Ocupado**
e. **Cerrado** (Example)
f. **Salida**
g. **Duchas**
h. **Caballeros**
i. **Salida de emergencia**
j. **No funciona**
k. **Prohibida la entrada**
l. **Caja**
m. **Señoras**
n. **Privado**

Listening 6 - At the sports centre/En el centro de deportes

a. Listen to the sports centre attendant requesting clients to comply with regulations and look at the corresponding signs below.

1.

2.

3.

4.

5.

6.

b. Now listen to the sports centre attendant requesting customers to comply with regulations and tick the corresponding sign in each case.

1.

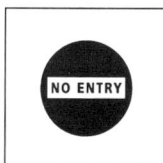

2.

3.

4.

5.

6.

HOW TO SAY IT

| Tiene | que | llevar gorro de baño. | You must | wear a swimming cap. |
| Hay | | salir por aquí. | | exit this way. |

| La ducha | es | obligatoria. | Shower | | obligatory. |
| El gorro | | obligatorio | Swimming cap | |

No se puede	fumar.	No	smoking.
Está prohibido	correr.		running.
Prohibido	sacar fotografías.		photographs.

| ¿Qué quiere decir | esto? | What | does | this | mean? |
| | eso? | | | that | |

| ¿Qué significa | este | cartel? | What does | this | sign | mean? |
| | ese | letrero? | | that | notice | |

| Quiere decir | aseos de señoras. | It means ladies toilets. |
| Significa | | |

LANGUAGE PRACTICE

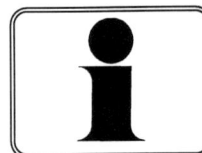

Exercise 1 - At the railway station/En la estación de ferrocarril

You are working at the information desk of the railway station (see map below). Listen to the tourists. Give them directions to the places they ask for.

(Remember to stop the tape at the signal. Once you have replied, switch it on again to hear a model answer and the next question.)

A. La estación de ferrocarril
B. Correos
C. La oficina de turismo
D. La agencia de viajes
E. El cine
F. La iglesia
G. El teatro
H. La estación de autobuses

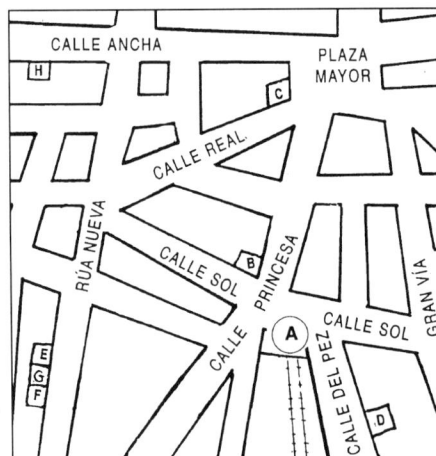

Exercise 2 - In town/En la ciudad

a. Look carefully at the map below and say which building is being referred to. Then write in the answers. You are standing outside the swimming pool in Calle Mayor.

1. Está a la derecha, al lado del cine: ....

2. Está a la izquierda, enfrente del supermercado: ....

3. Está entre el teatro y el hotel: ....

4. Está a la izquierda de la farmacia: ....

5. Está aquí mismo, a la derecha: ....

b. Complete the following sentences.

1. Correos está .... de la cafetería.

2. El museo está .... de la farmacia.

3. La piscina está .... , en la calle Mayor.

4. El banco está .... la librería y el supermercado.

5. La cafetería está .... , en la calle Real.

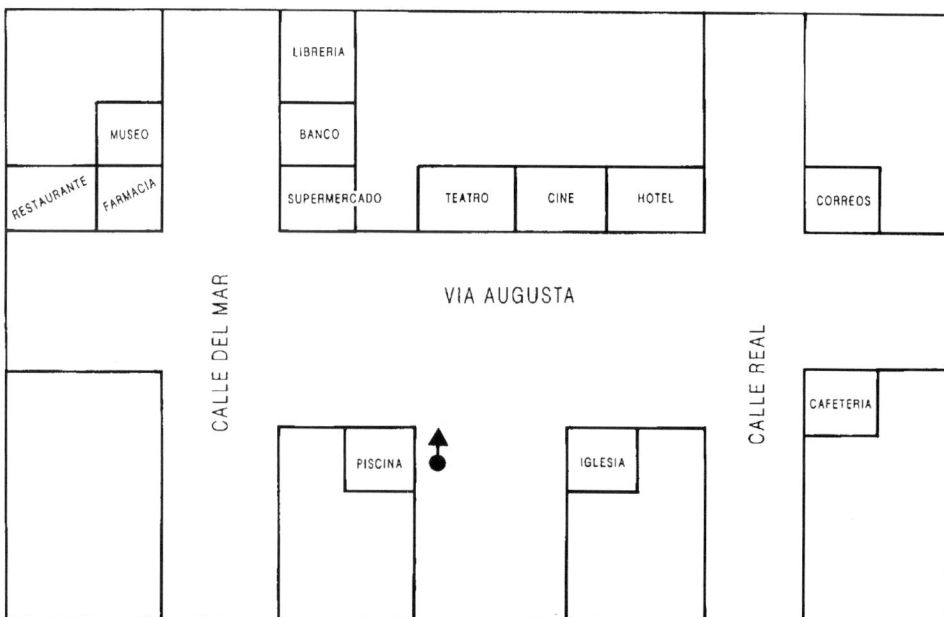

3

Exercise 3 - At the museum/En el museo

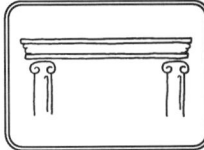

You are working at the information desk of a museum. (See map Listening 2).
Listen to the tape and reply to the questions asked by the tourists. (Remember to **stop** the tape at the signal.)

Exercise 4 - At the tourist office/En la oficina de turismo

You are working in a tourist office. Look at the map below and tell tourists how many kilometres each town is from Barcelona.

Example: **Zaragoza está a doscientos noventa y seis kilómetros de Barcelona.**

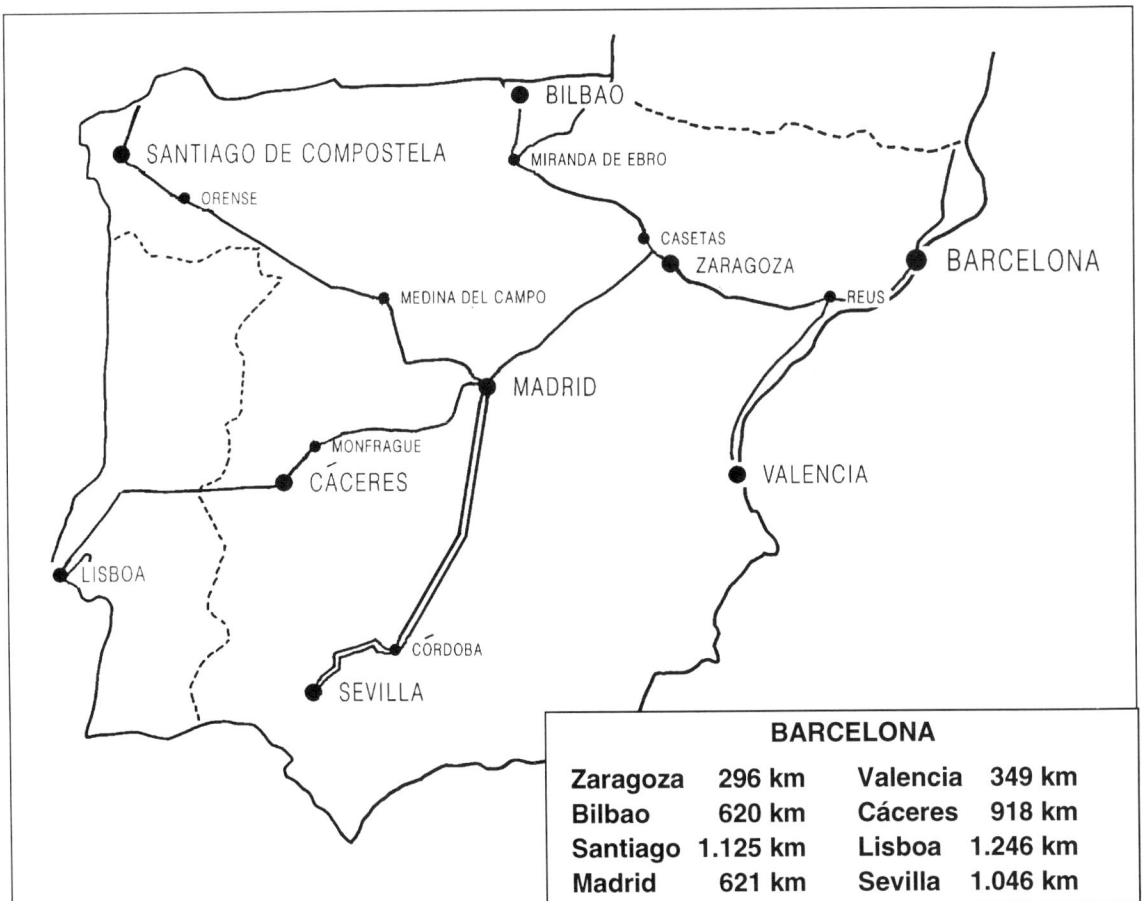

BARCELONA			
Zaragoza	296 km	Valencia	349 km
Bilbao	620 km	Cáceres	918 km
Santiago	1.125 km	Lisboa	1.246 km
Madrid	621 km	Sevilla	1.046 km

Exercise 5 - Look at the following signs and explain in Spanish what they mean.

1.   2.   3.   4.

Exercise 6 - At the leisure centre/En el centro recreativo

You are working as an attendant in a leisure centre. A Spaniard arrives at the reception desk. Answer his questions as prompted.

Visitor:	Buenas tardes.
Attendant:	*Greet the visitor and offer help.*
Visitor:	¿Hay piscina en este centro, por favor?
Attendant:	*Say that there is a swimming pool and that it is open all day.*
Visitor:	¿Dónde está?
Attendant:	*Tell the visitor to go to the end of the corridor and then turn left.*
Visitor:	¿Hay que llevar gorro?
Attendant:	*Tell him that he has to wear a swimming cap and that he must*
	take a shower.
Visitor:	¿Y dónde están las duchas?
Attendant:	*Tell him that the showers are at the end of the corridor, on the right.*
Visitor:	Muchas gracias.
Attendant:	*Say he is welcome and good-bye.*

Note: Check the answers on the tape but remember that they are model answers only.

WHICH SPANISH DO YOU SPEAK?

One of the great advantages of being able to speak some Spanish is that it also enables you to speak the language of Mexico, Argentina, Peru .... in fact, nearly all the countries of South and Central America. Spanish is the third most-spoken language in the world, so Spain itself is just the tip of the iceberg. However, Spain has four official languages: *castellano, catalán, gallego* and *vasco*.

Castellano is modern Spanish and is spoken throughout Spain, although of course there are regional variations just as there are between the English spoken in Dublin, Glasgow and London.

Catalán is a separate language - not just a dialect of Spanish, as any staunch Catalan will be quick to tell you. The region of *Catalunya* (Catalonia) centres on Barcelona in the north-east of Spain.

Gallego (Galician) is spoken in Galicia, in the north-west of Spain. Given the location, it not surprisingly shares some linguistic features with Portuguese.

Vasco (Basque) is also a completely different language: so much so that academics aren't even sure where it comes from! The *País Vasco* (Basque Country) is in the north of Spain. Its biggest city is Bilbao, although Vitoria is the capital.

The influence of Basque, Catalan and Galician is immediately visible in Spanish names, which can often seem strange and sometimes unpronounceable! Try *Goikoetxea* or *Etxebarria* — both Basque surnames. *Xavi* is the Catalan short form of *Javier* and is pronounced *"Chevi"*. *Xurxo* is the Galician form of *Jorge*. Many place names also have different forms in Basque, Catalan or Galician. For example, Lérida becomes Lleida in Catalan. San Sebastián becomes Donostia in Basque. Even the country itself isn't safe: *España* in *castellano* is *Espanya* in *catalán*.

Mind you, you don't need Catalan or Basque to have trouble with names: Spanish can be quite confusing enough, mainly due to the fact that Spaniards have two surnames. The first name is the father's and the second is the mother's. Most of the time people use both, although if only one is given, it is generally the first. If a Spaniard's mother and father both have the same name, then he or she will have two identical surnames — it's not unusual to meet an *Elena García García* or a *Juan Rodríguez Rodríguez*. Sometimes the surnames are linked by a **y, i** or **de** — for example, *Ruiz y Villarroel*.

Objectives

At the end of this unit you will be able to:

● Receive a telephone call

● Put someone through

● Ask for someone to hold the line

● Apologise

● Ask somebody's name and telephone number

● Say you do not understand

● Ask for repetition and/or slower delivery

(A.L.M.)

RECEIVING A SIMPLE TELEPHONE CALL

Listening 1 - At the hotel switchboard/En la centralita del hotel

Listen to the four telephone conversations on the tape. Then look at the scripts (below) and put the lines into the correct order.

1. a) Buenos días. Quisiera hablar con José Fernández.
    b) Hotel El Faro. Buenos días.
    c) Gracias.
    d) Un momento, por favor, ahora se pone.

2. a) Hotel Central. ¿Dígame?
    b) Un momentito, por favor, ahora se pone.
    c) ¿Podría hablar con Mónica López, por favor?
    d) Muchas gracias.

3. a) Sí. Diga.
    b) ¿Podría ponerme con la habitación 114?
    c) Un segundo, por favor. Le paso con la 114.
    d) Buenas tardes. ¿Hotel Atlántico, por favor?

4. a) Quería hablar con el Sr. Ríos Blanco, por favor.
    b) Sí. ¿Qué desea?
    c) Buenas noches. ¿Hotel Emperador?
    d) Un momentito, por favor. Ahora mismo le pongo con él.

Listening 2 - At the hotel switchboard/En la centralita del hotel

Listen to the four conversations on the tape and fill in the cards below.

Hotel Manila
Call for:
Room number:

Hotel Continental
Call for:
Room number:

Hotel Plaza
Call for:
Room number:

Hotel Las Vegas
Call for:
Room number:

How to say it

¿Dígame?	Hello!
Diga.	
Hotel Faro | **, buenos días.**	Hotel Faro | , good morning.
Hotel Central | **, buenas noches.**	Hotel Central | , good evening.
Un segundo | **, por favor.**	One moment | , please.
Un momentito	
Espere un momento.	Hold the line.
No cuelgue.	
Ahora se pone.	I'll transfer you to him/her.
Le pongo |**con**| **el señor Blanco.**	I'll put you through to | Mr Blanco.
Le paso | **la habitación 5.**	Room 5.
Perdone, ¿puede | **repetirlo?**	Sorry, can you | repeat that?
repetirlo más despacio?	repeat that more slowly?
deletrearlo?	spell it?
¿Cómo se escribe?	How do you spell that?
No comprendo.	I don't understand.
Quería hablar con la señora Río.	I'd like to speak to Mrs Río.
¿Podría hablar con Manuel Rama?	Could I speak to Manuel Rama?
¿Podría ponerme con | **la extensión 34?**	Could I put me through to | extension 34?
la habitación 15?	Room 15?
Con la habitación 110 | **, por favor.**	Room 110 | , please.
Extensión 58	Extension 58

Taking Simple Messages

Listening 3 - At the switchboard/En la centralita

a. Listen to the telephone conversation and answer the following questions.

1. The caller is telephoning

    a) a hotel
    b) a travel agency
    c) a bank

2. The caller wants to speak to

    a) Marta
    b) Marina
    c) Maite

3. The person being called is

    a) at a meeting
    b) out of the office
    c) on the phone

4. The caller will

    a) hold the line
    b) call back
    c) leave a message

5. What is the caller's name?

6. What does the operator ask him to repeat?

b. Listen to the conversation again and fill in the form below.

FICHA DE RECADOS TELEFÓNICOS
TELEPHONE MESSAGE

Para (To):

De parte de (From):

Teléfono (Tel No):

Volverá a llamar (will call again)   **a las** (at): _____

Desea que le llame (please call back)   **a las** (at): _____

Desea verle (wants to see you)   **a las** (at): _____

How to say it

Viajes Arenas. Dígame.	Viajes Arenas. Can I help you?
Lo siento, | **está comunicando.**	I'm sorry, | the line is engaged.
no contestan/no lo cogen.	there is no answer.
está reunido/reunida.	he/she is at a meeting.
¿Quiere | **dejar algún recado?**	Do you want to | leave a message?
volver a llamar?	call back?
esperar un momento?	hold the line a moment?
No se oye bien.	I can't hear.
Hay interferencias. **La línea está mal.**	It's a bad line.
¿Puede hablar más alto, por favor?	Can you speak louder, please?
¿De parte de quién?	May I say who is speaking?
De parte de Carmen Otero.	It's Carmen Otero.

Receiving a telephone call

Listening 4 - At the conference centre switchboard/En la centralita del Palacio de Congresos.

a. Listen to the four telephone conversations and match the following information according to what you hear.

1. Salón del Deporte
2. Feria del Mueble
3. Salón del Vehículo
4. Salón de la Informática

a) está comunicando
b) no contestan
c) ahora se pone
d) está en una reunión

b. Listen to the conversation again and complete the information grid below.

Salón/Feria Trade Fair	de from	para to	contacto establecido contact made	recado message
Deporte	/	representante de Adidas		
Mueble				Llamará más tarde
Vehículo	/		no	
Informática				

HOW TO SAY IT

¿Oiga?		Are you there?	
Luz García	**está en una reunión.** **no está en este momento.**	Luz García	is at a meeting. isn't here right now.
Volveré a llamar. **Llamaré más tarde.** **Dígale que me llame.**		I'll call back. I'll call later. Could you ask him/her to ring me?	
De acuerdo. **Ya se lo digo.**		That's fine. I'll tell him/her.	
El director/la directora. **El representante/la representante.**		The manager. The representative.	

L ANGUAGE PRACTICE

Exercise 1 - Word Search/**Sopa de letras**

Write down a telephone conversation using the 18 words which are hidden in the square. They read from left to right, from top to bottom and diagonally. You already have one word for each line.

-_____ Central. _____ .

-¿Podría _____?

-_____ , _____ , ahora _____ .

-_____ gracias.

```
A  V  Q  T  N  R  Y  E  I  K  A  J  D  B  S  A
C  N  P  R  O  I  E  M  P  M  N  E  U  A  G  D
C  E  C  O  N  A  H  N  O  L  A  Ñ  I  B  E  C
Q  J  N  A  G  H  A  B  R  R  N  C  Ñ  A  F  S
T  Y  O  T  P  O  D  R  I  A  A  O  P  Q  A  G
H  I  G  F  R  R  A  I  Q  R  K  U  T  H  A  I
R  O  A  P  N  A  T  N  G  L  K  N  C  R  O  N
A  M  T  N  G  J  L  M  I  A  J  U  O  Q  R  S
P  O  N  E  R  M  E  H  B  G  M  A  D  P  T  Y
L  M  A  D  L  N  D  N  M  F  N  E  C  O  A  B
E  E  R  U  H  A  B  I  T  A  C  I  O  N  E  T
D  N  N  H  A  T  I  N  N  V  U  F  I  G  Ñ  R
A  T  R  I  T  R  A  O  A  O  C  G  N  O  I  B
U  O  D  O  C  E  I  D  O  R  N  Y  U  A  R  O
```

Exercise 2

a. Listen to the two sample dialogues

-Quería hablar con la señora Fernández.
-*Un momentito, por favor, ahora* **se pone.**

-¿Podría ponerme con la extensión 528, por favor?
-*Espere un momento, ahora* **le paso con** *la extensión 528.*

b. Listen to the tape and answer the callers using the above expressions. (Remember to **stop** the tape after each request.)

c. Write the answers below.

1. ¿Podría hablar con la directora, por favor?

....

2. El señor Amado, por favor.

....

3. ¿Podría ponerme con la habitación 147?

....

4. Extensión 583, por favor.

....

5. Quería hablar con Marina Ríos.

....

6. Con la habitación 74, por favor.

....

Exercise 3 - At a travel agency switchboard/En la centralita de una agencia de viajes

Fill in the missing words in the telephone conversation below.

- Agencia de viajes Bonanza. ....

- Buenas tardes. ¿ .... ponerme con la directora?

- Sí, ahora le ....

- Gracias.

- Lo .... , pero ahora mismo está ....

  ¿Quiere .... un momento?

- No, gracias. ¿Podría .... un recado?

- Sí, dígame.

- De .... de Blanca Puente, que me .... a las seis.

- De .... Adiós.

Listen to the dialogue on the tape to check your answers.

Exercise 4 - At a travel agency switchboard/En la centralita de una agencia de viajes

You are working in the Azul travel agency when the 'phone rings. Answer the questions as prompted below. You play the part of the switchboard operator.

Caller: Buenos días. ¿Agencia de viajes Azul?

Operator: *Answer the 'phone in Spanish.*

Caller: ¿Podría informarme sobre los vuelos de Aviaco a España, por favor?

Operator: *Say that you don't understand and ask him to repeat more slowly.*

Caller: Sí, mire. Quería información sobre los precios y los días de los vuelos a España de la compañía Aviaco.

Operator: *Apologise and say you don't understand.*

Caller: Por favor, ¿podría hablar con el director?

Operator: *Ask him to hold the line ... Say that the manager is out of the office and ask the caller if he would like to leave a message.*

Caller: Vale, dígale que me llame. Soy Ramón Díaz.

Operator: *Ask him what his telephone number is.*

Caller: Es el 872 54 91.

Operator: *Thank him and take your leave.*

Caller: De nada. Hasta luego.

Note: Check the answers on the tape but remember that they are model answers only.

GETTING IN TOUCH

Using the telephone is often one of the most difficult linguistic feats facing the foreign language speaker. All the props of communication are gone: no gesture, facial expression, eye-contact ... it's all down to you and a voice at the other end of the line. Learning some fixed expressions will get you through the preliminaries but once those are successfully negotiated things can get sticky, so remember to speak as clearly as possible and to be patient when problems arise: you may not be the only one in difficulty!

The communications system in Spain is modern and well developed. Telephone kiosks *(cabinas telefónicas)* are of both the coin and the card-operated varieties. The card *(tarjeta)* works out cheaper and is definitely worthwhile for international calls. To get the most out of your *tarjeta,* 'phone after 10pm, when cheap rates are in operation. If you have no card and no money, you can always make a *llamada a cobro revertido* (reverse charge call) via the operator.

If you don't know a number, look it up in the *Guía telefónica* (telephone directory) complete sets of which are available at *la telefónica,* the Spanish telecom centres. Be careful of international and national codes - they can vary. For example, the international code for Madrid is 1, but the code for Madrid within Spain is 91. Finally, don't forget the dialling tone in Spain is different and, when ringing, sounds rather like our engaged tone.

The easiest place to buy telephone cards, stamps etc. is at an *estanco,* a kind of cross between a post office and a tobacco shop. Post boxes are yellow and rectangular, or alternatively you can post your letters at *Correos* (the post office).

Exercise 1 - At the travel agency/En la agencia de viajes

You are working in a travel agency. Listen to clients giving you their names on the telephone and tick which way they spell them in the grid below:

FLORES	☐	FLÓREZ	☐
GARCÍA	☐	GRACIA	☐
PUENTE	☐	FUENTE	☐
SAIZ	☐	SÁEZ	☐
FRANCO	☐	BLANCO	☐

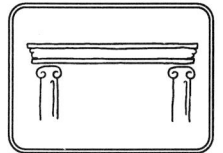

Exercise 2 - At the cloakroom/En el guardarropa

You are working at the cloakroom desk in a museum. Listen to tourists asking for their coats. Tick the number each one asks for.

1. 43 57 63 76 86 97

2. 23 54 75 82 92 104

3. 109 112 122 130 146 162

4. 215 227 267 296 315 386

5. 391 401 435 479 491 511

6. 534 552 567 577 589 590

Exercise 3 – At the reception desk/En la recepción

You are working in a hotel. Guests are ringing the reception desk to arrange their morning calls. Listen to the dialogues and fill in the grid below.

Guest	Room Number	Call Time
1.	....	....
2.	....	....
3.	....	....
4.	....	....

Exercise 4 - On the car ferry/En el transbordador de coches

Listen to the announcements made over the loudspeaker on a car ferry and write down when the following services are available.

1. La oficina de cambio está abierta de .... a ....

2. El cine abre a las ....

3. La tienda libre de impuestos abre de .... a ....

4. El restaurante está abierto de .... a ....

5. El bar está cerrado de .... a ....

6. La discoteca cierra a las ....

Exercise 5 - At the tourist office/En la oficina de turismo

a. Listen to the tourist information officer giving a customer the prices of various day trips available from Madrid and circle the correct price for each tour.

1.	Toledo	2.550 ptas	4.550 ptas	3.500 ptas
2.	Jardines de La Granja	3.300 ptas	5.200 ptas	6.320 ptas
3.	Valle de los Caídos	6.850 ptas	7.560 ptas	7.590 ptas
4.	Monasterio del Escorial	7.400 ptas	6.800 ptas	8.850 ptas
5.	Ciudad Encantada de Cuenca	9.150 ptas	8.050 ptas	10.300 ptas
6.	Palacio de Aranjuez	9.760 ptas	7.330 ptas	10.960 ptas

b. Now you give the following prices to a tourist.

Interplan Weekends (salida de Madrid - precio por persona)

Roma	61.450 ptas
Venecia	72.300 ptas
Praga	58.820 ptas
Túnez	43.900 ptas
Nueva York	92.500 ptas
Londres	39.780 ptas

Example: **El fin de semana en Roma cuesta 61.450 ptas por persona.**

Exercise 6 - At the tourist office/En la oficina de turismo

Listen to the dialogues you hear in a tourist office. Three tourists have come in looking for directions.

Look at the map below while listening to the tape and fill in **a)** the place each tourist wants to go and **b)** the letter on the map which marks its location.

	PLACE	LETTER
1.	....	....
2.	....	....
3.	....	....

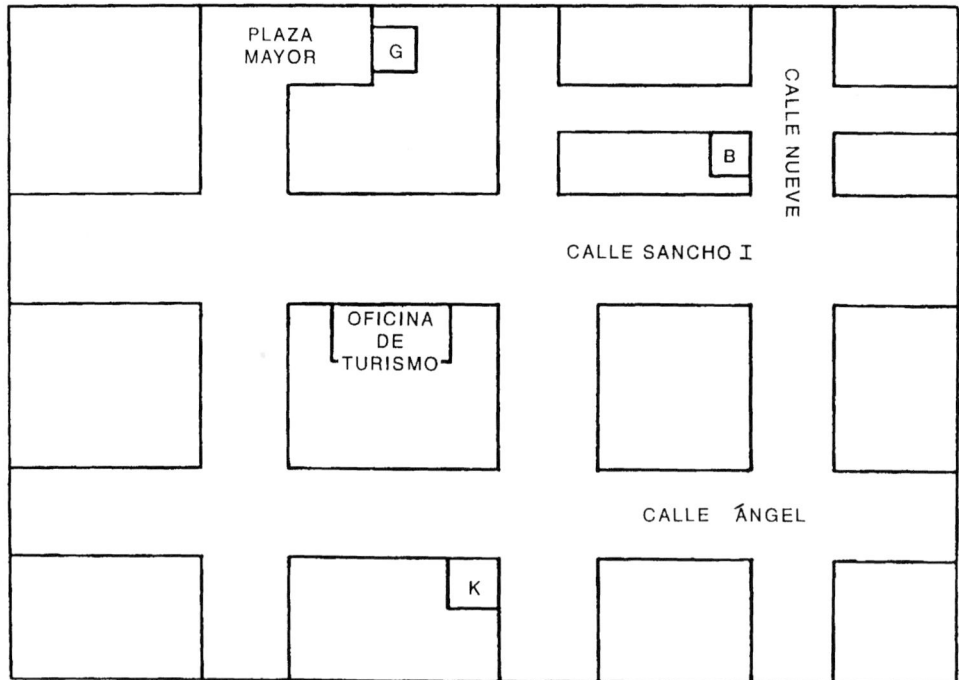

PLAZA MAYOR   G

CALLE NUEVE

B

CALLE SANCHO I

OFICINA DE TURISMO

CALLE ÁNGEL

K

Exercise 7 - In a tourist office/En una oficina de turismo

You are working in a tourist office. Tourists come in enquiring about various places in the town. Look at the map below and give them the directions they require. (Remember to **stop** the tape at the signal.)

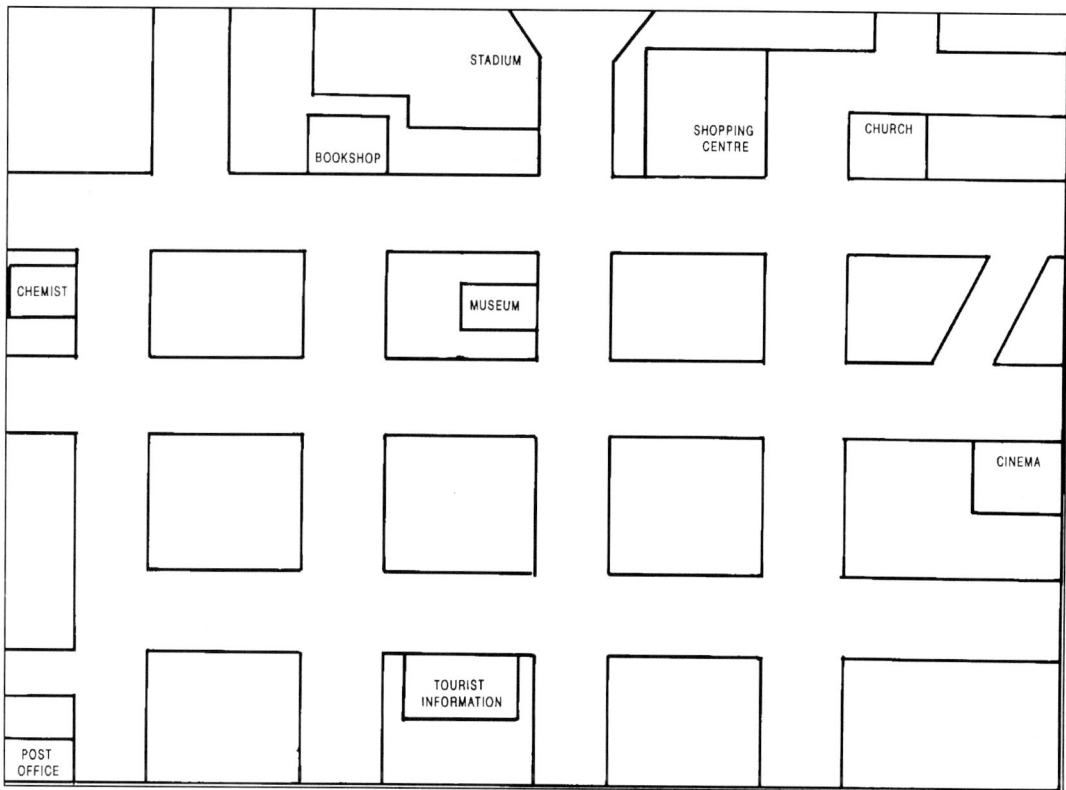

```
                                    STADIUM

                                                    SHOPPING        CHURCH
                                                    CENTRE
                          BOOKSHOP


    CHEMIST
                                        MUSEUM




                                                                        CINEMA




                          TOURIST
                          INFORMATION


    POST
    OFFICE
```

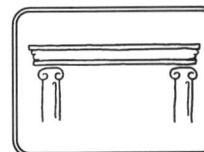

Exercise 8 - At the National Gallery/En la Galería Nacional

Listen to the tourist information officer directing people to the places they are looking for in the National Gallery and indicate with arrows on the floor plan which areas are referred to and in what order.

All directions are given from the information desk.

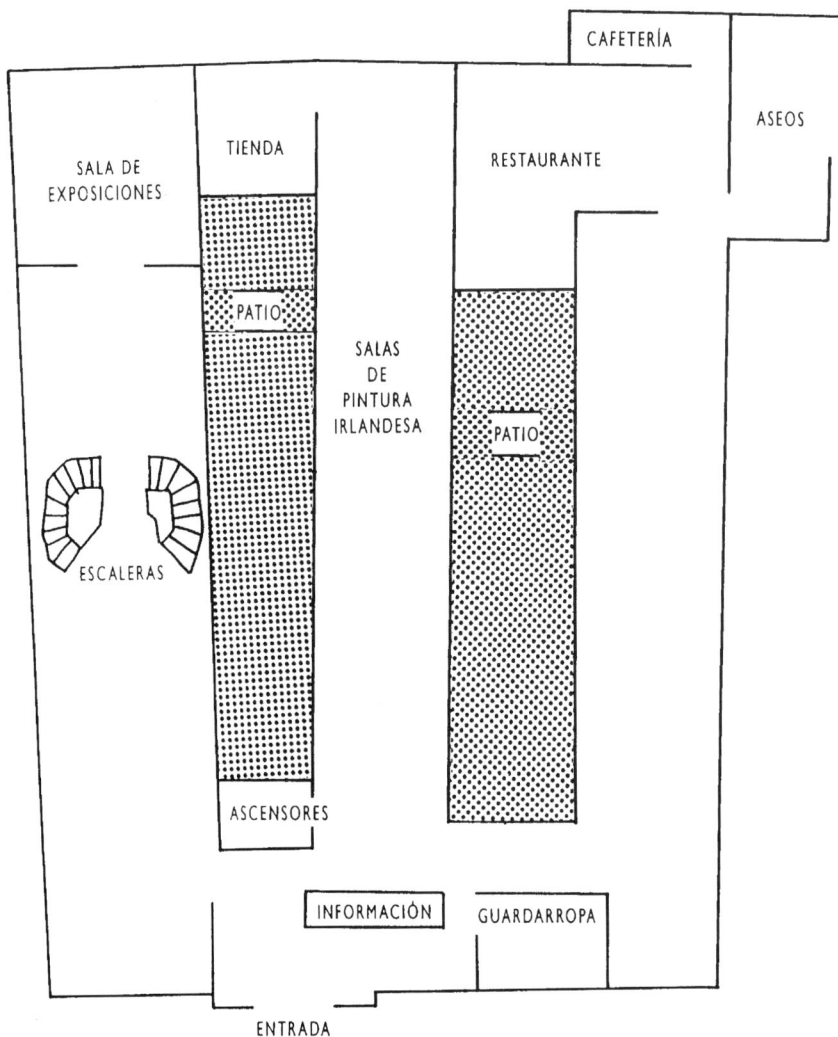

SALA DE EXPOSICIONES	TIENDA		RESTAURANTE	CAFETERÍA

PATIO

SALAS DE PINTURA IRLANDESA

PATIO

ASEOS

ESCALERAS

ASCENSORES

INFORMACIÓN   GUARDARROPA

ENTRADA

H E L P !

sala de exposiciones	exhibition room
salas de pintura irlandesa	The Irish Rooms
patio	courtyard

Exercise 9

a. Match the following symbols with the corresponding sentences in Spanish.

1.   A.   Prohibido sacar fotografías.
                                                          Prohibidas las cámaras fotográficas.

2.   B.   La ducha es obligatoria.
                                                          Hay que ducharse.

3.   C.   No se puede correr.
                                                          Prohibido correr.

4.   D.   No se admiten animales.
                                                          No se puede entrar con animales.

5.   E.   No se puede fumar.
                                                          Está prohibido fumar.

6.   F.   El gorro de baño es obligatorio.
                                                     Hay que llevar gorro de baño.

b. When you have checked your solutions in the Answer Key section, cover the sentences above (right hand side of page) and give the instruction corresponding to each symbol.

Exercise 10 - At a travel agency/En una agencia de viajes

Tourists in a travel agency are booking flights to various destinations.

Listen to the travel agent giving them the details of their dates of departure, times of departure and arrival and fares for the return flight. Then circle the correct information for each tourist on the computer screens below.

1.

MADRID - LONDRES

Fecha/ Date	Salida/ Departure	Llegada/ Arrival	Precio ida y vuelta/ Return fare
15/5	6,45	8,05	26.800
13/5	6,15	7,35	26.500
5/5	6,25	7,45	27.500

2.

MADRID - IBIZA

Fecha/ Date	Salida/ Departure	Llegada/ Arrival	Precio ida y vuelta/ Return fare
10/11	10,50	12,10	20.740
6/11	12,30	13,50	13.750
3/11	11,20	12,40	17.650

3.

MADRID - LISBOA

Fecha/ Date	Salida/ Departure	Llegada/ Arrival	Precio ida y vuelta/ Return fare
13/2	16,00	17,00	54.630
3/2	18,30	19,30	44.650
30/2	19,20	20,20	65.630

4.

MADRID - LA HABANA

Fecha/ Date	Salida/ Departure	Llegada/ Arrival	Precio ida y vuelta/ Return fare
10/12	20,15	19,05	88.900
2/12	22,05	20,55	97.300
20/12	23,25	22,15	109.900

Objectives

At the end of this unit you will be able to:

- Greet and offer your help.

- Provide information and advice about local tourist attractions.

- Provide and sell information and publicity material.

- Describe attractions and craft items.

- Make reservations for tourist events, restaurants and hotels.

- Provide information about prices.

(R.S.)

PROVIDING INFORMATION AND ADVISING TOURISTS

Listening 1 - At the tourist information office/En la oficina de turismo

Listen to the tourist information officer giving information to a tourist about attractions and places of interest in the Spanish town of Morella. On the list below tick the places mentioned in the dialogue:

la basílica	el ayuntamiento	el convento	la plaza de toros
el castillo	el polideportivo	la Cruz Roja	la gasolinera
la farmacia	la Casa Ciurana	la Puerta del Rey	la Fábrica Giner

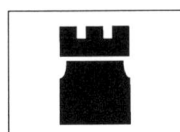

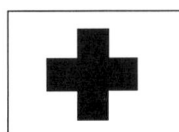

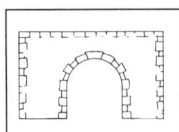

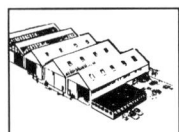

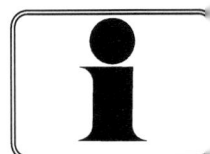

Listening 2 - At the tourist information office/En la oficina de turismo

Listen to the end of the conversation in the same tourist office and answer the questions below.

1. For each of the following towns, tick the correct distance from Morella:

Peñíscola	20 km	30 km	80 km
Catí	20 km	30 km	80 km
Castellfort	20 km	30 km	80 km
Herbés	20 km	30 km	80 km

2. Look at the list below and circle the places recommended by the tourist information officer.

> Hotel Cardenal Ram. Cuesta Suñer, 1. Tel.: 16 00 00.
> - 19 habitaciones con baño.
> Hotel Rey D. Jaime. Juan Giner, 6. Tel.: 16 09 11.
> - 44 habitaciones con baño.
> Hostal Elías. Colomer, 7. Tel.: 16 00 92.
> - 17 habitaciones con baño.
> Hostal El Cid. Puerta de San Mateo, 3. Tel.: 16 01 25.
> - 15 habitaciones con baño y 14 con lavabo.
> Fonda Moreno. San Nicolás, 12. Tel.: 16 01 05.
> - 7 habitaciones con lavabo.
> Habitaciones La Muralla. Muralla, 12. Tel.: 16 02 43.
> - 15 habitaciones con baño.
> Vivienda Turismo Rural, José Trullenque. Tel.: 17 31 90.
> - 7 habitaciones.

---

3. What does the tourist ask for: a) a leaflet?

   b) a map?

   c) a guide book?

4. Does she have to pay for it? YES ☐ NO ☐

HOW TO SAY IT

Hay	un castillo.			There	is a castle.
	jardines.				are gardens.
No hay	gasolinera.			There	is no petrol station.
	museos.				are no museums.
Tenemos	un campo de golf.			We have a	golf course.
	una piscina.				swimming pool.
Puede	hacer deporte.			You can	play sports.
	visitar la región.				visit the region.
Le	aconsejo	el	restaurante.	I recommend the	restaurant.
	recomiendo		monasterio.		monastery.

H O W   T O   S A Y   I T

Aquí tiene	**un**	**mapa.**		Here is	a	map.
Tome		**folleto.**		Take		leaflet.

Es gratuito.   It is free.

¿Hay	**club de squash?**		Is there a squash club?
	pistas de tenis?		Are there tennis courts?

¿Hay algo interesante que	**ver?**		Is there anything interesting to	see?
	hacer?			do?
	visitar?			visit?

¿Se puede hacer	**deporte?**	Can one	play sports?
	visitar la iglesia?		visit the church?

¿Puede	**aconsejarme**	**un**	**restaurante?**	Can you recommend a	restaurant?
	recomendarme		**hotel?**		hotel?

¿Tiene un	**mapa?**	Have you a	map?
	folleto?		leaflet?

D E S C R I B I N G   A T T R A C T I O N S   A N D   C R A F T   I T E M S

Listening 3 - At the local tourist information office/En la oficina de turismo

a. Listen to the tourist information officer giving information about some places of interest.

Match the following places with their descriptions:

1. La basílica   a. precioso/a
2. El castillo   b. de estilo gótico
3. El museo   c. impresionante
4. El palacio   d. visita obligada

b. Listen again and fill in the grid below:

	días de apertura opening days	**horario de apertura** opening hours
Basílica		
Castillo		
Museo		
Palacio		

Listening 4 - In the souvenir shop/En la tienda de recuerdos

A shop assistant is explaining the various food and craft items from the Valencia region.

a. Listen to the explanations given and circle the items mentioned by the shop assistant:

vinos   mantas   abanicos

alfombras   cerámica   queso

cristal   muebles   prendas de lino

jerseis   aceite de oliva   jamón

b. Listen to the dialogue again and indicate whether the statements below are true or false.

	TRUE	FALSE
1. The best best-known Valencian wine is Rioja		
2. The most famous pottery is from Onda		
3. The customer buys cheese		
4. The total bill comes to 2,380 ptas		
5. The customer wants to pay by credit card		

H O W   T O   S A Y   I T

Tiene | **el palacio.** | **jardines.**	You have | the palace. | gardens.
El museo es una visita obligada.	The museum is not to be missed.
¿Quiere | **el paquete para regalo?** | **los bombones?**	Do you want | gift wrapping? | the chocolates?
Que lo pase bien.	Have a nice stay.
¿Cuánto | **cuesta el queso?** | **cuestan las tazas?**	How much | does the cheese | cost? | do the cups |

MAKING RESERVATIONS AND PROVIDING INFORMATION ABOUT PRICES

Listening 5 - At the tourist information office/En la oficina de turismo

a. Listen to the tourist information officer making a reservation for a hotel room and complete the booking form below.

HOJA DE RESERVAS

Hotel El Fuerte. Marbella.

Número de personas: ....

Número de noches: ....

Tipo de habitación: ....

Nombre del cliente: ....

---

b. Listen again and answer the following questions:

1. How much is the room?
   - a) 5,800 ptas
   - b) 6,700 ptas
   - c) 7,800 ptas

2. Is breakfast included in the price?

   YES ☐   NO ☐

3. What category does the Hotel El Fuerte belong to? Circle the correct answer.

   ★   ★ ★   ★ ★ ★   ★ ★ ★ ★   ★ ★ ★ ★ ★

4. What does the sum of 2,300 ptas refer to?

   ....

Listening 6 - At the hotel reception/En la recepción del hotel

a. Listen to the hotel receptionist making a reservation for a flamenco show and indicate whether the statements below are true or false.

	TRUE	FALSE
1. The show is on every day		
2. Reservation in advance is required		
3. The show ends at 12.45 am		
4. The customer wants to make a group booking		
5. There are two options for the show		
6. The customer wants to pay by cheque		

b. Listen again and fill in the the form below with the correct information:

Name of customer: ....

Booking for: ....

Amount paid: ....

Method of payment: ....

H OW TO SAY IT

¿Para cuántas	**personas**	**es?**	How many	people	is it for?
	noches			nights	
¿Para	**qué fecha es?**		What date	is it for?	
	cuándo?		When		
¿Puedo	**pagar con talón/cheque?**		Can I	pay by cheque?	
	reservar una	**habitación?**		book a	room?
		entrada?			ticket?
Quería	**hacer una reserva.**		I would like	to make a reservation.	
	reservar una suite.			book a suite.	

L ANGUAGE PRACTICE

Exercise 1

a. Match each word with the corresponding picture.

1.	Una iglesia		a.	
2.	Un castillo		b.	
3.	Un museo		c.	
4.	Un puente		d.	
5.	Una piscina		e.	

b. Complete the following table from this list of Spanish terms.

Un mapa, un plano, un folleto, gratuito/a, una habitación, con baño, una cena, un desayuno, un espectáculo, una entrada, esta noche, todos los días.

a map	**un mapa**	every day	
a show		a street map	
a brochure		tonight	
a room		with bath	
free		a dinner	
a ticket		a breakfast	

Note: If you are uncertain about the meaning of a word, you can check it in the glossary at the back of the book.

Exercise 2

Listen to the examples.

La iglesia - muy bonita   La iglesia **es** muy bonita.
Los jardines - muy grandes   Los jardines **son** muy grandes.

Listen to the cues on the tape and build up sentences as in the examples above:

1. El puente - romano

2. El palacio - impresionante

3. Las tiendas - muy típicas

4. Las habitaciones - muy cómodas

5. La chaqueta - de lana

Exercise 3

Listen to the examples.

Examples:

Pista de tenis   **Hay** pista de tenis.

Duchas de agua caliente   **Hay** duchas de agua caliente.

Listen to the cues on the tape and use the signs below to provide information on what is available at this campsite.

Bar/bar   **Tiendas**/shops

Sauna/sauna   **Lavandería**/laundry

Parque infantil/playground   **Restaurante**/restaurant

Playas/beaches   **Aparcamientos**/car parks

Río/river   **Campo de golf**/golf course

Exercise 4 - At the tourist office/En la oficina de turismo

You are working as a tourist officer in Spain. A tourist comes in to book a hotel room in San Roque (Cádiz). Based on the extract below, you give him/her as much information as possible on the Suites Hotel.

HOTEL

GOLF EXCLUSIVO

Cada vez hay menos lugares donde desconectar del trabajo, la mujer, el jefe, la publicidad, el tráfico y la corbata. Una terapia eficaz para insolidarizarse con el mundo es el golf, un deporte relajante y entretenido –aunque de dificultoso aprendizaje– que

cada vez cobra más adeptos. Suites Hotel, un conjunto de casitas o *bungalows* en torno a una silenciosa piscina, posee su propio campo. Perteneciente al circuito europeo, discurre entre densas arboledas de alcornoques y arroyos, lo que complica seriamente el juego. Sus

acogedoras *suites* y sus seis kilómetros y medio de praderas son razón suficiente para alojarse –y no salir– de este paradisíaco rincón gaditano. Las *suites* poseen baño lujurioso, salón, comedor, terraza, aire climatizado, minibar, TV vía satélite y todos los extras de un hotel de lujo.

Nombre: Suites Hotel.
Categoría: Cuatro estrellas.
Situación: Carretera Nacional 340. Km., 126,5. San Roque (Cádiz).
Telefono: (956) 61 30 30.
Precios: 14.000 (habitación doble), 19.000 (*suite*) y 29.000 (*suite* de dos dormitorios).
Desayuno: *Buffet* americano.
Instalaciones: Campo de golf propio, piscina y jardines.
Capacidad: 100 habitaciones.
Cierra: Nunca.

Note: Check the answers on the tape but remember that they are model answers only.

Exercise 5 - At the tourist office/En la oficina turística

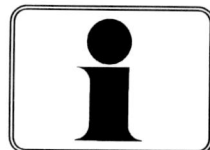

You are working in a tourist information office in Dublin. A Spanish visitor asks you for information. Answer the questions as prompted below.

Visitor:	Buenas tardes.
TI Officer:	*Greet the visitor and offer help.*
Visitor:	¿Tiene un plano de la ciudad, por favor?
TI Officer:	*Give the visitor a map and say that it is free.*
Visitor:	Gracias. ¿Podría aconsejarme algo que ver en la ciudad o alguna excursión por los alrededores de Dublín?
TI Officer:	*Tell the visitor that there is a tour of the city every morning at 10.00 am. There are also excursions to the monastic site in Glendalough and to the medieval city of Kilkenny.*
Visitor:	Muy bien. ¿Cuánto cuesta la excursión a Glendalough?
TI Officer:	*Tell the visitor that the trip to Glendalough costs £11 and ask if he or she wants to book for the tour.*
Visitor:	Mejor... déme dos billetes, por favor.
TI Officer:	*Say that two tickets cost £22 and ask when he or she wants to go on the tour.*
Visitor:	Mañana, si es posible.
TI Officer:	*Say yes, give the visitor the tickets and wish him or her a pleasant stay.*

Note: Check the answers on the tape but remember that they are model answers only.

NO ROOM AT THE INN?

Spain's vast tourist industry is supported by an equally vast array of places to stay. From the pampered pleasures of luxury hotels to the more ascetic qualities of a mountain hut, and with just about every step in between, travellers in Spain should always be able to find a bed that suits their pockets.

Hotels in Spain are graded from one to five stars. Among the best known of the four or five star establishments are the *Paradores.* These are state-owned hotels, usually found in castles, monasteries or other old buildings which have been converted to provide high-class hotel accommodation. There is one for every *provincia* (county) in Spain and, while not cheap, they represent good value at the very top of the market.

At the other end of the scale is a host of budget accommodation with different classifications but often little difference between them! *Fondas, Casas de Huéspedes* and *Pensiones* usually offer cheap and functional rooms all of a similar standard. Bars will also sometimes offer *camas* (beds) or *habitaciones* (rooms).

The gap between the above options and the hotels is filled by the *hostales. Hostales* are graded from one to three stars and often have a good *comedor* (dining room) on the premises. As in the rest of Europe, the cheapest accommodation of all is usually in the *Albergues Juveniles* (Youth Hostels). A similar type of accommodation is provided in the mountain regions of Spain by the *refugios,* simple huts which offer a bed, cooking facilities, and very little else!

Finally, for those who prefer to bring their own accommodation, there are many *Campings* (campsites) in Spain, usually found close to the main tourist areas. Away from such areas, the natural generosity of most Spaniards will be enough to secure you space for your tent. Needless to say, it's best to check with the locals before pitching your tent — courtesy apart, you don't want to be performing a *pasodoble* with the resident bull before breakfast!

Objectives

At the end of this unit you will be able to:

- Greet and offer help

- Advise on and make travel arrangements

- Provide information about departure and arrival times and the duration of journeys

- Describe the locations of airports, stations, ferry terminals and give directions to them

- Sell and book package tours and individual travel

- Issue travel documents such as 'plane, train and ferry tickets

(A.L.M.)

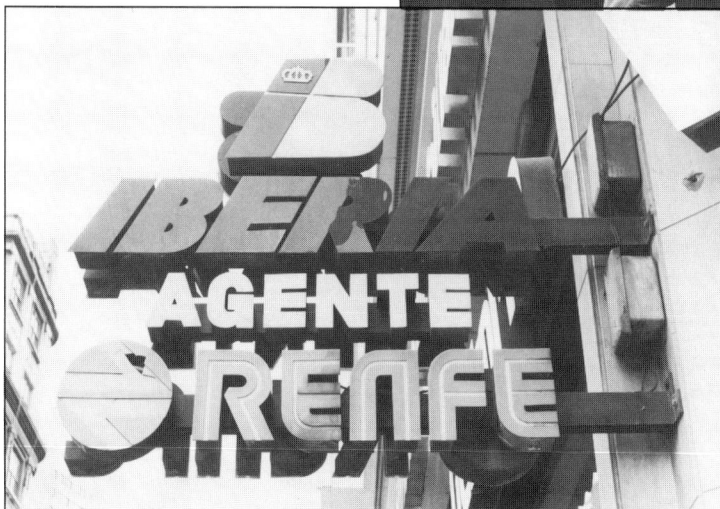

(A.L.M.)

ADVISING ON AND MAKING TRAVEL ARRANGEMENTS
DESCRIBING THE LOCATIONS OF STATIONS AND FERRY TERMINALS

Listening 1 - At the travel agency/En la agencia de viajes

a. Listen to the travel information officer providing information to a customer about the various travel options between Spain and Ireland when travelling by car.

Indicate on the map below the various possible ferry crossings between Spain and Ireland either via Great Britain or via France.

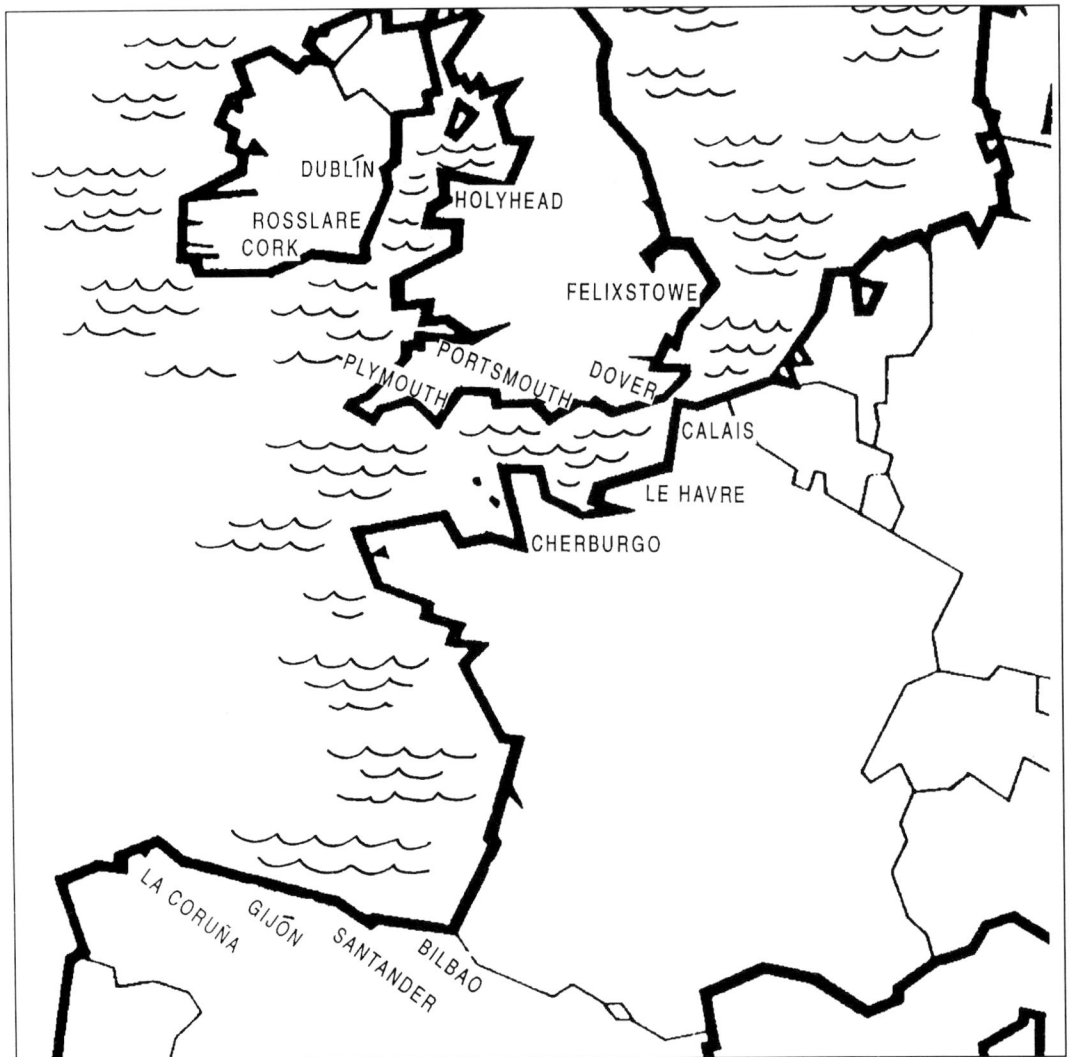

b. Listen to the tape again and take down further details. Mark on the table below the various crossings mentioned, their duration and price (see example 1).

Ruta/ Route		Duración de la travesía/ Duration of crossing	Precio/ Price
Vía Gran Bretaña/via Great Britain			
1. de: Bilbao	a: Portsmouth	30 horas	74.600 ptas
2. de:	a:	.... horas	.... ptas
3. de:	a:	.... horas	.... ptas
Vía Francia/via France			
1. de:	a:	.... horas	.... ptas
2. de:	a:	.... horas	.... ptas

c. Listen once more to the dialogues and choose the correct answers below:

1. The tourist would like to go to Ireland
   - a) on the 2nd of June
   - b) on the 12th of July
   - c) on the 22nd of July

2. The tourist would prefer to go to Ireland
   - a) directly
   - b) via Great Britain
   - c) via France

3. The tourist will be travelling with
   - a) 2 other people
   - b) 3 other people
   - c) 4 other people

4. The prices quoted are
   - a) single fares
   - b) return fares
   - c) APEX

Listening 2 - At the travel agency/En la agencia de viajes

a. Listen to the travel information assistant replying to three customers and indicate in which order the dialogues are heard by numbering the maps below.

A

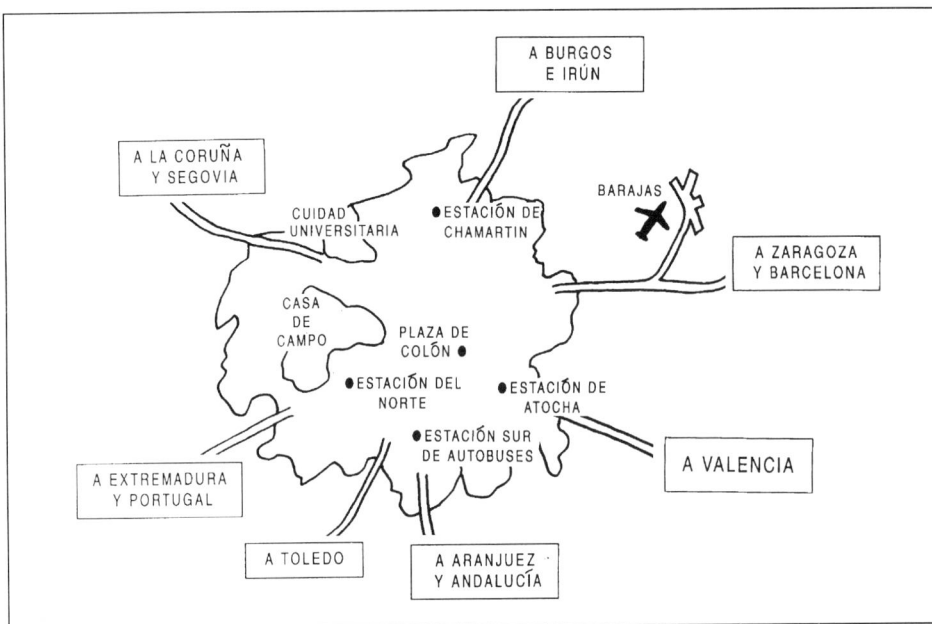

Aeropuerto de Barajas, Madrid

B

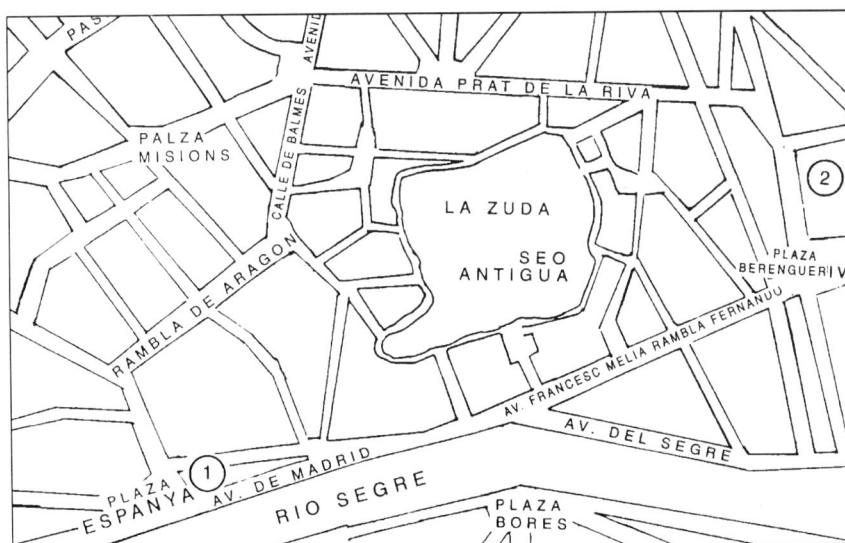

Estación de ferrocarril y estación de autobuses de Lérida (Lleida).

C **VALENCIA**

Playa de la Malvarrosa

Mar Mediterráneo

Playa de Levante

Pza Armada Española

C. Doctor Lluch

Docto J. Dominé

Avda del Puerto

MUELLE DEL GRAO

DARSENA INTERIOR

ESTACION MARITIMA

ESTACION DEL GRAO

Puente de

Astilleros

DARSENA DE LEVANTE

TERMINAL DE CONTENEDORES

DARSENA SUR

DARSENA NORTE

DIQUE SUR

Camino del Canal

N O E S

ESCALA GRAFICA

0   200   400   600 m

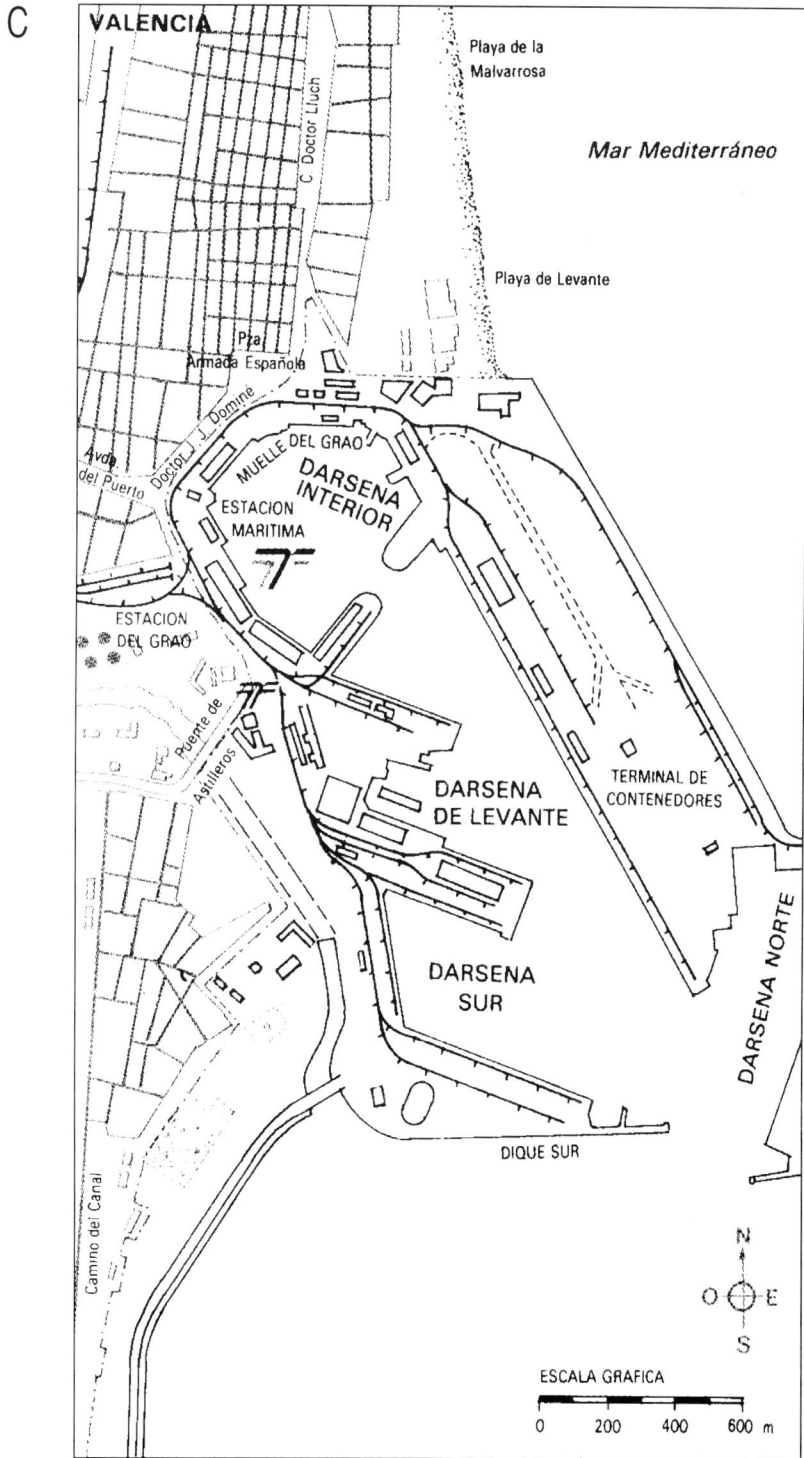

Estación marítima de Valencia

b. Now listen to the three dialogues again and fill in the gaps in the texts below with the appropriate words taken from the list below:

al lado; tomar; enfrente; cómo se va; dónde está; en coche; al final; de nada; al este; todo recto; al este; tome.

1. - Oiga, ¿............................ la estación marítima, por favor?

   - *La estación marítima está .... de la ciudad. Tome la Avenida del Puerto y siga hasta el final. Allí, ... de la estación del Grao, está la estación marítima.*

   - Gracias.

   - *No hay de qué.*

2. - Oiga, por favor. ¿............................ al aeropuerto de Barajas?

   - *Lo mejor para ir al aeropuerto es .... un autobús en la plaza de Colón, está en el centro de Madrid. Hay autobuses continuamente. También se puede ir .... Barajas está al este de la ciudad, a 16 km por la carretera de Zaragoza.*

   - Gracias.

   - ....

3. - Por favor, ¿Para ir a la estación del tren?

   - *La estación de ferrocarril está .... de la ciudad. .... la avenida Francesc Meliá, continúe .... por la Rambla Fernando y ...., en la plaza Berenguer IV, está la estación.*

   - ¿Y la estación de autobuses?

   - *Está en el centro. .... del río, en la plaza de Espanya.*

   - Muchas gracias.

   - *De nada. Adiós*

HOW TO SAY IT

¿Cuánto tiempo	**dura**	**el viaje?**		How	long	does the journey	take?
¿Cuántas horas	**lleva**				many hours		

El viaje	**dura**	**doce horas.**	The	journey	takes twelve hours.
La travesía	**lleva**			crossing	

Puede ir	**directamente.**	You can go	directly.	
	por **Inglaterra.**		via	England.
	vía **Francia.**			France.

¿Dónde está	**la estación marítima?**	Where is	the ferry terminal?
	el aeropuerto?		the airport?

Está	**en el centro**	**de la ciudad.**	It is in the city centre.
	al sur		to the south of the city.

¿Cómo se va a la estación de ferrocarril (RENFE)?	How do I get to the train station?

PROVIDING INFORMATION ABOUT DEPARTURE AND ARRIVAL TIMES
ISSUING TRAVEL DOCUMENTS

Listening 3 - At the travel agency/En la agencia de viajes

Listen to the travel agent telling tourists how to get from Madrid to various European cities and fill in the grid below.

De Madrid a:	en autocar-en autobús/ by coach duración/duration	en tren/by train duración/duration	en avión/by plane duración/duration
1. París			
2. Roma			
3. Lisboa			

Listening 4

a. Now listen to the end of the conversations between the travel agent and the tourists. In the following time-tables tick the departure and arrival times of the train, 'plane or coach they are going to take.

1.

RENFE	MADRID - PARÍS	
Madrid - Chamartín	18,15	19,30
Vitoria	23,41	
Irún	02,03	02,50
Burdeos	05,51	04,35
París - Austerlitz	10,30	08,30

	PARIS - MADRID	
París - Austerlitz	20,00	18,05
Burdeos	00,29	22,23
Irún	02,56	01,05
Vitoria		03,52
Madrid - Chamartín	08,32	09,50

2.

IBERIA

MADRID (Barajas) — ROMA (Fiumicino)

Salida		Llegada	
	09,30		11,50
	15,20		17,40
	15,50		18,05
	20,10		22,25

ROMA (Fiumicino) — MADRID (Barajas)

Salida		Llegada	
	08,00		10,20
	12,50		15,10
	19,05		21,25
	19,30		22,00

3.

```
AUTOBUSES PENÍNSULA

           MADRID - LISBOA

Itinerario              horario

Madrid            10,00      22,00
Badajoz           15,30      03,30
Elvas             16,00      04,00
Estremoz          16,45      04,45
Setúbal           18,15      06,15
Lisboa            19,00      07,00

           LISBOA - MADRID

Itinerario              horario

Lisboa            10,00      22,00
Setúbal           10,45      22,45
Estremoz          12,15      00,15
Elvas             13,00      01,00
Badajoz           13,30      01,30
Madrid            19,00      07,00
```

b. Listen again to the end of the conversations and complete the following tickets with the missing details.

1.

RENFE	Billete + litera		Clase: 2
IDA	**Hora**	**VUELTA**	**Hora**
Salida: Madrid - Chamartín	....	**Salida**:	....
Llegada:	08,30	**Llegada**: Madrid - Chamartín	08,32
Fecha:		**Fecha**:	
Reserva de literas: No. 31			
No. 32			
		Pesetas:	

2.

IBERIA			
Nombre:			
	Fechas	**Horas**	
		Salida	Llegada
De: MADRID - Barajas	17/5	....	18,05
A:			
A: MADRID - Barajas	....	19,05	....
Tarifa: .... ptas.			

3.

AUTOBUSES PENÍNSULA			
MADRID - LISBOA - MADRID			

Ida	Fecha	Hora	**Vuelta**	Fecha	Hora
Salida de Madrid:	....	....	Salida de Lisboa:	6/12	....
Llegada a Lisboa:		07,00	Llegada a Madrid:		....
Precio: .... ptas.					

HOW TO SAY IT

Hay varios vuelos.	There are several flights.
Hay | **un tren** | **a las** | **diez.** | **otro** | | **dos.**	There is | one train | at | ten. | another | | two.
El primer | **avión** | **sale a las doce.** **El último** | **autobús** |	The first | 'plane | leaves at twelve. The last | bus |
El autocar | **sale** | **el** | **sábado.** | **llega** | | **viernes.**	The coach | leaves | on | Saturday. | arrives | | Friday.
El barco | **sale de Santander.** | **llega a Plymouth.**	The boat | leaves from Santander. | arrives in Plymouth.
Usted | **sale** | **el veinte.** | **va** | **en barco.**	You | leave | on the twentieth. | go | by boat
Usted | **vuelve** | **el doce.** | **regresa** |	You come back on the twelfth.

SELLING AND BOOKING TRAVEL AND TOURS

Listening 5 - At the travel agency/En la agencia de viajes

Listen to a tourist enquiring about holidays in Cuba and tick the correct answers below.

1. The only way to travel from Spain to Cuba is with Iberia.

   TRUE ⬜   FALSE ⬜

2. Iberia has a flight to Cuba on:

   a)   Friday, Saturday and Sunday

   b)   Tuesday, Thursday and Sunday

   c)   Monday, Wednesday and Sunday

3. The tourist wants to stay in Cuba for:

   a)   7 days

   b)   8 days

   c)   9 days

4. The trip costs:

    a)   119,300 ptas
    b)   119,600 ptas
    c)   117,300 ptas

5. Which of the following meals are included in the price of the trip?

    a)   breakfast
    b)   lunch
    c)   dinner

6. What does **pensión completa** mean?

    a)   accommodation with one meal
    b)   accommodation with two meals
    c)   accommodation with three meals

7. Which of the following means of transport are included in the price?

    a)   'plane and car
    b)   'plane and coach
    c)   'plane and train

8. Which of the following excursions are optional?

    a)   Cayo Largo and Santiago de Cuba
    b)   Cayo Largo and Varadero
    c)   Cayo Largo and Cayo Coco

HELP!

volar	to fly
alojamiento	accommodation
la comida	the meal
la comida/el almuerzo	lunch

Listening 6

Listen to the end of the conversation between the same travel agent and tourist and complete the registration form below.

AGENCIA DE VIAJES AZUL

HOJA DE INSCRIPCIÓN

RELLÉNESE CON MAYÚSCULAS (*)

Destino: CUBA

Salida de: MADRID

Fecha de salida: ....   **Fecha de vuelta:** ....

Viaje: AL CORAZÓN DE CUBA

Participantes:

Apellidos	Nombre	Fecha de nacimiento	Nacionalidad	Profesión

Dirección: ....

....

Teléfono particular: ....   Teléfono del trabajo: ....

Cantidad a pagar   ....

☐ en efectivo   ☐ con tarjeta de crédito   ☐ con talón

(*) complete in block capitals

LANGUAGE PRACTICE

Exercise 1

a. Replace the drawings below with the corresponding Spanish word.

1. -Puede ir a Italia en .... o en ....

   -¿Se puede ir en .... ?

   -Sí, también es posible.

2. -¿Prefiere visitar la zona en .... o a .... ?

   -Prefiero visitarla en ....

   -De acuerdo. ¡Buen viaje!

b. Now fill in the following sentences with **en, a** or **de**.

1. El viaje .... barco dura unas catorce horas. .... avión sólo lleva dos horas.

2. El autocar sale .... Barcelona .... las 8,00 .... la tarde y llega .... Bruselas al día siguiente.

3. .... Sevilla .... Madrid es posible viajar .... el AVE (Tren de Alta Velocidad). Se puede ir .... noche o .... día.

Exercise 2

Listen to the examples.

a.

ir - Ginebra:	Usted **va a** Ginebra.
llegar - la estación:	Usted **llega a la** estación.
llegar - el aeropuerto:	Usted **llega al** aeropuerto.

Note: a + el = al

Listen to the cues on the tape and build up sentences as in the examples.

1. ir - Colombia
2. llegar - el puerto
3. ir - el hotel
4. llegar - San Sebastián
5. llegar - la ciudad

b.

volver - Berlín	Usted **vuelve de** Berlín
salir - el hotel	Usted **sale del** hotel
regresar - la excursión	Usted **regresa de la** excursión

Note: de + el = del

1. salir - el centro
2. volver - Argentina
3. regresar - Suiza
4. salir - la estación
5. volver - Marruecos
6. regresar - el viaje

Exercise 3 - At the tourist office/En la oficina de turismo

You are working at the information desk of a major tourist office. Give the following information to tourists enquiring about transport.

Then check the answers on the tape.

1.

RENFE	
AVE No. 214	
Madrid - Estación Puerta de Atocha	14,00
Sevilla - Santa Justa	16,25

2.

SPAINAIR MADRID (Barajas) - BARCELONA (Prat del Llobregat)		
	Salida Madrid	Llegada Barcelona
De lunes a viernes	07,00	08,00
	17,30	18,30
	22,45	23,45
Sábado	07,00	08,00
Domingo	14,15	15,15
	17,45	18,45
	22,45	23,45

3.

AUTOBUSES MADRID - LA CORUÑA		
	Salida Madrid	Llegada La Coruña
Diario	10,15	19,15
	* 14.00	23,00
	21,30	06,30
* Excepto los domingos y festivos		

Exercise 4 - At the travel agency/En la agencia de viajes

The travel agency **Arenas** has just published its new brochure. Before you can advise tourists, check if you understand the description of following hotel options in Spain by answering **en inglés** (in English) the questions below.

1. HOTEL TORREQUEBRADA

HOTEL TORREQUEBRADA
H *****   Benalmádena-Costa
Situación: Al borde del Mar Mediterráneo. A pocos mts. del campo de golf de Torrequebrada.
Habitaciones: Con baño. TV color con conexión vía satélite. teléfono, mini-bar. aire acondicionado y terraza vista al mar.
Complementos: Centro de convenciones, restaurantes. cafeterías. casino. Peluquería, sauna, masajes, squash, jacuzzi, tenis. piscina climatizada.

PRECIOS POR PERSONA Y DIA EN HABITACION DOBLE

HOTELES	TEMPORADAS	REGIMEN DE ESTANCIA			OBSERVACIONES
		HABITACION Y DESAYUNO	MEDIA PENSION	PENSION COMPLETA	
BENALMADENA					
TORREQUEBRADA H***** AGP 5 BENALMADEN TORREQUEBRADA (HA)	1/11 al 25/3 y 6/4 al 30/4	7.560	10.710	13.230	Niños: hasta 14 años gratis alojamiento y desayuno. 2 niños (solos en doble) 25% dcto.

a) List three sports named in the brochure. ....

b) What does the sum of 13,230 ptas relate to? ....

c) What is free for children under 14? ....

d) Does the hotel have a swimming pool? ....

e) What is situated a few metres away from the hotel? ....

f) In which town is the hotel situated? ....

2. HOTEL KENIA NEVADA

HOTEL KENIA NEVADA****

Hotel de nueva construc-ción, en el más puro estilo alpino y de ambiente fami-liar. Cuenta con 68 habita-ciones dobles exteriores con baño, teléfono, radio, TV con antena parabólica y vídeo, minibar y caja de seguridad, y algunas con terraza y salón privado. Complementa sus instala-ciones con 2 restaurantes, bar, cafetería, piscina climatizada, gimnasio, pista de squash, jacuzzi, sauna, sola-rium, garaje y parking.

PRECIO POR PERSONA DE DOMINGO A SABADO 7 DIAS/6 NOCHES				
	REG ALOJAMIENTO	DOBLE	TRIPLE	CUADRUPLE
Apertura-17-12,	AD	28.990	25.400	22.600
9/4 -Cierre	MP	46.250	42.750	38.400
9/1-12/2	AD	-	-	-
20/2-26/3	MP	54.650	50.500	45.400
18/12-8/1, 13-19/2	AD	-	-	-
27/3-9/4	MP	67.950	62.900	56.500

DESCUENTO NIÑOS: Menores de 12 años 50%. **CENA DE FIN DE AÑO:** Obli-gatoria a liquidar en su agencia de viajes. Adultos 14.400, niños 7.200

* AD = Alojamiento y Desayuno
* MP = Media Pensión

a) How many bedrooms are there in this hotel?

b) Is it a new building?

c) How much is the discount for children?

d) Give the opening and closing dates of the season.

e) What does the amount of 14,400 ptas refer to?

f) The rates quoted are for how many nights?

Exercise 5 - At the travel agency/En la agencia de viajes

You are working at the information desk of a travel agency in Dublin when a Spanish client arrives. Answer the questions as prompted below. You play the part of the assistant.

DUBLÍN - BILBAO (vía Barcelona)				
Diario	Hora		Hora	* Precio
Salida Dublín	12,25	Llegada Barcelona	15,45	£285
Salida Barcelona	16,30	Llegada Bilbao	17,30	
* Tasas de aeropuerto £5 no incluidas en el precio.				

Visitor: Buenas tardes.

Assistant: *Greet the client and offer help.*

Visitor: Quisiera ir a Bilbao a finales de este mes.

Assistant: *Ask the client if she wants to travel by 'plane or by boat.*

Visitor: ¿Podría decirme cuánto dura la travesía en barco?

Assistant: *Tell her that the crossing takes 30 hours.*

Visitor: Ya. ¿Y cuánto cuesta el viaje?

Assistant: *Tell her that it costs £225.*

Visitor: Creo que prefiero ir en avión. ¿Podría informarme de los precios y las fechas de los vuelos?

Assistant: *Give her the information (see information sheet).*

Visitor: ¿Están las tasas de aeropuerto incluidas en el precio?

Assistant: *Give the client the information (see information sheet).*

Visitor: Muy bien. ¿Puedo reservar un billete para el 30 de marzo, por favor?

Assistant: *Ask her name.*

Vistor: María Moreno. M-O-R-E-N-O.

Assistant: *Give the client her reservation, thank her and say good-bye.*

Note: Check the answers on the tape, but remember that they are model answers only.

ON THE MOVE

Spain has a well-developed network of train and coach services, both of which offer a reliable and not too expensive mode of getting from A to B. The coach is generally a bit cheaper, and is probably preferable for short journeys, while for the long haul the comfort of the train makes it worth the extra few pesetas. Choose the railway, and you'll meet RENFE.

RENFE is the Spanish railway company. The variety of different train services they offer can be bewildering, so check carefully how long each journey takes before reserving a seat. Normal trains are called — somewhat undeservedly — *expreso* or *rápido.* The most common express trains are called *talgo,* and are correspondingly more expensive. Another possibility, especially for a long journey, is to travel overnight. If you do so it's a good idea to take a *litera*, a kind of shelf-bed, with six per compartment. More expensive *coche-camas* (beds) sleep two to a compartment.

If you're really in a hurry, then the best option is the high-speed AVE *(tren de alta velocidad).* There's only one problem: you have to be travelling from Madrid to Seville or vice versa!

Don't forget to check for any discounts when planning your journeys - carefully chosen departure times can make for big reductions in ticket prices. *Días Azules* (blue days) are discount days on the RENFE calendar. Also be careful to check the service if you are travelling on a Sunday or a public holiday. These days are marked *Domingos y Festivos* and have a very different timetable to working days *(laborables).* If you are travelling on a holiday weekend, be sure to book in advance or risk being disappointed at the station.

Driving

Much of "real Spain" is best got at by car - the small *pueblos* and the hidden interior which the majority of tourists will never see. Car hire is relatively inexpensive in Spain, so if possible it's worth hiring one and getting off the beaten track. However, if you're planning on driving in one of the big cities like Madrid or Barcelona, steel your nerves - it is not for the faint-hearted.

Fortunately both the above cities have good metro systems, which are cheap and easy to use. Taxis too are a good option, as they are much cheaper than you would expect and are in plentiful supply.

Objectives

At the end of this unit you will be able to:

● Greet and welcome visitors

● Provide information on activities and facilities

● Provide information on regulations and safety rules

● Ask someone what he or she would like to do

● Suggest doing something

● Ask about medical conditions and symptoms

● Respond to requests for assistance

(R S)

PROVIDING INFORMATION ON ACTIVITIES, FACILITIES AND REGULATIONS

Listening 1 - In a holiday village/En una ciudad de vacaciones

a. Listen to the leisure assistant greeting and welcoming a group of tourists who have just arrived at the holiday village of Castlegregory. On the vocabulary list below, tick the activities available in the village.

	Piscina cubierta/Indoor swimming pool	☐
	Piscina exterior/Outdoor swimming pool	☐
	Vela/Sailing	☐
	Windsurf (plancha a vela)/Windsurfing	☐
	Esquí naútico/Water skiing	☐
	Submarinismo/Scuba diving	☐
	Piragüismo en canoa/Canoeing	☐
	Piragüismo en kayak/Kayaking	☐
	Campo de golf/Golf course	☐

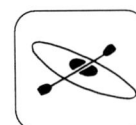

Pesca/Fishing ❏

Senderismo/Hill walking ❏

Montañismo/Mountaineering ❏

Escalada/Rock climbing ❏

Paseos en bicicleta/Cycling ❏

Bicicleta todo terreno (BTT)/Mountain biking ❏

Equitación/Horse riding ❏

Paseos en caballo/Pony trekking ❏

Tiro con arco/Archery ❏

Musculación/Weight training ❏

Baile/Dancing ❏

b. Listen again and indicate whether the statements below are true or false.

	True	False
1. There is a bureau de change in the village.		
2. It is only 7 minutes walk from sandy beaches.		
3. There are two 18-hole golf courses.		
4. Pets are not allowed.		
5. There is a children's play area.		
6. There are laundry facilities.		

Listening 2 - At the hotel leisure centre/En el hotel club

Listen to the receptionist at the desk of this hotel leisure centre and try to list all the rules and regulations he is indicating to the visitor by completing the sentences below **en español** (in Spanish).

The following words will help you to do so:

fumar, el gimnasio, la entrada, los animales, el gorro de baño.

1. .... es obligatorio.

2. .... no pueden entrar en la piscina.

3. Los niños pueden usar ....

4. .... en la discoteca está prohibida a los menores de 16 años.

5. Solamente se puede .... en la sala de juegos.

PROVIDING INFORMATION ON ACTIVITIES AND REGULATIONS AND SUGGESTING ACTIVITIES.

Listening 3 - At the adventure centre/En el centro de aventuras.

a. Listen to the leisure assistant suggesting possible activities to a group of visitors and fill in their programme for the day's activities.

> **TIGLIN ADVENTURE CENTRE**
> LUNES 13 DE MAYO
>
> Mañana: ....
>
> 12,30 - 14,00: Almuerzo
>
> Tarde: ....
>
> 20,30: Cena
>
> 22,00: ....

b. Now listen again and list **en español** all six activities mentioned in the conversation.

1. ....

4. ....

2. ....

5. ....

3. ....

6. ....

HOW TO SAY IT

¿Podría | ayudarle en algo? **¿Puedo** |	Can I help you?
¿Qué | **le gustaría** | **hacer?** | **prefiere** |	What would you | like | to do? | prefer |
No | **olvide** | **el chaleco salvavidas.** | **olviden** |	Don't forget your life | jacket. | jackets.
Lleve | **el gorro de baño.** **Lleven** | **la raqueta.**	Take your | swimming cap. | racquets.

Listening 4 - At the outdoor pursuit centre/En el centro de aventuras.

a. Listen to the receptionist giving information to a newly arrived visitor about some activities and the equipment required for each. Match the sport with the required equipment.

1. Natación

2. Equitación

3. Esquí acuático

4. Vela

5. Tenis

6. Windsurf

7. Submarinismo

8. BTT (Bicicleta Todo Terreno)

a) esquíes

b) raqueta

c) chaleco salvavidas

d) botella

e) tabla o plancha

f) gorro de baño

g) casco

h) botas

b. Listen again and indicate whether or not you must hire (**alquilar**) the items listed below.

	YES	NO		YES	NO
1. Los esquíes	☐	☐	5. La tabla	☐	☐
2. La raqueta	☐	☐	6. El gorro de baño	☐	☐
3. El chaleco salvavidas	☐	☐	7. El casco	☐	☐
4. La botella	☐	☐	8. Las botas	☐	☐

ILLNESSES AND INJURIES

Listening 5 - At the information session/En la reunión informativa

A tour guide is discussing health-related issues with a group of tourists who are planning a holiday in Colombia. Listen to the conversation and select the correct answers from the list below.

HELP!

cabeza
ojo
boca
garganta
mano
dedo
espalda
estómago
tobillo
los pies

tábano
mosca
mosquito

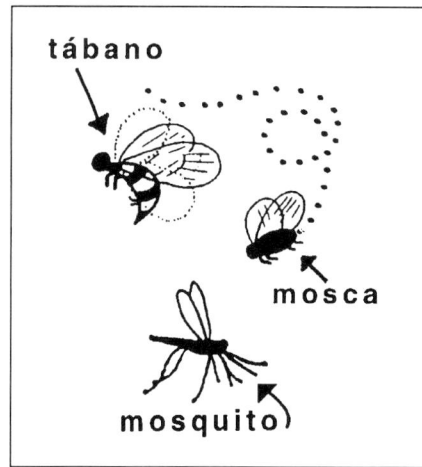

1. The group is going on a
  a. hill-walking holiday
  b. pony trekking holiday
  c. cycling holiday

2. One of the participants suffers from
  a. malaria
  b. hepatitis
  c. diabetes

3. Another participant is allergic to
  a. horses
  b. pollen
  c. mosquitoes

4. Another participant has problems with his
  a. throat
  b. back
  c. eyes

5. In Colombia there are lots of

a. flies
b. mosquitoes
c. wasps

6. The recommended vaccinations are

a. anti-tetanus
b. anti-malaria
c. anti-polio

Listening 6 - At the campsite/En el camping

a. The participants are now in The Andes and they have stopped at a campsite for the first night of their tour. Listen to the dialogues where the participants complain about a variety of ailments and indicate in which order the complaints are made by numbering each illustration as in example A.

A . (Cut finger) 4

B . (Broken ankle)

C . (Headache)

D. (Upset stomach)

E . (Mosquito bites)

F. (Toothache)

b. Listen to the same passages again and choose the answer which matches the statement or question on the left.

1. Me encuentro mal del estómago.
2. Me duele mucho la cabeza.
3. Tengo un dolor de muelas.
4. Me he cortado un dedo.
5. Creo que me he roto el tobillo.
6. ¿Tiene algo para las picaduras de mosquitos?

a. Voy a llamar una ambulancia.
b. Si quiere, llamo a un dentista.
c. Tome estas pastillas.
d. Hay que desinfectarlo.
e. Use esta crema.
f. Tenga una aspirina.

¿Está bien de salud?	Are you in good health?
¿Tiene | algún problema de salud? | alguna | enfermedad? | alergia?	Have you any | health problems? | illnesses? | allergies?
¿Qué le duele?	Where does it hurt you?
Tome | esta crema. | estas pastillas. | una tirita. | un algodón.	Take | this cream. | these tablets. | a sticking plaster. | some cotton wool.
Voy a llamar | al médico. | Si quiere, llamo | a una ambulancia.	I'll call | a doctor. | If you want, I'll call | an ambulance.
No se preocupe.	Don't worry.
Me encuentro mal.	I feel ill.
Me duele la cabeza. | Tengo dolor de cabeza.	I have a headache.
Me duelen las muelas. | Tengo dolor de muelas.	I have a toothache.

LANGUAGE PRACTICE

Exercise 1

Listen to the examples.

Hacer aerobic   **Puede** hacer aerobic.

Jugar al golf   **Puede** jugar al golf.

Listen to the cues on the tape and build up sentences based on the examples.

(Remember to **stop** the tape at the signal.)

1. Hacer footing
2. Hacer senderismo
3. Jugar al tenis
4. Jugar al squash
5. Hacer escalada

6. Hacer equitación
7. Jugar al fútbol
8. Jugar al baloncesto
9. Hacer orientación
10. Hacer submarinismo

Exercise 2

Here you have a list of activities and facilities available in **Cala Montjoy** in Cataluña. With the help of the extract from the Cala Montjoy brochure, write the Spanish equivalents of the words below.

1. Scuba diving ....

2. Laundry ....

3. Children's playground ....

4. Archery ....

5. Windsurfing ....

6. Bureau de change ....

7. Weight training ....

8. Fishing ....

9. Tennis ....

10. Car park ....

BAR Y TERRAZA JUNTO AL MAR
BOUTIQUE SHOPPING
CAJA FUERTE
CAMBIO DE MONEDAS
DISCOTECA
ENFERMERIA
ESTANCIA EN BUNGALOW
BAR KARAOKE
LAVANDERIA
MINI-GOLF
PARKING
PARQUE INFANTIL
PENSION ALIMENTICIA COMPLETA
PESCA DEPORTIVA
PISTAS PARA COMPETICIONES DEPORTIVAS
PLANCHAS A VELA
PLAYA VIGILADA
PRENSA DIARIA
SALA PING-PONG
SERVICIO DE MONITORES
SQUASH
TEATRO AL AIRE LIBRE (ESPECTACULOS)
TENIS
TIRO AL ARCO - TIRO CARABINA
SUBMARINISMO
SALA DE MUSCULACION

PRECIOS ESPECIALES
PARA GRUPOS Y
TERCERA EDAD

Cala Montjoy

Exercise 3

Study the leaflet of the activity holiday offered by **Estación de Montaña Manzaneda,** in **Galicia,** and answer the questions **en inglés** (in English).

JORNADAS DE MONTAÑA

DURACION: Un día y un máximo de cinco días. Domingo noche a viernes tarde. Temporada baja.	**EMPLAZAMIENTO:** Estación de Montaña Manzaneda.	**ALOJAMIENTO:** En Apartamentos "Galicia"

Para hacer más agradable la estancia en la Estación, los acogidos a esta oferta podrán disfrutar, cada día de estancia, de dos horas de una de las actividades siguientes: Tenis, baloncesto, bicicletas, caballos, piscina cubierta y climatizada o rocódromo, según las disponibilidades y programas de la Estación y en caso de que la climatología lo permita. Estas dos horas diarias podrán ser de esquí, incluyendo remontes, material y clases de esquí. También podrán disfrutar libremente de la montaña y el entorno de la Estación, haciendo footing y senderismo en caminos y circuitos señalizados y de nuestras instalaciones recreativas del Club Galleira (Sala de juegos, T.V., biblioteca, pub, discoteca y piscina climatizada).
Medios humanos: Monitores cualificados para el desarrollo de las actividades descritas.
Medios materiales: Los necesarios para estas actividades.

PRECIOS

4.210,-pts. persona/día, incluye: alojamiento, **media pensión alimenticia** (Desayuno y Almuerzo o Cena en Restaurante Autoservicio), utilización del Club Galleira y actividades descritas.
5.210,-ptas. persona/día, si se realiza alojamiento y **pensión alimenticia completa** (Desayuno, Almuerzo y Cena en Restaurante Autoservicio).

Suplemento ESQUI A TOPE

1.100,-pts. persona/día, cuando se condiciona la estancia a la nieve, realizando un cursillo específico de esquí. Pudiéndo anular en el caso de que no haya nieve esquiable.
FECHAS: Todas las semanas, excepto Temporada Alta.

1. What is the length of the special offer holiday?

....

2. Where do you stay on this holiday?

....

3. Name three sports referred to in the leaflet.

....

4. Which two activities take advantage of the mountain location?

....

5. What kind of swimming pool is available in Manzaneda?

....

6. Are the activities named in the brochure included in the prices quoted?

....

7. Which meals are included in the 4,210 pesetas price?

....

8. What does the rate of 1,100 pesetas refer to?

....

Exercise 4 - At the adventure centre/En el centro de aventuras

Look at the information sheet below and imagine you are working as a leisure assistant in Little Killary Adventure Centre. A group of Spanish holiday-makers has just arrived at the centre and you give them information about the activities and facilities available.

**LITTLE KILLARY
ADVENTURE CENTRE**

*Salruck, Renvyle, Co Galway
Tel: (095) 43411; Fax: (095) 43591*

Contact: Jamie and Mary Young

Open: February to November.

Activities: Sailing, canoeing, windsurfing, sea kayaking, water skiing, mountaineering, hill walking, rock climbing, orienteering, mountain biking, cycling, archery.

Age groups: 18 years plus

Courses: Multi-activity and specialist; weekend, mid-week and one week. Basic and advanced.

Rates: From 1/2 hour – week courses. Prices on application.

Accommodation: 34 in comfortable two or four-person rooms. Heating, showers, sauna, 2 lecture rooms and audio-visual aids.

General Information: All activities within walking distance of the centre. Wine Licence.

Adult centre in renovated farm building set around a courtyard beside Little Killary Bay.

Note: Check the answers on the tape but remember that they are model answers only.

Exercise 5 - In a holiday village/En una ciudad de vacaciones

You are a leisure assistant in a holiday village. A Spanish visitor is asking you about the various activities on offer in the village. Answer the questions as prompted below.

Visitor:	Hola. Buenos días.
Assistant:	*Return the greeting and offer your help.*
Visitor:	¿Qué actividades se pueden practicar por la mañana?
Assistant:	*Say that he can use the indoor swimming pool, do aerobics or windsurfing.*
Visitor:	¿Es obligatorio el gorro de baño en la piscina?
Assistant:	*Say that it is, but that he can hire one at the pool.*
Visitor:	Y por la tarde, ¿qué se puede hacer?
Assistant:	*Tell him that in the afternoon there is a mountain bike outing organised, or he can do horse riding or archery.*
Visitor:	¿Es necesario reservar plaza para la excursión en bicicleta todo terreno?
Assistant:	*Tell him that it is necessary.*
Visitor:	De acuerdo. Y por la noche, ¿hay algún espectáculo de luz y sonido?
Assistant:	*Tell him that, yes, there is a son et lumiére organised for 10.00pm but that he should buy tickets before 4.00pm.*
Visitor:	¿Cuánto cuestan las entradas?
Assistant:	*Tell him that the tickets are £8 each.*
Visitor:	Muy bien. Otra cosa, ¿tiene algo para el dolor de cabeza?
Assistant:	*Say yes and offer him aspirin tablets.*
Visitor:	Muchas gracias.
Assistant:	*Say he is welcome. Say good-bye and wish him a nice day.*

Note: Check the answers on the tape but remember that they are model answers only.

A COUNTRY OF SPORT

The Spanish have often been called a passionate people, and this is perhaps nowhere better illustrated than in their attitude to sport. Sport is followed with real intensity and successful sports figures are national heroes.

Fútbol is a good example. It is the most popular sport in Spain and a visit to one of the weekly matches is well worth experiencing. The two biggest clubs are Real Madrid and Barcelona. The natural rivalry is intensified by the regional tension between *Castilla* and *Catalunya,* and when the two meet the whole country tunes in to watch.

Although football is the biggest sport in Spain many other disciplines have become increasingly popular, often prompted by the international success of some Spanish sports person. *El ciclismo* (cycling) has benefited hugely from the Tour de France victories of Pedro Delgado and Miguel Induráin, with hordes of potential Pedros and Miguels pestering their parents for new bicycles to emulate their heroes.

Tennis too has benefited from the glory of its international stars among whom Sergi Bruguera, Arantxa Sánchez Vicario and Conchita Martínez have won major tournaments. Success breeds success and, in a country where sporting figures are so revered, such victories ensure a flood of new youngsters taking up the sport.

More traditional national sports have strong support too. The most famous — to some, infamous — indigenous sport is bull-fighting. While many find it deeply offensive, in Spain it is regarded as an art rather than a sport. To the aficionado there is nothing to replace the thrill of a good contest where the power and fury of *el toro* (the bull) is pitched against the skill and bravery of the *torero.* If a *torero* performs with exceptional courage and grace, he can be awarded the *orejas* (ears) of the bull as a trophy, while if the crowd considers the *torero* to have erred on the side of caution it's not uncommon for seat-cushions to be thrown into the *ruedo* (ring) in disgust. On very rare occasions a bull is spared if it has taken part in an exceptional *corrida* (bullfight).

Which brings us to ... bowls, or at least a version of it. *Bochas* is mostly the preserve of Spanish senior citizens, and is usually played in parks or indeed any place where a plot of common ground permits it. It's a leisurely pursuit, where metal or wooden balls are tossed to land near a marker, the winner being the player whose *bochas* (balls) lie closest to the marker. But don't be fooled - the look in the eyes of a contestant taking aim would probably make most *toreros* glad to get back to their bulls!

Objectives

At the end of this unit you will be able to:

- Provide information about excursions and tours

- Describe attractions, sights and scenery

- Make suggestions on places of interest, local crafts, and events

- Ask someone what he or she would like to do

- Suggest doing something

- Invite someone to do something

- Provide information and respond to enquiries about weather conditions

(R.S.)

PROVIDING INFORMATION ABOUT EXCURSIONS AND TOURS
DESCRIBING ATTRACTIONS, SIGHTS AND SCENERY

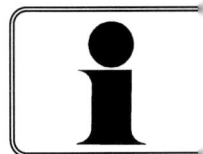

Listening 1 - At the local tourist office/En la oficina de turismo

The local tourist information officer in Santiago, in Galicia, is answering questions about possible tours in the area.

a. Listen to the first part of the dialogue so as to complete the following chart. Tick the correct information as you hear it.

1. The Santiago-Padrón-Noya tour takes

   a. one day
   b. two days
   c. three days

2. What length is the Santiago-Padrón-Noya tour?

   a. 40km
   b. 60km
   c. 70km

3. What distance is Vilagarcía from Santiago?

   a. 25km
   b. 35km
   c. 45km

4. What length is the Vilagarcía tour?

   a. 120km
   b. 150km
   c. 180km

5. Which is the most important harbour in this area?

   a. Catoira
   b. Vilagarcía
   c. Cambados

b. Listen again to the itineraries described by the tourist information officer, and fill in the gaps with the appropriate words from the following list:

famosas, está, alrededores, pueblos, cerca, zona, costa, mapa, total, gira.

- Hola, buenos días. Queremos quedarnos tres días por esta ....

    ¿Podría aconsejarnos alguna excursión interesante por los ....?

- Por supuesto. ¿Tienen un .... de la región?

- Sí, aquí tiene.

- Hay muchos sitios atractivos .... de Santiago. Pueden hacer, por

    ejemplo, una gira por Padrón y Noya. Es una excursión muy cómoda para

    hacer en un día, ya que recorren, en .... , unos 70km. También

    pueden hacer una .... por la ría de Vilagarcía, ... a

    45km de Santiago. Este recorrido lleva dos días porque es un poco más largo, unos

    180km en total. Es un viaje muy variado, en el que pueden visitar muchos pueblos

    pintorescos de la .... , como Catoira, con sus ....

    torres prerromanas; Vilagarcía, el puerto más importante de la ría; Cambados, un bello

    conjunto arquitectónico.

- ¿Hay playas en esos ....?

- Sí, desde luego. Es una costa llena de playas preciosas.

- Parece un viaje interesante. ¿Podría describirnos las rutas con más detalle? Es decir,

    qué lugares y monumentos se pueden visitar.

Listening 2 - At the local tourist office/En la oficina de turismo

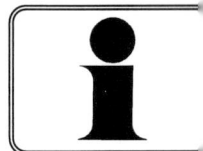

Listen to the second part of the dialogue, where the tourist information officer gives more details about the attractions in the Santiago area.

a. Tick the attractions listed below as often as you hear them.

	1	2	3	4
Iglesia *(Example)*	✔	✔	✔	✔
Isla				
Palacio				
Torre				
Panorámica				
Vino				
Playa				
Puente				
Pescado				
Balneario				

b. First, identify the meaning of the symbols below. Then, listen to the itineraries again. Looking at the map, identify which attractions correspond to each place on the route, and cross off the symbols that have been placed on the map by mistake.

Panorámica/ Viewing point

Iglesia/ Church

Balneario/ Spa

Palacio/ Palace

Torre/ Tower

Playa/ Beach

Puente/ Bridge

Pescado/ Fish

Vino/ Wine

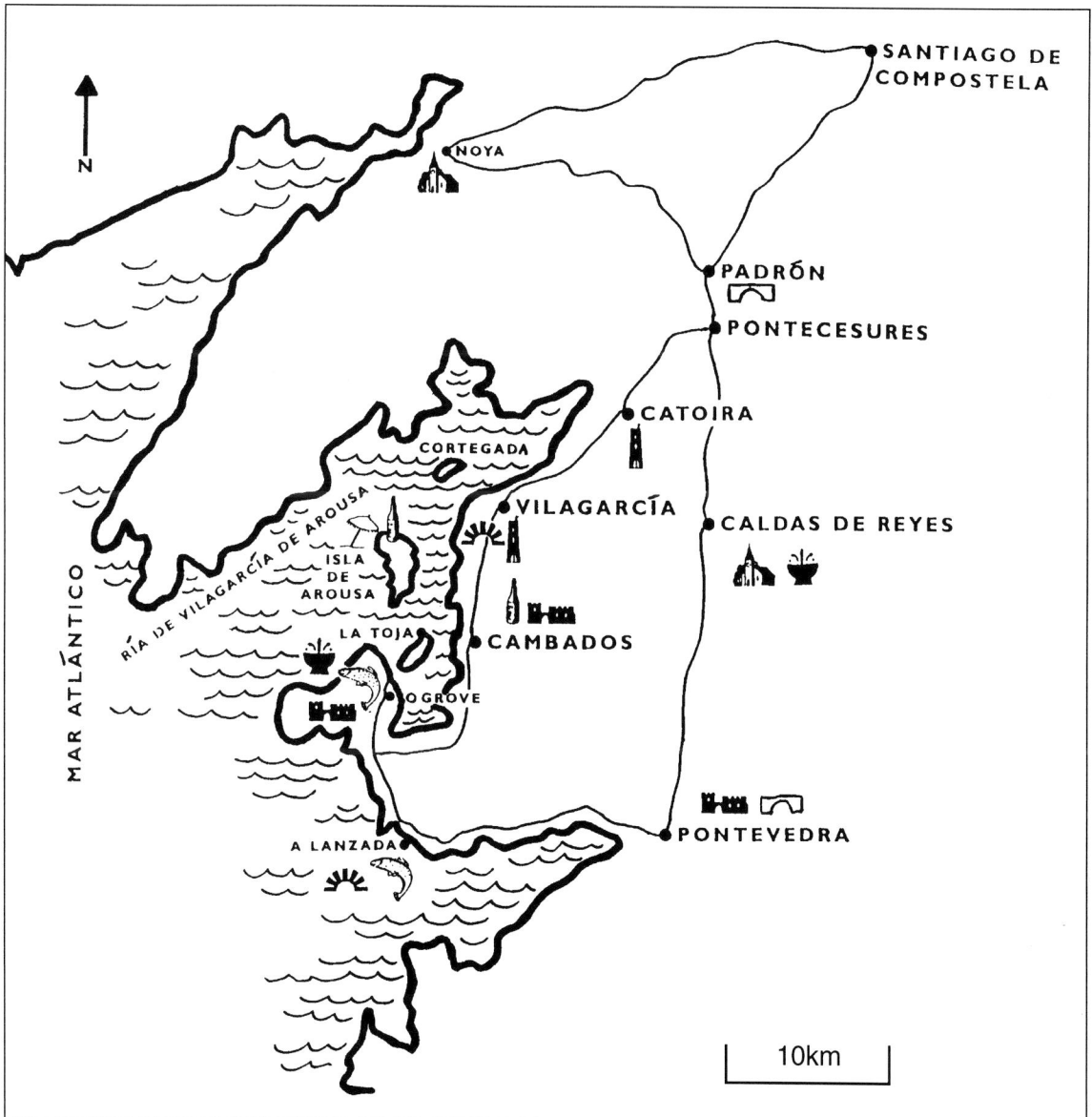

c. Listen again to the itineraries described by the tourist information officer and fill in the gaps with the following verbs or expressions, which may be used several times in the dialogue (replay the tape if you find it helpful). Then check your answers in the tapescript.

ver, volver, la siguiente, en dirección sur, hay, a la salida, ofrece, tomar, una visita obligada, se encuentra.

- Por supuesto. Para la primera excursión ustedes salen de Santiago por la carretera

   nacional 550, ... , y a 20km ....

   Padrón, en cuyo casco antiguo pueden visitar el Palacio del Obispo de Quito, la casa-

   museo de Rosalía Castro y un puente medieval que separa este pueblo de

   Pontecesures. .... de Padrón pueden.......................................

   la carretera de la derecha que lleva a Noya, donde hay varias iglesias y edificios de

   estilo románico. De allí pueden .... directamente a Santiago por

   una carretera comarcal.

- Y en la otra ruta, ¿cuáles son los pueblos más típicos?

- Bueno, para ir a Vilagarcía tienen que tomar la misma carretera, la de Padrón, y girar a

   la derecha a la salida de Pontecesures.

   El primer pueblo por el que pasan es Catoira, donde puede...

   las torres prerromanas. Vilagarcía es .... parada. Aparte del

   puerto pesquero, la ciudad .... muchas visitas interesantes,

   en particular los pazos o

   palacios de sus alrededores, la vista panorámica desde el monte Lobeira y dos islas:

   Cortegada y la Isla de Arousa, famosa por sus playas y cuevas.

   A unos 8km de Vilagarcía, ... Cambados, tal vez el pueblo

   más bonito de la ría. El palacio o Pazo de Fefiñanes es .... , *e igualmente imprescindible es probar el exquisito vino de la comarca, el Albariño,*

visitar las bodegas y ver las ruinas de la iglesia de Santa Mariña.

Más adelante, en O Grove, pueden degustar los diferentes platos de pescado y

marisco y pasar, por el puente, a la isla de La Toja, donde ....

un famoso balneario.

Muy cerca de O Grove tienen una de las playas más grandes de Galicia: A Lanzada.

Allí pueden .... una pequeña iglesia en un promontorio desde

el que se contempla, además, una bonita panorámica.   Desde A Lanzada es posible

... a Santiago pasando por Pontevedra, donde pueden

visitar numerosas iglesias y palacios, típicas tabernas y el puente del Burgo.

Por último, en la carretera de vuelta a Santiago, pueden parar en Caldas de Reyes,

donde hay otro conocido balneario.

HOW TO SAY IT

¿Cuál es la ruta más interesante? **¿Cuáles son los pueblos más típicos?**	Which | is the most interesting tour? | are the most typical towns?
Es imprescindible probar el vino.	You must try the wine.
¿Qué | lugares | se pueden | visitar? **| monumentos | | ver?**	Which | places | can you | visit? | monuments | | see?
Se | puede visitar el monasterio. **pueden visitar las bodegas.** **puede pasar por | Pontevedra.** **| el puente.**	You can | visit | the monastery. | the wine cellars. pass through Pontevedra. cross the bridge.
¿Dónde se puede | pescar? **| comer?**	Where can one | fish? | eat?
¿Qué | le | interesa | ver? **| les | | hacer?**	What are you interested in | seeing? | doing?

Listening 3 - At the travel agency/En la agencia de viajes

Listen to a travel agent giving information about a 2-week package tour in Mexico.

a. Indicate, on the map below, the itinerary of the tour called **"México paso a paso"**.

```
TIJUANA

                          EL PASO
                          CUIDAD
                          JUÁREZ              MÉXICO

                        CHIHUAHUA
      CUIDAD OBREGÓN

           CULIACÁN
                          MONTERREY      GOLFO DE
                                          MÉXICO

                     SAN LUIS DE POTOSÍ

             GUADALAJARA
                    CIUDAD DE MÉXICO            MÉRIDA
   OCÉANO PACÍFICO                                     CANCÚN
                      CUERNAVACA   VERACRUZ       CHICHÉN
                    TAXCO                          ITZÁ

                                      VILLAMERMOSA
                        ACAPULCO
                                                  MAR
                                                CARIBE
```

b. Listen again to the travel agent and tick the correct answer.

1. On the first day, you fly from Madrid to:
    a.   Ciudad de México
    b.   Cuernavaca
    c.   Acapulco

2. On the second day, you stay in a:
    a.   2 star hotel
    b.   3 star hotel
    c.   4 star hotel

3. On the third day, you go to Cuernavaca by:
    a.   train
    b.   coach
    c.   'plane

4. On the fourth day, you stay overnight in:
   a. Ciudad de México
   b. Taxco
   c. Cuernavaca

5. On the fifth day, you visit:
   a. a museum
   b. an island
   c. a casino

6. On the sixth day, in Acapulco, you go on:
   a. a tour of the city
   b. a cruise
   c. a visit to the museum

7. On the seventh day, you have a 'plane journey of:
   a. 2 hours
   b. 2 hours 30 mins
   c. 2 hours 15 mins

8. On the eighth day, you taste which local specialities?
   a. vegetables
   b. wine
   c. fish

9. On the ninth day, you visit:
   a. an archaeological site
   b. a cathedral
   c. a monastery

10. On the tenth day, you travel by:
   a. car
   b. train
   c. coach

11. On the eleventh day, you spend the night in:
   a. Cancún
   b. Chichén Itzá
   c. Uxmal

12. On the twelfth day, there is:
   a. a guided tour of Cancún
   b. a guided tour of Uxmal
   c. shopping in Cancún

13. On the thirteenth day, you visit:
   a. beaches
   b. villages
   c. mountains

14. On the fourteenth day, you arrive in Madrid:

    a.   in the morning

    b.   in the afternoon

    c.   at night

MAKING SUGGESTIONS ON PLACES OF INTEREST, LOCAL CRAFTS AND EVENTS

Listening 4 - On the coach/En el autocar

a. Listen to the guide answering questions about evening entertainment in Santiago, and tick the options in which the tourists express an interest:

1. un paseo tranquilo ☐
2. un restaurante muy famoso ☐
3. un concierto de música clásica ☐
4. un festival de música folclórica ☐
5. una actuación de ballet ☐
6. un recital de poesía ☐
7. una obra de teatro ☐
8. una discoteca ☐

b. Listen again to the dialogues and complete the table below with the corresponding entertainment:

A. **enfrente de la universidad** (Example)   (**2**) **un restaurante muy famoso**

B. en la catedral   ( )

C. por el casco antiguo   ( )

D. en las afueras de la ciudad   ( )

E. al lado de la catedral   ( )

c. Listen once more and write down the times at which the following events start:

1. el concierto de música clásica   ....

2. la actuación de ballet   ....

3. el recital de poesía   ....

4. la obra de teatro   ....

Listening 5 - In the hotel lobby/En el vestíbulo del hotel

a. Listen to the guide advising tourists on local crafts and specialities in Galicia and match the comments with the appropriate items as in the example below.

Example:

1.

> la artesanía de cuero
> la perfumería
> la platería — es muy original
> la cerámica — es famosa
> la alfarería
> la cestería

2.

> la tarta de almendra
> la tarta de manzana
> la tarta de queso   es exquisita
> la tarta helada   es deliciosa
> la tarta de chocolate
> la tarta de fresa

3.

> las prendas de lino
> los trabajos en madera
> los artículos de cristal   son típicos
> las muñecas de porcelana   son de excelente calidad
> los encajes
> los tapices

4.

> los vasos
> los objetos de plata
> las flores secas   son de diseño exclusivo
> las mantas   son un buen recuerdo
> los platos   son baratos y muy bonitos
> los cuencos

b. Listen to the four dialogues again and identify where the items in the dialogues can be found by circling the appropriate number(s) as in the example below.

Location	Dialogues			
en el mercado (Example)	1	2	3	④
al lado del hotel	1	2	3	4
en la Rúa del Villar	1	2	3	4
en la Rúa Nueva	1	2	3	4
por toda la ciudad	1	2	3	4
alrededor de la catedral	1	2	3	4
en el casco antiguo	1	2	3	4

GIVING INFORMATION AND REPLYING TO QUERIES ABOUT WEATHER CONDITIONS

Listening 6 - Weather forecast/El pronóstico del tiempo

a. Look at the map below and listen to the weatherwoman giving the weather forecast for Spain this morning. The symbols will help you to know what the weather forecast is for each area.

A

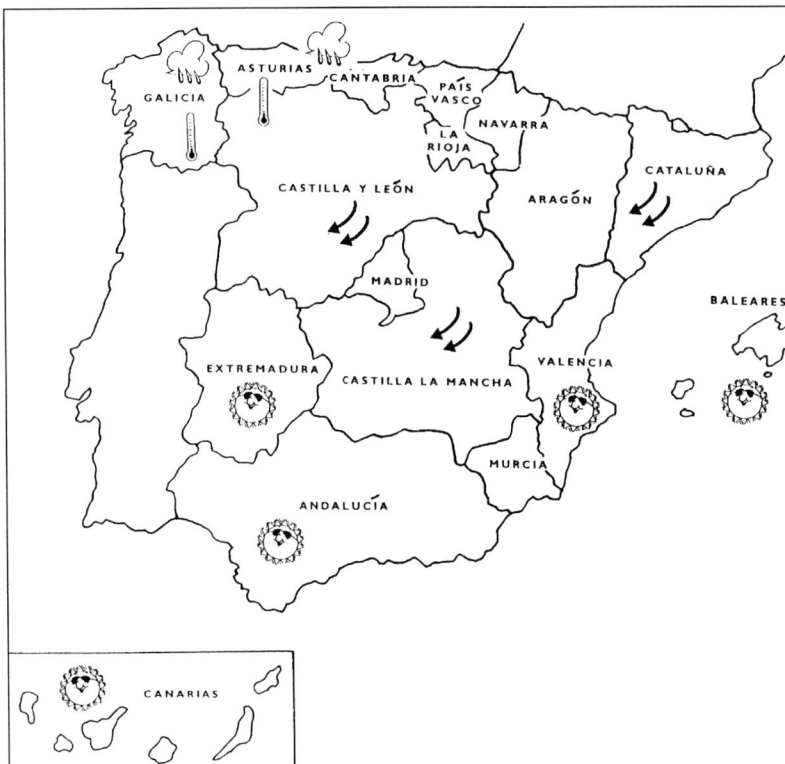

lluvias

frío

viento

buen tiempo

120

Now, complete these sentences using words from the key on the right of map A.

Esta mañana hace   ....   Esta mañana hay   ....

         ....

         ....

b. Look at this map and listen to the weather forecast for this evening. Then complete the sentences below the map.

B

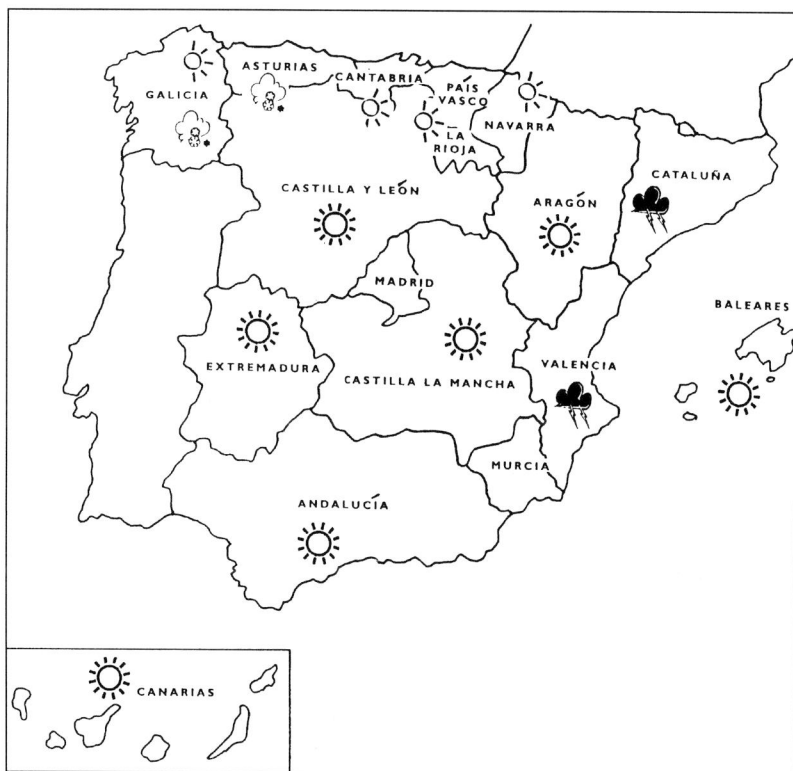

☀	sol
❄	nieve
⛈	tormentas
☼	fresco

Esta tarde hará   ....   Esta tarde habrá   ....

         ....

c. Look at this map and listen to the weather forecast for tomorrow. Then complete the sentences below the map.

C

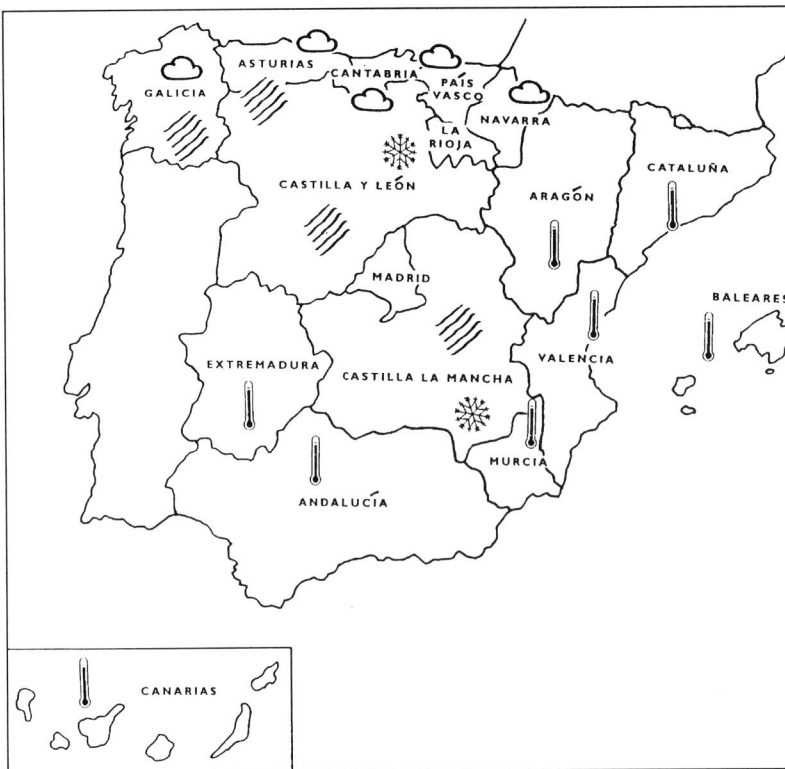

nubes	
calor	
heladas	
nieblas	

Mañana va a hacer ....   Mañana va a haber ....

....

....

d. Now, listen to the end of the weather forecast which covers the rest of Europe, and place the appropriate symbols in the spaces provided.

[Map of Europe with cities: Dublín, Londres, Amsterdam, Bruselas, Berlín, Praga, París, Viena, Berna, Madrid, Lisboa, Roma, Atenas, and weather symbol key on the right]

H OW TO SAY IT

¿Qúe tiempo hace?		What is the weather like?		
Hace	**buen tiempo.**	It is	fine.	
Va a hacer	**frío.**	is going to be	cold.	
Hará	**sol.**	will be	sunny.	
Hay	**tormenta.**	There is	a storm.	
Va a haber	**niebla.**	is going to be	fog.	
Habrá	**heladas.**	will be	frost.	
Llueve.		It is raining.		
Va a llover.		going to rain.		

Listening 7 - In the travel agency/En la agencia de viajes

a. Listen to the travel agent replying to enquiries about the weather in various holiday destinations in July. Tick the weather conditions and fill in the temperatures that you hear mentioned on the chart below.

Destino/ destination	Tiempo/weather					Temperaturas/temperatures		
	🌡	🌡	☀	🌧	🌬	Media/ average	Min	Max
1. Francia	✔			✔		22	12	34
2. Irlanda								
3. Grecia							—	—
4. Venezuela								
5. Canadá							—	—
6. Filipinas								
7. Islandia							—	
8. Egipto							—	—

b. Listen to the dialogues again and tick the recommended seasons to go to the following places:

	Primavera	Verano	Otoño	Invierno
1. Irlanda				
2. Venezuela				
3. Canadá				
4. Egipto				

LANGUAGE PRACTICE

Exercise 1

Listen again to the itineraries around **Padrón** and **Vilagarcía** in Listening 1 and 2 of this unit, and match the attractions mentioned with the corresponding descriptions (1-14).

Attractions: **sitios, excursión, recorrido, viaje, pueblos, torres, playas, iglesia, puente, edificios, visitas, vino, balneario, tabernas.**

1. .... de la comarca

2. .... de estilo románico

3. .... un poco más largo

4. típicas ....

5. .... interesantes

6. .... atractivos

7. famoso ....

8. .... medieval

9. .... preciosas

10. .... muy cómoda

11. pequeña ....

12. .... pintorescos

13. .... muy variado

14. .... prerromanas

Exercise 2

a. With the help of the map and key below, describe the following tour starting from **San Sebastián** (known is Basque as **Donostia**).

b. Now, use a map of your local area and describe aloud possible tour routes and visits.

Exercise 3

a. Describe the weather on the following weather map: **El tiempo en España.**

b. Use the weather map in today's newspaper to give the weather forecast.

Exercise 4

The document below presents a package holiday in Ireland. Study it and answer the questions which follow:

IRLANDA: GRANJAS

Un atractivo sistema de alojamiento en BED & BREAKFAST: "GRANJAS DE IRLANDA", que ofrecen habitaciones dobles con baño privado en unas instalaciones llenas de tradición y ambiente familiar.

Una forma original y nueva de hacer turismo por éste país.

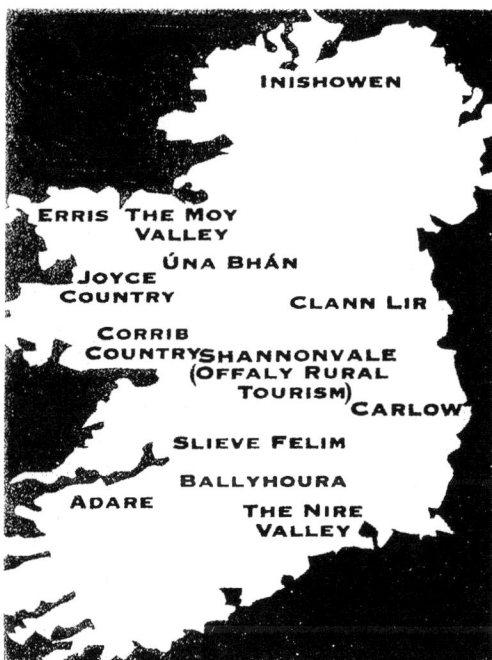

LAS REGIONES QUE INCLUYE EL PROGRAMA

Un total de trece regiones en donde es posible alojarse en una granja:

1.—**Inishowen,** extremo norte del Condado de Donegal.
2.—**Erris,** Noroeste del Condado de Mayo.
3.—**The Moy Valley,** valles del sur del Condado de Sligo.
4.—**Una Bhan,** ocupa el sur del Condado de Roscommon.
5.—**Joyce Country,** península de Connemara, en Gallway.
6.—**Corrib Country,** sur de Gallway y Lago Corrib.
7.—**Clann Lir,** Condado de los Lagos de Offaly.
8.—**Shannon Vale,** Valle del rio Shannon, en Offaly.
9.—**Carlow,** Condado del mismo nombre, al sur de Dublin.
10.—**Slieve Felim,** en el Condado de Tipperary.
11.—**Ballyhoura,** ocupa el sur del Condado de Limerick.
12.—**Adare,** ocupa el norte del Condado de Kerry.
13.—**Nire Valley,** la costa del Condado de Waterford.

COMO RESERVAR

Un sencillo sistema de reserva que le permitirá configurar su viaje a Irlanda "a medida".

Se eligen las regiones que se quieren visitar y el número de noches en cada una, con el número de habitaciones que se precisen.

En 48 horas tendrá la confirmación de cada una de las Granjas de los lugares seleccionados.

La estancia mínima en una Granja es de dos noches y el número mínimo de noches en un programa es de siete noches.

Precio: 5.000 pts. por persona en habitación doble/noche, e incluye:

— alojamiento en hab. doble con baño.
— desayuno irlandés.
— guía turística de las regiones y mapa.
— té de bienvenida.
— café irlandés de despedida.
— entradas gratuitas (una en cada región) para atracciones turísticas.
— tasas e impuestos.

EJEMPLO DE PROGRAMA A MEDIDA EN GRANJAS DE IRLANDA
DURACION 8 DIAS/7 NOCHES EN BASE A 2 PERSONAS

Día 1.º: Llegada a la 1.ª Granja, en el Condado de Nire Valley. Té de bienvenida. Alojamiento.
Día 2.º: Desayuno. Entrada gratuita a la fábrica de vidrio de Waterford. Alojamiento.
Día 3.º: Desayuno. Salida de la 1.ª Granja. Llegada a la 2.ª Granja en el Condado de Ballyhoura. Alojamiento.
Día 4.º: Desayuno. Día libre. Alojamiento.
Día 5.º: Desayuno. Entrada gratuita al Museo de Kilmallock. Alojamiento.
Día 6.º: Desayuno. Salida de la 2.ª Granja. Llegada a la 3.ª Granja en el condado de Offaly.
Día 7.º: Desayuno. Entrada gratuita al castillo de Birr. Alojamiento.
Día 8.º: Desayuno. Mañana libre. Café irlandés de despedida.
Precio: 35.000 pts. por persona.

1. What is the name of this tour? ....

2. What does the package include?

   a. ....   e. ....

   b. ....   f. ....

   c. ....   g. ....

   d. ....

3. Do guests spend each night in a different place? ☐ yes ☐ no

4. Which of the following attractions are mentioned in the brochure?
   a) visit to a crystal factory
   b) visit to a museum
   c) visit to a forest park
   d) visit to a castle

Exercise 5 - In the hotel lobby/En el vestíbulo del hotel

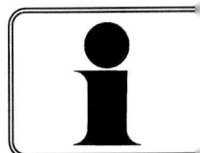

You are working as a guide. Some visitors are enquiring about evening entertainment and shopping in Dublin. Answer the questions as prompted below. You play the part of the guide.

Visitor 1: ¿Qué se puede hacer en Dublín por la noche?

Guide: *Say that there are many things to do. Ask the visitor what interests him.*

Visitor 1: Me gustaría ir a un restaurante y después escuchar música irlandesa.

Guide: *Say that there are many good restaurants near Grafton Street and that there are many pubs where you can listen to Irish music near the hotel.*

Visitor 1: ¿A qué hora cierran los pubs?

Guide: *Say that pubs close at 11.30pm*

Visitor 1: Vale. Gracias.

Guide: *Tell the visitor he is welcome and wish him a pleasant evening.*

Visitor 2: Me gustaría ir de compras mañana. ¿Hay alguna tienda cerca del hotel donde vendan artículos típicos de Irlanda?

Guide: *Tell the visitor that there are several shops near the hotel; that you recommend pottery, Aran jumpers (los jerseis de Arán) and Waterford Crystal (el cristal de Waterford).*

Visitor 2: Me gustaría encontrar algo original y no muy caro.

Guide: *Suggest he buy a tape (una cinta) of Irish music.*

Visitor 2: Me parece una buena idea. Muchas gracias.

Guide: *Tell the visitor he is welcome.*

Note: Check the answers on the tape, but remember they are model answers only.

FOOD, GLORIOUS FOOD

"Hunger is the best sauce in the world"

Miguel de Cervantes (Don Quixote Part II Chapter 5)

Spain is a good country in which to be hungry! With a wealth of fresh natural ingredients from land and sea and a variety of recipes and regional specialities, the hunger rarely lasts for long.

For example, when you order a drink you will usually get a small *tapa* — maybe a few olives or nuts, or a small piece of fish or meat. If you find a good bar, you can have a meal just by having a few glasses of beer! The quality and quantity of tapas is certainly not uniform throughout Spain. The big cities tend to give little for free, while the *tapas* bars of Granada, for instance, can be much more rewarding!

However, if you want a more substantial snack you usually have to pay for it. These bigger portions are called *raciones.* They can vary as much as the *tapas,* from the humble *tortilla* or Spanish omelette, (containing only egg, potato and onion contrary to popular belief) to freshly fried *calamares* (squid) or *gambas* (prawns).

Mariscos (sea food) is often the most expensive item on a Spanish menu. The people of Spain are renowned for their love of seafood, and special transport arrangements ensure that fish landed at port is rushed to the interior — Madrid in particular — to arrive beautifully fresh at the market place.

Although Spain doesn't have an immediately recognisable national cooking style like France or Italy, it has numerous special dishes which more than compensate. *Paella valenciana,* a dish of saffron rice with chicken and whatever else takes the cook's fancy, comes originally from Valencia on the Mediterranean coast. *Gazpacho,* a cold vegetable soup from Andalusia, is the perfect dish for hot southern summers while *Caldo gallego,* a soup of beans and potatoes cooked in the water of boiled bacon and cabbage, is more what you'd want on a winter's day in the north-west of Spain.

The variety is endless, and it would be a choosy palate indeed that got bored at the dinner table in Spain. There is one exception to the happy diner, however: vegetarians can have a tough time. Spaniards like their meat and, while fish-eaters will usually have an alternative, pure vegetarians have a greatly reduced choice in most Spanish restaurants.

Those partial to a big breakfast will also be a bit disappointed — many Spaniards content themselves with just a coffee, few have more than an accompanying *tostada* (bread toasted on an hot plate) or *churros* (strips of dough deep fried and sprinkled with sugar) which are dipped into coffee or hot chocolate before being eaten.

In any case, the rumbling tummy is rarely far from the safe haven of a *tapas* bar, which brings us back to our first point: appetites have short but happy lives in Spain!

Objectives

At the end of this unit you will be able to:

- Register delegates

- Provide information on programme events and other services

- Direct delegates and visitors inside and outside the centre or fair

- Provide information material

- Provide information on starting and finishing times of events

(A.L.M.)

DIRECTING DELEGATES INSIDE AND OUTSIDE THE CONFERENCE CENTRE
GIVING INFORMATION ON SERVICES

Listening 1 - At the conference centre/En un centro de congresos

Listen to one of the organisers at the conference reception desk answering queries from Spanish delegates, either on the phone or directly at the desk.

Listen carefully and tick the correct answers.

A. 1. The distance from the airport to the university is:
    a. 3km
    b. 5km
    c. 6km

   2. Which bus can you take from the airport to the university?
    a. 41A
    b. 41C
    c. 40

   3. The taxi fare from the airport to the university is:
    a. £12
    b. £10
    c. £10-12

B. 1. Which bus can you take from the airport to the city centre?
    a. 41
    b. 21
    c. 40

   2. How far is the bus stop from the hotel?
    a. 5 minutes' walk
    b. 10 minutes' walk
    c. 15 minutes' walk

C. 1. Which of these buses can you not take from the university to the city centre?
    a. 11
    b. 11A
    c. 13
    d. 19

2. How much is the bus fare from the university
   to the city centre?
   - a. 85 pence
   - b. 90 pence
   - c. 95 pence
   - d. £1.05

3. At what time is the last bus?
   - a. 11.00pm
   - b. 11.15pm
   - c. 11.30pm
   - d. 11.45pm

D. 1. How long does it take to get from the airport
      to the university by car?
      - a. 15 minutes
      - b. 25 minutes
      - c. 30 minutes

   2. Which is the nearest entrance coming from the airport?
      - a. Ballymun Road
      - b. Griffith Avenue
      - c. Collins Avenue

E. 1. What are the telephone numbers of Airport Express Taxis?
      - a. 836 01 11
      - b. 826 01 11
      - c. 827 55 37
      - d. 837 55 37

   2. To telephone Spain, what is the international country
      code?
      - a. 34
      - b. 24
      - c. 00

   3. What is the telephone number for international
      directory enquiries?
      - a. 1197
      - b. 1168
      - c. 1198

Listening 2 - At the conference centre/En un centro de congresos

a. Listen to one of the organisers at the reception desk answering queries from Spanish delegates. Then number on the map below the order in which the various places are mentioned.

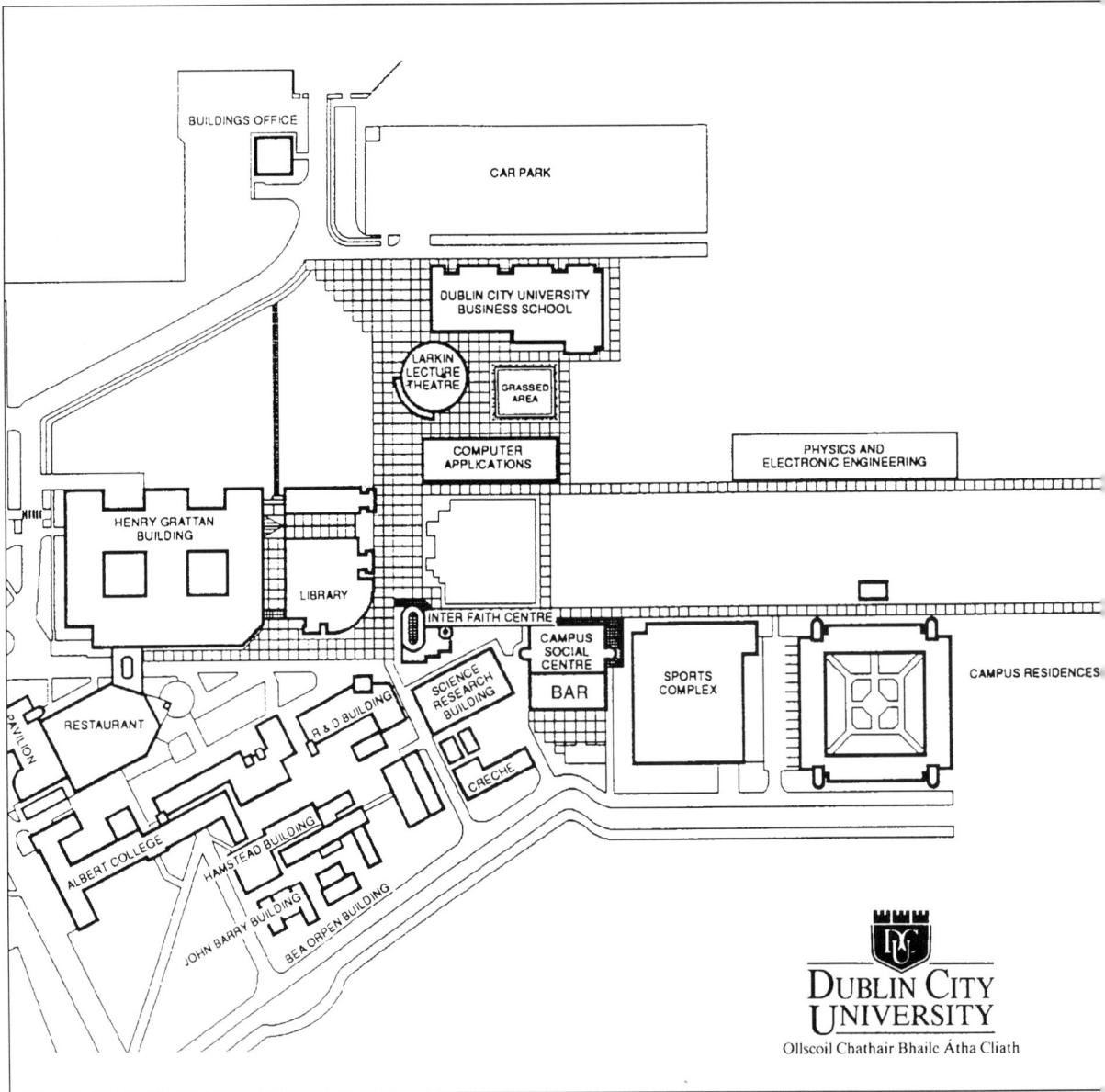

BUILDINGS OFFICE

CAR PARK

DUBLIN CITY UNIVERSITY BUSINESS SCHOOL

LARKIN LECTURE THEATRE

GRASSED AREA

COMPUTER APPLICATIONS

PHYSICS AND ELECTRONIC ENGINEERING

HENRY GRATTAN BUILDING

LIBRARY

INTER FAITH CENTRE

CAMPUS SOCIAL CENTRE

BAR

SPORTS COMPLEX

CAMPUS RESIDENCES

PAVILION

RESTAURANT

R & D BUILDING

SCIENCE RESEARCH BUILDING

CRECHE

ALBERT COLLEGE

HAMSTEAD BUILDING

JOHN BARRY BUILDING

BEA ORPEN BUILDING

DUBLIN CITY UNIVERSITY
Ollscoil Chathair Bhaile Átha Cliath

b. Listen again to the same dialogues. Then fill in the missing details below:

BAR

Opening hours:

Closed (days):

RESTAURANT

Lunch served from:

to:

LIBRARY

Opening hours:

Closed (days):

Location:

STUDENT SHOP

Opening hours:

Closed (days):

Location:

SPORTS COMPLEX

Opening hours:

Location:

Fee for each visit:

RESIDENCE OFFICE

Opening hours:

Telephone number:

Fax number:

REGISTERING DELEGATES AND GIVING INFORMATION ON PROGRAMME OF EVENTS

Listening 3 - At the conference centre/En un centro de congresos

Listen to one of the organisers registering the Spanish participants at the International Conference for Tourism Studies. Check the information in the grid below. If it is not correct, amend the document accordingly. Then fill in the last column.

INTERNATIONAL CONFERENCE FOR TOURISM STUDIES MAY 5-6-7						
Nombre	Temple Bar Hotel	Student Residences	Extra Nights	Accompanying Persons	Amount Paid	Amount Due
ALONSO Manuel	✔		1	2	£708	—
DÍAZ Carmen	✔		0	0	£236	—
MORENO Alicia		✔	0	0	£185	
PÉREZ Alberto	✔		2	1	£472	—
SOTO Ana	✔		0	0	£185	
VÁZQUEZ Fernando	✔		2	2	£708	

REGISTRATION AND ACCOMMODATION FEES

Student Residences:	(3 nights with full board: 5-6-7 May) £185 per person
Additional nights:	£19.50 per night per person
Temple Bar Hotel:	(3 nights with full board: 5-6-7 May) £236 per person
Additional nights:	£36 per night per person

H OW TO SAY IT

Para ir del aeropuerto al hotel.	To get from the airport to the hotel.
Quisiera saber | **cuánto cuesta el billete.** | **cómo se va al centro.**	I'd like to know | how much the ticket costs. | how to get to the city centre.
(Usted) ha | **pagado 185 libras.** **(Ustedes) han** | **reservado una habitación.**	You have | paid £185. | booked a room.
¿Cuánto le debo?	How much do I owe you?
(Usted) | **debe** **1.500 pesetas.** | **tiene que pagar** |	You | owe | 1,500 pesetas. | have to pay |
(Ustedes) | **deben** **la cena.** | **tienen que pagar** |	You | owe | for the dinner. | have to pay |
¿Cómo | **va a** | **pagar?** | **quiere** |	How are you going to pay?
¿Cómo | **van a** | **pagar?** | **quieren** |	How are you going to pay?

Listening 4 - At the conference centre/En un centro de congresos

Listen to one of the organisers announcing changes in the conference programme for the first day of the conference and amend the programme of events below accordingly.

CONGRESO INTERNACIONAL DE TURISMO
5, 6 y 7 de MAYO

INTERNATIONAL CONFERENCE FOR TOURISM STUDIES
MAY 5-6-7

Viernes 5 de mayo/Friday, 5 May

Horario/Time	**Actividades**/Activity	**Lugar**/Location
9.00 - 9.30am	**Registro y entrega de documentación**/Registration and presentation of documentation	**Recepción**/Reception
9.30 - 11.00am	**Sesión plenaria**/Plenary session **Ceremonia de inauguración y bienvenida**/Welcome and opening	**Auditorio Larkin**/ Larkin Lecture Theatre
11.00 - 11.30am	**Pausa-café**/Coffee-break	S210
11.30 - 1.00pm	**Grupos de trabajo A - D**/ Workshops A - D	A: S230 C: S232 B: S231 D: S233
1.00 - 2.30pm	**Almuerzo**/Lunch	**Restaurante**/Canteen
2.30 - 3.30pm	**Debate general**/General discussion	**Auditorio Larkin**/ Larkin Lecture Theatre
3.30 - 4.00pm	**Pausa-café**/Coffee-break	S210
4.00 - 5.30pm	**Grupos de trabajo E - H**/ Workshops E - H	E: S210 G: S212 F: S211 H: S213
5.30 - 6.30pm	**Debate general**/General discussion	**Auditorio Larkin**/ Larkin Lecture Theatre
7.00pm	**Autobús al centro**/Bus to town	**Aparcamiento**/Car park
7.30pm	**Recepción ofrecida por el alcalde**/Reception hosted by Lord Mayor	Mansion House

PROVIDING INFORMATION ON THE TRADE FAIR DIRECTING VISITORS AROUND THE TRADE FAIR

Listening 5 - At the trade fair/En la feria de muestras

Listen to one of the organisers of the 10th World Fair for Tourism giving information about the fair and fill in the fact sheet below (in Spanish).

10ª EDICIÓN DE LA FERIA INTERNACIONAL DE TURISMO

10TH WORLD FAIR FOR TOURISM

Lugar/Location: ....

Fechas/Dates: ....

Jornadas técnicas para profesionales/Trade only: ....

Horario de apertura/Opening hours: ....

Días de apertura al público/Open to the public: ....

Horario de apertura/Opening hours: ....

Expositores/Exhibitors: ....

Extranjeros/Foreign: ....

Españoles/Spanish: ....

Superficie ocupada/Total surface area: ....

Número de visitantes esperados/Expected number of visitors: ....

Número de teléfono de información/
      Information telephone number: ....

Listening 6 - At the exhibition centre/En el recinto ferial

Listen to the receptionist at the information desk (on the main floor) of the 10th World Trade Fair for Tourism telling visitors where various stands and facilities are. Then fill in the missing information in the floor plans below:

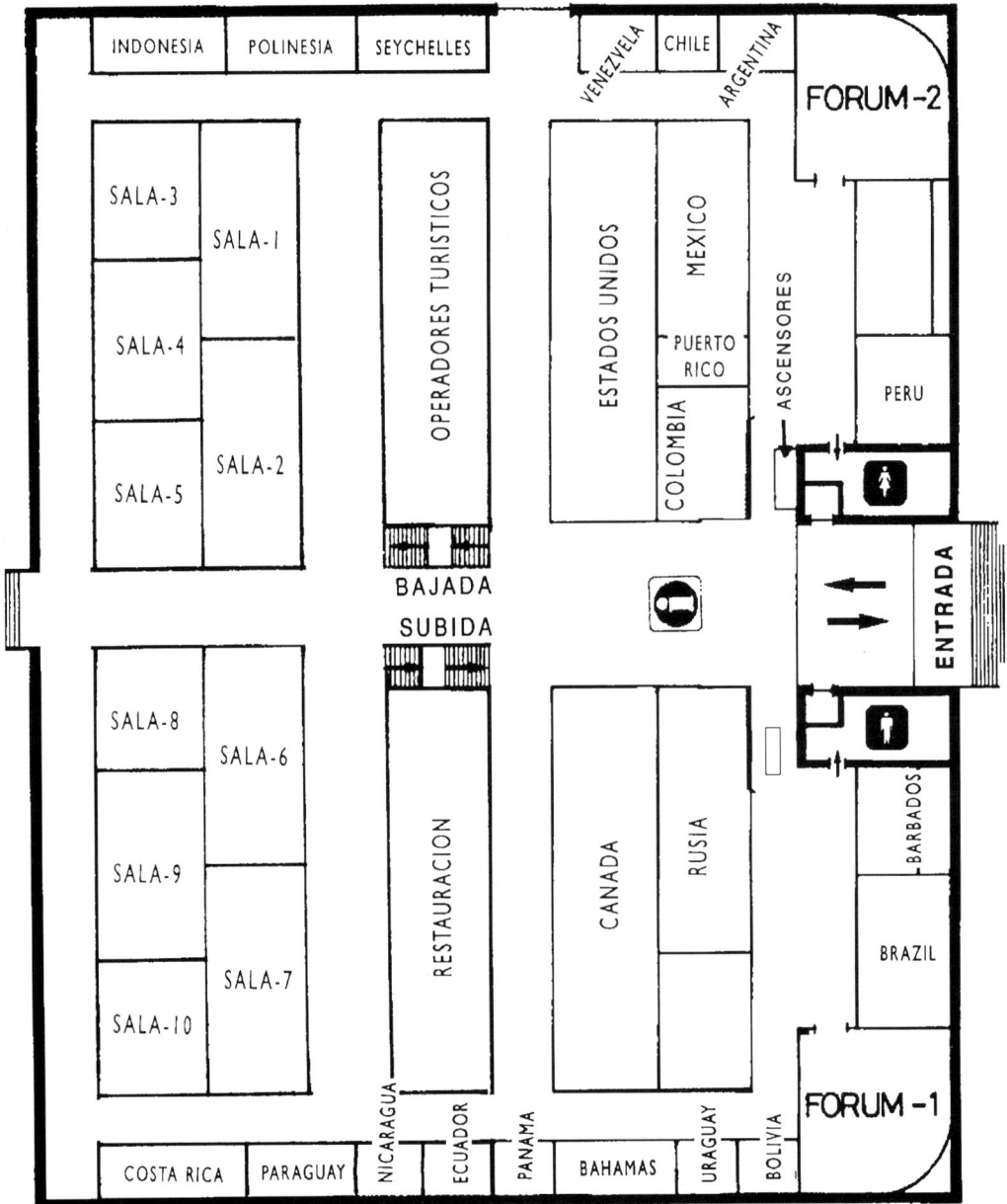

INDONESIA	POLINESIA	SEYCHELLES

VENEZUELA | CHILE | ARGENTINA

FORUM -2

SALA-3

SALA-1

SALA-4

SALA-5

SALA-2

OPERADORES TURISTICOS

BAJADA

SUBIDA

ESTADOS UNIDOS

MEXICO

PUERTO RICO

COLOMBIA

ASCENSORES

PERU

ENTRADA

SALA-8

SALA-6

SALA-9

SALA-7

SALA-10

RESTAURACION

CANADA

RUSIA

BARBADOS

BRAZIL

FORUM -1

NICARAGUA

ECUADOR

PANAMA

URUGUAY

BOLIVIA

COSTA RICA	PARAGUAY			BAHAMAS		

MAIN FLOOR

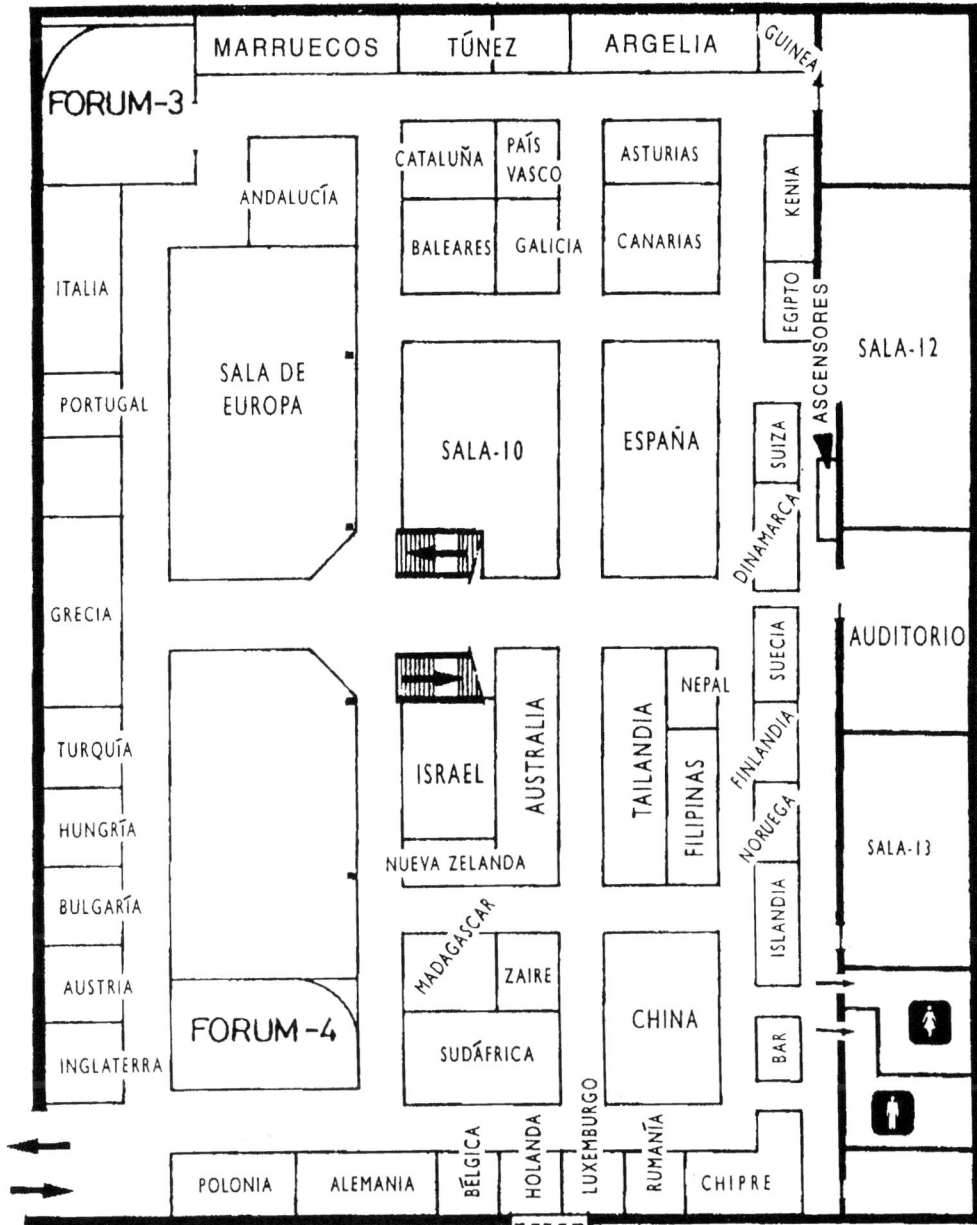

FORUM-3

MARRUECOS | TÚNEZ | ARGELIA | GUINEA

ANDALUCÍA

CATALUÑA | PAÍS VASCO | ASTURIAS

BALEARES | GALICIA | CANARIAS

KENIA

EGIPTO

ASCENSORES

SALA-12

ITALIA

SALA DE EUROPA

SALA-10

ESPAÑA

SUIZA

DINAMARCA

PORTUGAL

GRECIA

AUDITORIO

SUECIA

FINLANDIA

NORUEGA

ISLANDIA

TURQUÍA

ISRAEL | AUSTRALIA

NEPAL

TAILANDIA | FILIPINAS

SALA-13

HUNGRÍA

NUEVA ZELANDA

BULGARÍA

AUSTRIA

FORUM-4

MADAGASCAR | ZAIRE

SUDÁFRICA

CHINA

BAR

INGLATERRA

POLONIA | ALEMANIA | BÉLGICA | HOLANDA | LUXEMBURGO | RUMANÍA | CHIPRE

GROUND FLOOR

HELP!

baje	las escaleras en el ascensor	take the	stairs lift	to the ground floor
	subida	way up		
	bajada	way down		
ahí	mismo al lado	right there		
	detrás de	behind		

Listening 7 - At the trade fair/En la feria

Listen to the same receptionist giving the programme of presentations to be held in **"Sala de Europa"** and complete the document below:

SALA DE EUROPA

Tuesday 24th May

16.00 :   Presentation on   ....

.... :   Presentation on   ....

Wednesday 25th May

.... :   Presentation on   ....

.... :   Presentation on   ....

.... :   Presentation on   ....

.... :   Presentation on   ....

LANGUAGE PRACTICE

Exercise 1

Listen to the examples.

Examples:

usted - pagar - 500 libras	Usted **ha pagado** 500 libras.
ustedes - reservar - dos plazas	Ustedes **han reservado** dos plazas.
usted - deber - 80 libras	Usted **debe** 80 libras.
ustedes - tener que pagar - la cena	Ustedes **tienen que pagar** la cena.

Listen to the cues on the tape and build up sentences as in the examples. (Remember to **stop** the tape at the signal.)

1. usted - deber - 10.000 ptas

2. ustedes - pagar - 450 libras

3. usted - tener que pagar - 6.700 ptas

4. ustedes - deber - las entradas

5. usted - reservar - una habitación

6. ustedes - tener que pagar - 196 libras

Exercise 2

Listen to the example.

Example: Bélgica - 15   El stand de Bélgica **es el 15**.

Listen to the cues on the tape and build up sentences as in the example.

1. Polonia - 12

2. Grecia - 19

3. Perú - 27

4. Venezuela - 30

5. Estados Unidos - 38

6. Costa Rica - 46

Exercise 3 - At the exhibition centre/En el recinto ferial

You are working at the information desk of the 10th World Trade Fair for Tourism (on the main floor, facing the entrance). Listen to visitors asking you where various stands and facilities are. Use the floor plans in Listening 6 to answer their queries.

Remember to stop the tape at the signal.
Check your answers in the Answer Key section.

Exercise 4

Listen to the information given on the tape and with the help of the document on page 138 (Listening 4), complete the programme of events below in Spanish.

**CONGRESO INTERNACIONAL DE TURISMO
5, 6 y 7 de MAYO**

INTERNATIONAL CONFERENCE FOR TOURISM STUDIES
MAY 5-6-7

Sábado 6 de mayo/Saturday, 6 May

Horario/Time	**Actividades**/Activities	**Lugar**/Locations
9.30 - 11.00am	**Sesión plenaria**/Plenary session	**Auditorio Larkin**/ Larkin Lecture Theatre
11.00 - 11.30am	....	....
11.30 - 1.00pm	....	I : ....
		J : ....
		K : ....
		L : ....
1.00 - 2.30pm	....	....
2.30 - 3.30pm	....	....
3.30 - 4.00pm	....	....
4.00 - 5.00pm	....	M: ....
		N: ....
5.00 - 6.00pm	....	....
6.30pm	**Autobuses para la recepción en el Castillo**/Buses to the reception in Dublin Castle	....

Exercise 5 - At the conference centre/En el palacio de congresos

You are working at the reception desk of a conference centre. A Spanish participant arrives. Answer the questions as prompted below.

Participant: Buenos días.

Assistant: *Greet the participant and ask her if she is taking part in the Conference on Tourism.*

Participant: Sí, participo en el congreso.

Assistant: *Ask her name and the name of her company.*

Participant: Yo me llamo Manuela Vicente y trabajo para Ociotur. ¿Podría decirme cuál es el programa del congreso?

Assistant: *Tell her that the conference programme is as follows:*

Today, Monday, at 10.30am - Seminar (seminario) on travel agencies.

Tuesday at 9.30am - Seminar on agri-tourism (turismo rural).

Wednesday at 11.00am - Seminar on tour operators (operadores turísticos)

Thursday at 10.00am - Seminar on leisure centres.

All the seminars finish at 4.30pm and they are held in the Conference Room on the ground floor, at the end of the corridor on the left.

Participant: ¿Hay restaurante en el centro?

Assistant: *Tell her that there is no restaurant in the Conference Centre but that there is one fifty metres away opposite the railway station.*

Participant: ¿Podría decirme donde están los servicios y el guardarropa, por favor?

Assistant: *Tell her that the ladies' toilets are on her left next to the lifts.*

The cloakroom is next to the reception desk.

Participant: Muchas gracias.

Assistant: *Tell the participant that she is welcome and wish her a good day.*

Note: Check the answers on the tape but remember that they are model answers only.

CAPITAL!

Spain has, by European standards, a relatively young capital. When Felipe II decided to move his government there in 1561, it was little more than a dusty town, and with little to recommend it at that.

Situated high on a plateau and as far from the sea as it is possible to get in the Iberian Peninsula, it seems an unlikely spot to have chosen as a first city. However it was its very equidistance from all parts of his kingdom that recommended Madrid to Felipe. With his administration in the centre of the county, most places could be reached quickly. And thus it was that a small unknown town became today's bustling, thriving city of five million people.

While Madrid does not have the architectural attractions of some of its rivals, for example Paris, Rome or Athens, it does have many of the trappings of the capital of a once-great empire. Principal among these is the **Museo del Prado,** one of the world's greatest art galleries. Although it houses works of huge diversity, it is best known for its collection of the Spanish masters, especially Velázquez and Goya. The most famous painting in the national collection however is in the modern art museum **Museo Nacional Centro de Arte Reina Sofía** (*Reina Sofía* for short), and records one of Spain's most terrible memories: the bombing of the Basque town of *Guernica* by German warplanes in the Spanish Civil War. During Franco's reign *Guernica* was kept in New York with instructions from Picasso that it be returned to Spain when the country was a democracy. It finally arrived back to join the national collection in 1981.

Franco's death signalled more than a painting's return. It was like a starting pistol for the emergence of today's Madrid. Reacting against decades of conservatism, Madrid became one of Europe's most exciting and lively cities. Madrileños — the city's "natives" — set about the serious business of enjoying themselves, and *la marcha madrileña* — the Madrid night life — became synonymous with style, fashion and, above all, fun. *Madrileños* will find any excuse to party, and when they start are unlikely to stop until the small hours of the *madrugada.*

A more traditional aspect of Madrid life is the *paseo* — a stroll for a little exercise, to see and, of course, to be seen! One of the favourite places to *pasear* is in the **Parque del Buen Retiro,** Madrid's biggest city-centre park. On Sundays its a pleasant chaos of leisurely strollers interspersed with fortune-tellers, buskers, puppet-masters and other types of street performers. Respite can be taken at one of the many *quioscos* (open air bars) to be found within its gates.

Madrid's other great Sunday activity is a visit to the *Rastro,* a huge, sprawling flea-market near Lavapiés, an old working-class district. Here you can buy anything from designer furniture to a parrot to a carpet to a single boot or a set of keys with no lock! It seems an apt symbol for the city itself: a bit chaotic, a mixture of old and new, at times bizarre, but above all, fun!

Note:

Exercises 1 to 6 are for grammar revision.
The remaining exercises are based on Units 5 to 9 and in each case there is a written comprehension exercise and an oral production exercise.

Exercise 1

Fill in the blanks in the column as shown in the examples (and see Grammar section 3):

a. Example: un museo **bonito**   una iglesia **bonita**

       1. un puente **antiguo**   una torre ....

       2. un recuerdo **original**   una chaqueta ....

       3. un pueblo **pintoresco**   una ciudad ....

       4. un recuerdo **interesante**   una visita ....

       5. un turista **alemán**   una turista ....

b. Example: un monumento **bonito**   unos monumentos **bonitos**

       1. una playa **preciosa**   unas playas ....

       2. un restaurante **grande**   unos restaurantes ....

       3. un balneario **famoso**   unos balnearios ....

       4. una especialidad **local**   unas especialidades ....

       5. un barco **irlandés**   unos barcos ....

Exercise 2

Write the numbers in letters as shown in the example (and see Grammar section 4):

21 libras	**veintiuna** libras
1er piso	**primer** piso

1. 4ª planta   ....

2. 31.000 pesetas   ....

3. 720 libras   ....

4. 3er día ....

5. 500 pesetas   ....

6. 10ª edición   ....

7. 1 dólar   ....

8. 4º pasillo   ....

9. 21 museos   ....

10. 7º piso   ....

11. 250 libras   ....

12. 834 marcos   ....

Exercise 3

Use the words given to build up sentences as shown in the examples (and see Grammar section 9 (a) and 9 (g)):

a. Examples: usted - visitar el convento   ¿**Le interesa** visitar el convento?
                  ustedes - ver el pueblo   ¿**Les interesa** ver el pueblo?

1.   ustedes - escuchar música   ....

2.   usted - viajar en tren   ....

3.   ustedes - reservar las entradas   ....

4.   usted - jugar al tenis   ....

5.   usted - hacer submarinismo   ....

6.   ustedes - comprar algo   ....

b. Examples: usted - hacer una excursión   ¿**Le gustaría** hacer una excursión?
                  ustedes - salir por la noche   ¿**Les gustaría** salir por la noche?

1.   usted - comer pescado   ....

2.   ustedes - dar un paseo   ....

3.   ustedes - visitar el museo   ....

4.   usted - probar el vino   ....

5.   ustedes - montar a caballo   ....

6.   usted - hacer un crucero   ....

Exercise 4

Transform the following sentences as shown in the examples (and see Grammar section 9 (c) and 9 (d)):

Example: El avión saldrá a las 12.   El avión **va a salir** a las 12.

Hará buen tiempo.   **Va a hacer** buen tiempo.

1. Usted llegará por la mañana.   ....

2. Habrá niebla.   ....

3. Los turistas visitarán el palacio.   ....

4. A la izquierda verá la iglesia.   ....

5. Ustedes volverán mañana.   ....

6. Hará frío.   ....

Exercise 5

Transform the following sentences as shown in the examples (and see Grammar section 9 (f) and 9 (g)):

a. Example: Tome el autobús.   **Puede tomar** el autobús.

1. Llame más tarde.   ....

2. Baje en el ascensor.   ....

3. Compre algún recuerdo.   ....

4. Gire a la izquierda.   ....

5. Siga todo recto.   ....

6. Salga por la planta baja.   ....

b. Example: Tiene que volver al pueblo. **Vuelva** al pueblo.

1. Tiene que esperar un momento ....

2. Tiene que continuar todo recto ....

3. Tiene que pasar por León ....

4. Tiene que escribir su dirección ....

5. Tiene que decir su nombre ....

6. Tiene que ir por la carretera ....

Exercise 6

Ask questions appropriate to the answers given as shown in the examples (and see Grammar section 10)

Examples: Voy a viajar el 15. **¿Cuándo** va a viajar?
  Quiero comer en el hotel. **¿Dónde** quiere comer?

1. Prefiero la más barata. ....

2. Quiero beber vino. ....

3. Me gustaría ir en tren. ....

4. Quiero 5 botellas. ....

5. El visitante va a la catedral. ....

6. El perfume cuesta 35 libras. ....

Parque Nacional
de la montaña de Covadonga

Foto ALVARO

«DESCENSO DEL ALTO SELLA»

Caño   Cangas   Arriondas

Piragüimo
Montaña
Pesca
Esquí...

Foto: SALMER

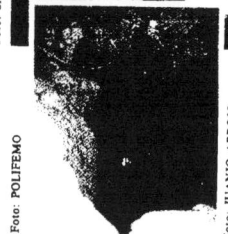

Foto: POLIFEMO

Foto: JUANJO ARROJO

INFORMACION
- Macizo Occidental de los Picos de Europa.
- 16.925 Hectáreas.
- Altura máxima: Peña Santa de Castilla, 2.596 metros.
- Lagos: Enol y Ercina a más de 1.000 m.
- Geología: Glaciar y Karst sobre caliza de montaña.
- Clima: Semialpino.
- Bosques templados caducifolios.
- Fauna: Rebeco, corzo, jabalí, ciervo, lobo, urogallo, águila.
- Refugio Municipal: Vega de Enol, 26 camas, comidas, abierto todo el año.
- Zonas de camping y baños limitadas.
- Fiesta del Pastor: 25 de julio, declarada de interés turístico.
- Información: ICONA y Oficina de Turismo en Cangas de Onís.

Foto ALVARO

5 EXCURSIONES DE MONTAÑA

1.–Lagos-Vega de Ario. Seis horas. Fácil.
2.–Lagos-Vega Redonda-Ordiales. Seis horas. Fácil.
3.–Covadonga-Valle de Orandi. Cuatro horas. Fácil.
4.–Ruta del Cares. Siete horas. Fácil.
5.–Lago Enol-Torre Santa de Enol. Ocho horas. Difícil.

Todas estas rutas son fácilmente recorribles por cualquier persona, sin necesidad de material específico, excepto la que se señala como difícil. Información: Compañía de Guías de Montaña, c/ Emilio Laria, 2, 2.º, Apartado 82, Cangas de Onís, Asturias. Teléfono 848799.

ITINERARIO TURISTICO

1.–En Cangas:
 a) Puente Romano, época medieval.
 b) Capilla y Dolmen de Santa Cruz, Edad del Bronce. (Llave en la Oficina de Turismo).
 c) Palacio de Cortés, s. XVI.
2.–Monasterio de San Pedro de Villanueva, s. XII.
3.–Ermita de San Bartolomé, s. XII. (Las Rozas).
4.–Salto salmonero. (Caño).

5.–Río Dobra: Puente medieval y entorno ecológico.
6.–Cueva del Buxu. (Cardes). Solutrense y Magdaleniense. Visitas: Máxima 25 personas/día.
7.–Covadonga: Cueva y Basílica.
8.–Los Lagos, Enol y Ercina, a 1.060 m. Macizo Occidental de los Picos de Europa.
9.–Santa Eulalia de Abamia, iglesia románica. (Corao).
10.–Palacio de Labra, s. XVII. (Labra).
11.–Molinos antiguos. (Peruyes).

Exercise 7

Read the document on 'Covadonga' and answer the following questions:

1. This document is a brochure on:

    a. a town

    b. a national park

    c. an adventure centre

2. Which four sports are named in the brochure?

    a. ....

    b. ....

    c. ....

    d. ....

3. Are there areas designated for camping?   YES ☐   NO ☐

4. When do the local celebrations take place?

    ....

5. Which of the following geographical features are mentioned in the brochure?

    a. a beach   d. a waterfall

    b. a river   e. a mountain

    c. a lake

6. Write beside each item below the names of the towns or places in which they are
    situated according to 'ITINERARIO TURISTÍCO'.

    a. a church   ....

    b. a palace   ....

    c. a bridge   ....

    d. a dolmen   ....

    e. a cave   ....

Exercise 8 - At the tourist office/En la oficina de turismo

You are working as a tourist information officer in Dublin. Spanish-speaking tourists come in looking for information on the 'James Joyce Tower' and 'George Bernard Shaw's House'. Based on the document below, you give them as much information as possible on these two places (access, opening hours, admission charges, facilities).

THE SHAW BIRTHPLACE

33 Synge Street, Dublin 8
Telephone: (01) 4750854 (May to October) or (01) 8722077
Fax: (01) 8722231

1994

OPENING HOURS:
May - October inclusive:

Monday - Saturday	10.00 - 17.00 hours
Sundays & Public Holidays	10.00 - 18.00 hours
Closed for Lunch	13.00 - 14.00 hours

OPEN ON REQUEST FOR GROUPS OUTSIDE OF ABOVE HOURS

ADMISSION	INDIVIDUAL	GROUPS
Adults (18 yrs. & over)	£1.90	£1.40
Senior Citizens & Students (12 - 17 yrs.)	£1.50	£1.20
Children (3 - 11 yrs.)	£1.00	£0.80

Family Ticket: £5.50p (2 Adults & 3/4 children)

Facilities: Bookshop

Combined Dublin Writers Museum/James Joyce Tower (April/October) or George Bernard Shaw Birthplace tickets available (May/October)

Adults (18 yrs. & over)	£3.80	£3.30
Senior Citizens & Students (12 - 17 yrs.)	£2.80	£2.30
Children (3 - 11 yrs.)	£1.40	£1.20

Family Ticket: £8.50 (2 Adults & 3/4 children)

TOURS AVAILABLE IN FOREIGN LANGUAGES.
Designed & Printed by C.R.C. Workshops

JAMES JOYCE TOWER

SANDYCOVE

Tel. (01) 2809265/2808571   Fax (01) 2802641
(8 miles from Dublin – Bus No. 8 & Dart Rail Service)

1994

OPENING HOURS
April - October inclusive

Monday - Saturday	10.00 - 17.00 hours
Sundays & Public Holidays	14.00 - 18.00 hours
Closed for Lunch 13.00 - 14.00 hours	

OPEN ON REQUEST FOR GROUPS OUTSIDE OF ABOVE HOURS

ADMISSION	INDIVIDUAL	GROUPS
Adults (18 yrs. & over)	£1.90	£1.40
Senior Citizens & Students (12 - 17 yrs.)	£1.50	£1.20
Children (3 - 11 yrs.)	£1.00	£0.80

Family Ticket: £5.50 (2 Adults & 3/4 children)

Facilities: Bookshop

Combined Dublin Writers Museum/James Joyce Tower (April - October) or George Bernard Shaw Birthplace tickets available (May - October)

TOURS AVAILABLE IN FOREIGN LANGUAGES

James Joyce

Note: Check the answers on the tape, but remember that they are model answers only.

Exercise 9 - At the tourist office/En la oficina de turismo

You are working as a tourist information officer in Galway. Spanish-speaking tourists come in looking for information on the Aran Islands. Based on the information below, you give them as much information as possible on how to get to the Aran Islands:

INISHMORE

Location: The most northly and largest island is located 48km from Galway and 16km from Ros a'Mhil (Rossaveal) in Connemara.

Access: BY FERRY: From Galway 3 sailings daily returning 5.00pm. Aran Ferries. Tel: (091) 68903 office hours; (091) 92447 after hours.

From Ros a'Mhil (Rossaveal) 38km west of Galway. There are 3/4 sailings daily. Aran Ferries.

BY AIR: From Galway Airport (8km east of Galway at Carnmore). Several flights daily. Contact: Aer Arann. Tel: (091) 55437.

INISHMAAN

Location: Inishmaan - the middle island - lies to the south east of Inishmore across Gregory's Sound.

Access: BY FERRY: From Spiddal - 18km west of Galway which operates 3 crossings daily from June to 9 September. Connecting bus operates from Galway station. For further details: Tel (091) 62131.

BY AIR: From Galway Airport and from Inishmore and Inishere. Several flights daily. Contact: Aer Arann.

INISHERE

Location: The smallest of the Aran Islands lies 8km north west of Doolin in County Clare.

Access: BY FERRY: From Doolin - 12 more return sailings daily - leaving Doolin on the hour and returning from Inishere on the 1/2 hour.
Crossing takes 25/30 minutes.
Contact: Doolin Ferries. Tel: (065) 74189
From Spiddal - 18km west of Galway. 3 crossings daily from June to 9 September. Connecting bus operates from Galway station. For further details: Tel (091) 62131.
BY AIR: From Galway Airport and from Inishmore and Inishmaan. There are several flights daily. Contact: Aer Arann.

Note: Check the answers on the tape, but remember that they are model answers only.

Exercise 10

Read the document on 'Guatemala' and answer the questions which follow:

GUATEMALA

ITINERARIO

Dia 1º: ESPANA-BOGOTA

Presentación en el aeropuerto (2 horas antes) y salida en vuelo regular a Bogotá. Asistencia y traslado al hotel Tekendama. Alojamiento.

Dia 2º: BOGOTA-GUATAMALA

Desayuno. Mañana libre en la que se recomienda visitar: Palacio Nacional, Museo del Oro, Monserrate, Quinta de Simón Bolivar... Traslado al aeropuerto y salida en vuelo regular a Guatemala, país en el que destaca su gran riqueza paisajista: lagos, volcanes, playas, selvas tropicales... así comos sus gentes y ciudades, en donde una de sus curiosidades son los mercados semanales con más de 500 variedades en trajes de los indígenas, sin olvidar las iglesias en cuyo interior se realizan una mezcla de ritos mayas y católicos. Llegada y traslado al hotel.

Dia 3º: GUATAMALA-FLORES

Traslado al aeropuerto y salida en avión a Flores, situada junto al Lago Peten Itza. Visita al Parque Nacional de Tikal, donde se encuentra la ciudad más importante del Imperio Maya. Entre sus numerosos monumentos, templos y palacios destaca el Templo del Gran Jagüar, el Templo de la Serpiente Bicéfala, etc., que forman el centro religioso y político del pueblo Maya de la antigüedad.
Durante la visita se efectuará el almuerzo en el Parque. Alojamiento en el Hotel.

Dia 4º: FLORES-GUATAMALA

Mañana libre. Se recomienda efectuar una excursión opcional a las ruinas Mayas de Ceibal. A una hora determinada traslado al aeropuerto para salir en vuelo regular hacia la ciudad de Guatemala.
Llegada y traslado al hotel seleccionado. Alojamiento.

Dia 5º: GUATAMALA-ANTIGUA CHICHICASTENANGO

Salida por carretera hacia la ciudad de Antigua, declarada por la Unesco patrimonio cultural de la Humanidad y visita de la misma. Continuación del viaje por carretera efectuando un breve recorrido por el altiplano guatemalteco hacia Chichicastenango. Se visitarán las Iglesias del Calvario y de Santo Tomás situadas en la Plaza Mayor. Alojamiento en el hotel.

Dia 5º: CHICHICASTENANGO LAGO ATITLAN-GUATEMALA

Mañana libre en la que se recomienda visiten el colorista Mercado. Salida hacia la región de Solola en donde se encuentra el Lago Atitlan, rodeado por los volcanes de San Pedro, Toliman y Atitlan. Continuación hacia Guatemala. Llegada y alojamiento.

Dia 5º: GUATEMALA-ESPANA

Traslado al aeropuerto de Guatemala y salida hacia España vía Bogotá. Noche a bordo.

Dia 6º: ESPANA

Llegada al aeropuerto de origen y FIN DEL VIAJE.

Selección HOTELERA

CIUDAD	TURISTA ★★★	PRIMERA ★★★★	LUJO ★★★★★
GUATEMALA	RITZ/PANAMERICAN	RAMADA	CAMINO REAL/ EL DORADO
FLORES	DEL PATIO	VILLA MAYA	CAMINO REAL
ANTIGUA	POSADA D. RODRIGO	RAMADA	CASA STO. DOMINGO/ANTIGUA
CHICHICASTENANGO	VILLA GRANDE	STO. TOMAS	STO TOMAS/ MAYA INN
LAGO ATITLAN	VILLA SANTA	DEL LAGO	ATITLAN

PRECIO POR PERSONA EN HABITACION DOBLE.

DICIEMBRE 4/11	★★★	MAD	212.500	22.700
		BCN	225.000	
	★★★★	MAD	220.400	28.700
		BCN	232.900	
	★★★★★	MAD	227.500	33.400
		BCN	240.000	
ENERO 1/8	★★★	MAD	237.500	22.700
		BCN	250.000	
	★★★★	MAD	245.400	28.700
		BCN	257.900	
	★★★★★	MAD	252.500	33.400
		BCN	265.000	
MARZO 26/ ABRIL 2	★★★	MAD	212.500	22.700
		BCN	225.000	
	★★★★	MAD	220.400	28.700
		BCN	232.900	
	★★★★★	MAD	227.500	33.400
		BCN	240.000	

MAD. Madrid/BCN: Barcelona.
Suplemento para otras ciudades peninsulares a añadir a los precios de Madrid: **12.500 Ptas.**

1. Do you have to pay a supplement if you go from Madrid?:   YES ☐   NO ☐

2. Which of the following attractions are mentioned in the document?
   - a.   a castle
   - b.   a palace
   - c.   a church
   - d.   a market
   - e.   a monastery
   - f.   a lake

3. Where do you have lunch on the third day?
   - a.   in a park
   - b.   in a hotel
   - c.   by a lake.

4. On the fourth day you travel by:
   - a.   car
   - b.   coach
   - c.   'plane

5. On the sixth day you are advised to visit:
   - a.   a lake
   - b.   a market
   - c.   a volcano

6. On the seventh day you spend the night:
   - a.   on a 'plane
   - b.   on a boat
   - c.   on a coach

Exercise 11

Study the document on '**Naturaleza y deporte en Soria**' and answer the following
questions:

1. Which of the following facilities are available   a. children's playground
    in **Berlanga de Duero**?   b. swimming pool
                                                       c. sports centre
                                                       d. tennis court

2. Which of the following sports are mentioned   a. fishing
    in the brochure?   b. climbing
                                                       c. sailing
                                                       d. swimming
                                                       e. archery
                                                       f. hill walking
                                                       g. mountain biking

3. In which season are you advised to do   a. summer
    canoeing?   b. spring
                                                       c. autumn
                                                       d. winter

4. Where can you ski?   a. in Valle del Alto Duero
                                                       b. in Picos de Urbión
                                                       c. in Tierras de Berlanga

5. Which of the following courses is available?   a. mountaineering
                                                       b. skiing
                                                       c. canoeing

6. Do all the activity holidays last the same   YES ☐   NO ☐
    length of time?

NATURALEZA Y DEPORTE EN SORIA

CAMPAMENTOS DE VERANO

Mediante las actividades desarrolladas en los campamentos, se pretende conocer los aspectos culturales, paisajísticos y ecológicos de esta comarca:

Hoces y cañones, páramos, extensos pinares, sabinares, ríos, etc.

Castillos medievales, atalayas, arquitectura y costumbres populares, etc.

Vegetación, ornitología, geología, etc.

El núcleo donde se van a desarrollar las actividades es Berlanga de Duero, población situada al pie de un espléndido castillo y al inicio de la hoz que forma el río Escalote, afluente del Duero y próximo a este.

ESTANCIA: 14 días

Instalaciones y servicios perfectamente equipados, piscina, polideportivo, ecomuseo, ...

ACTIVIDADES: piragüismo, bicicleta de montaña, senderismo, iniciación a la montaña, talleres, natación, etc.

PIRAGUISMO DE APRENDIZAJE Y AVENTURA

Es una buena manera de conocer lo que el río Duero en su curso alto nos ofrece a su paso: Vegetación selvática, bosques de ribera, aves acuáticas, antiguos molinos, presas, construcciones abandonadas y parcialmente sumergidas, etc.
ESTANCIA: Fin de Semana
Cinco Días

FECHA: Primavera (Mayo-Junio).
ACTIVIDADES: Cursos de iniciación y perfeccionamiento. Descensos turísticos por el Duero.

Escalada, bici de montaña, piragüismo, senderismo, parapente, ... , son algunas de las actividades que podrás hacer a lo largo de fascinantes rutas en el Valle del Alto Duero, Picos de Urbión y Tierras de Berlanga.
ESTANCIA: Fin de Semana
Semanas Escolares
Cinco Días
FECHA: Primavera y Otoño

BICI DE MONTAÑA POR TIERRAS DE SORIA

Es un medio para acercarnos a nuestro entorno natural, transitar por caminos que recorren olvidados pueblos, atravesar por sendas espesos bosques, acceder a picos de espléndida panorámica, recorrer junto a ríos sus cañones y gargantas habitadas por multitud de rapaces.

ESTANCIA: Fin de Semana
Cinco Días
Semanas Escolares

FECHA: Primavera y Otoño.
ACTIVIDADES: Atractivos recorridos por sendas, pistas forestales, caminos carreteros, etc.

ESQUI DE FONDO EN PICOS DE URBION

Llega el invierno y la nieve lo transforma todo, las montañas ahora son un lugar distinto al que conocimos en otras

estaciones. El esquí de fondo es una forma perfectamente adaptada para adentrarnos hasta lugares poco practicables a pie, una buena manera de conocer los extensos bosques que cubren los Picos de Urbión.

ESTANCIA: Fin de Semana
Cinco Días
Semanas Escolares

FECHA: Invierno.

Exercise 12

Read the document below on 'Lough Muckno Leisure Park' and give as much information as possible to a Spanish-speaking tourist who would like to spend a short break at the centre. Give him or her information about its location, type of accommodation, facilities, activities and cost.

LOUGH MUCKNO LEISURE PARK

Castleblaney, Co. Monaghan
Tel: (042) 46356, Fax: (042) 46610

Adventure/multi-activity holidays for adults. Accommodation in rooms for 2, 4 or 6 persons. Cutstone coachhouse set in 360 ha. Hope Castle bar, restaurant and conference facilities. Brochure on request.

ACTIVITIES:
Boardsailing, canoeing, sailing, orienteering, golf, tennis, mountain biking, water skiing (extra). Wetsuits/life jackets provided for water based activities. Activities supervised by fully qualified instructors.

PRICES QUOTED IN IR£

G T	1 FEB – 30 JUN	JUL & AUG
WEEK – FULL BOARD (7 B&B/7 DINNERS/7 LUNCHES)	201.00	250.00
WEEKEND (2 B&B/1 DINNER/2 LUNCHES)	80.00	90.00
MID-WEEK – FULL BOARD (3 B&B/3 DINNERS/3 LUNCHES)	89.00	110.00
PUBLIC HOLIDAY WEEKENDS (3 B&B/3 DINNERS/3 LUNCHES)	130.00	

Note: Check the answers on the tape, but remember that they are model answers only.

Exercise 13

Read the following descriptions of suggested routes in the Andalucía region.

a. Number each of the maps according to the number of the corresponding description below (see Example: Map A).

1.   La ciudad de *Carmona*, antigua **Carmo**, conserva la **Puerta de Sevilla**, fortificación cartaginesa, con arcos de entrada romanos, al igual que la **Puerta de Córdoba**. El interesante **Conjunto Arqueológico de Carmona** incluye una necrópolis hipogea romana y un anfiteatro, con museo monográfico. Merecen también atención dos grandes ciudades de campiña, con sendos museos: *Ecija*, **Astigi** romana y *Osuna*, antes **Urso**, con restos de una notable necrópolis.

2.   El itinerario 2 nos lleva a *Carmona*, donde se conservan restos de una mezquita almohade en el Patio de los Naranjos de la **Iglesia de Santa María**. Del recinto amurallado, de origen romano, perviven lienzos, torres y la **Puerta de Sevilla**. Restos de construcciones islámicas hay también en los dos **Alcázares** de la ciudad. *Marchena* tiene aún gran parte de la cerca del siglo XI, embutida a veces en construcciones posteriores, con numerosos torreones, arcos y puertas. Un caso similar de ciudad amurallada es el de *Palma del Río*.

3.   **Carmona** con sus restos de defensas romanas y musulmanas (Puertas de Sevilla y Córdoba, Alcázares de Abajo y de Arriba); **Alcalá**, con los restos de su castillo y, en las afueras, el de Marchenilla (s. XIV)

4. SEVILLA | **Casa de las Dueñas**
Arte Suntuario.

Dueñas, 5 ☎ 422 09 56

Casa de Pilatos
Pintura. Escultura. Alicatados mudéjares.

Plaza Pilatos, 1 ☎ 422 52 98

GERENA | **Colección Taurina**
Carteles. Documentos. Divisas de ganaderías.

Pablo Picasso, 19.

A.

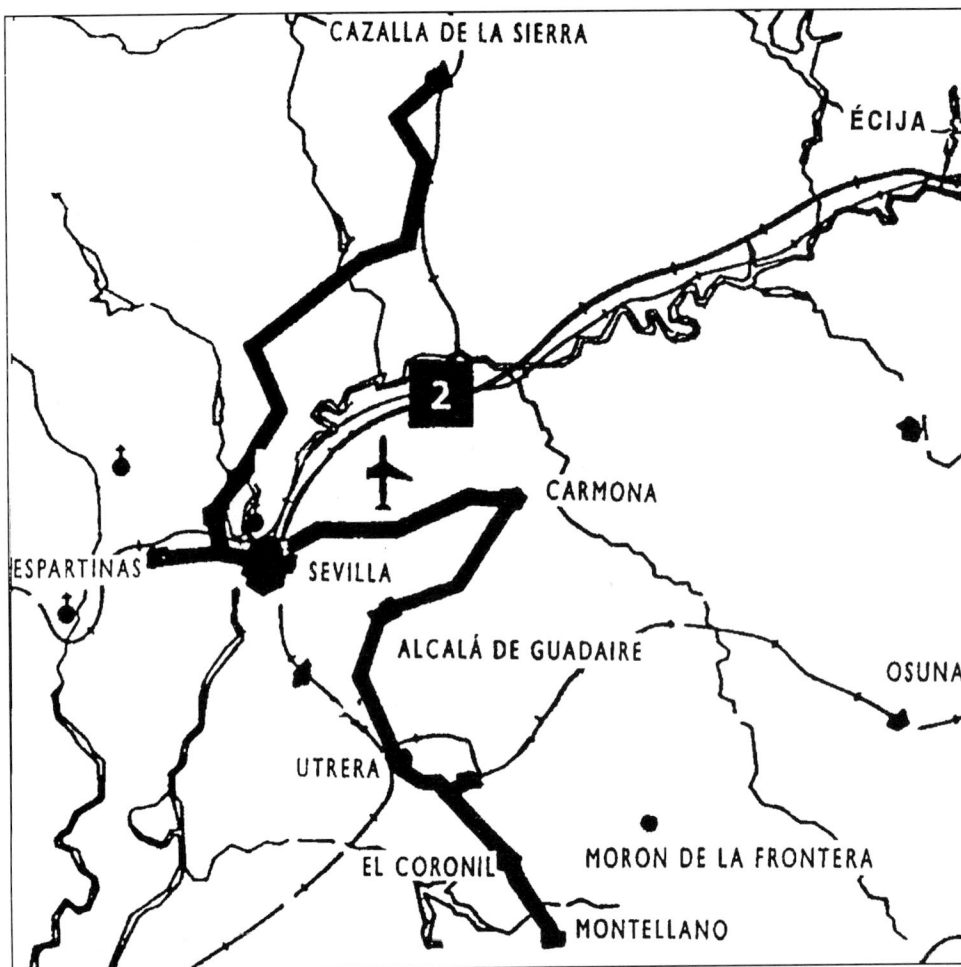

CAZALLA DE LA SIERRA

ÉCIJA

2

CARMONA

ESPARTINAS

SEVILLA

ALCALÁ DE GUADAIRE

OSUNA

UTRERA

MORÓN DE LA FRONTERA

EL CORONIL

MONTELLANO

Example

3

Ruta de los Castillos de Andalucía

B.

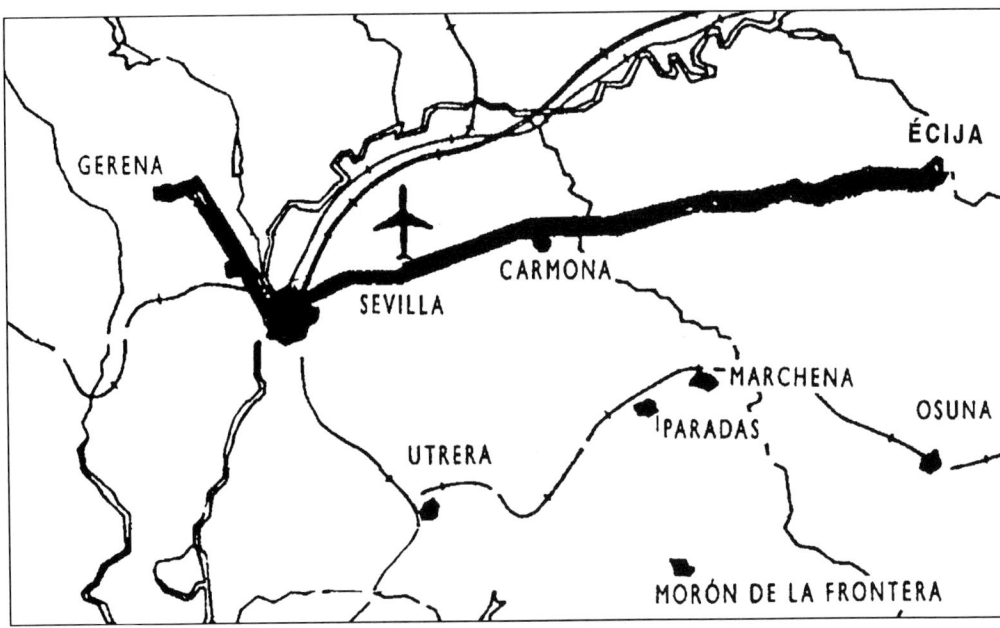

ÉCIJA

GERENA

CARMONA

SEVILLA

MARCHENA

PARADAS

OSUNA

UTRERA

MORÓN DE LA FRONTERA

C.

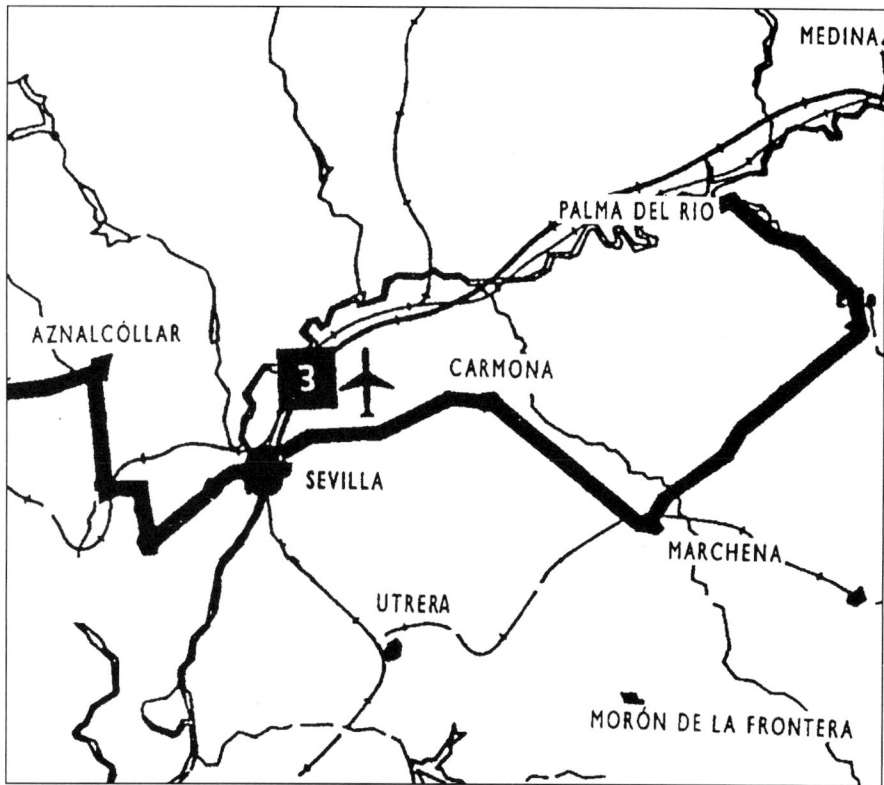

MEDINA

PALMA DEL RIO

AZNALCÓLLAR

3 ✈

CARMONA

SEVILLA

MARCHENA

UTRERA

MORÓN DE LA FRONTERA

D.

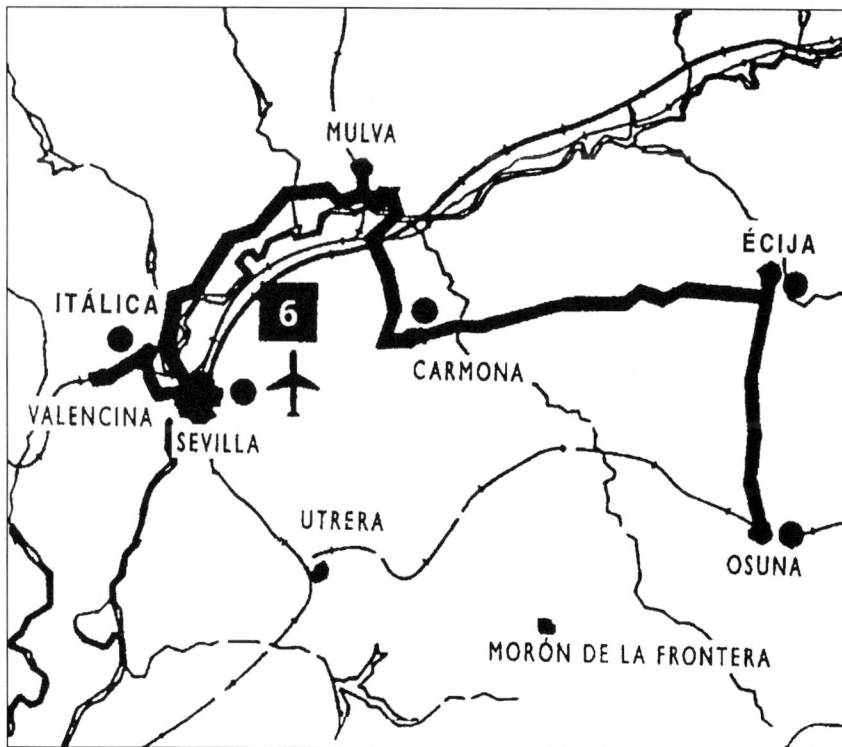

MULVA

ÉCIJA

ITÁLICA

6 ✈

VALENCINA

CARMONA

SEVILLA

UTRERA

OSUNA

MORÓN DE LA FRONTERA

b. From the list below, choose the appropriate name for each map of the area around Seville above and fill in the blank space under each one (see example: Map A).

'Rutas de ANDALUCÍA ISLÁMICA'

'Rutas de ANDALUCÍA ANTIGUA'

'Rutas de los Museos de ANDALUCÍA'

'Rutas de los Castillos de ANDALUCÍA'

Exercise 14 - At the information desk/En el mostrador de información

You are working at the information desk of 'Bus Eireann'. Spanish-speaking tourists come looking for information on day-tours from Dublin. Based on the document below, give them as much information as possible on day-tours available on Sundays and then on Fridays.

BUS EIREANN

	TOUR	DEPART	RETURN	DAYS OF OPERATION	DATES OF OPERATION	FARES
C.D.1	GLENDALOUGH & WICKLOW PANORAMA	10.30	17.45	SAT AND SUN DAILY	MAR 5th - MAR 27th & OCT 1st - OCT 30th APRIL 2nd - SEPT 29th	ADULT £13.50 CHILD £6.50
D.D.1	GLENDALOUGH & WICKLOW PANORAMA (Operates from Dun Laoghraie Tourist Office)	11.00	17.45* *Returns to Busaras	SAT AND SUN DAILY	MAR 5th - MAR 27th & OCT 1st - OCT 30th APRIL 2nd - SEPT 29th	ADULT £13.50 CHILD £6.50
C.D.2	AVONDALE, GLENDALOUGH & WICKLOW HILLS	09.30	16.30	FRIDAYS ONLY	JUNE 3rd - SEPT 23rd	ADULT £13.50 CHILD £6.50
C.D.3	NEW GRANGE & BOYNE VALLEY	10.00	17.45	TUESDAY, THURSDAY & SUNDAYS	APRIL 17th - OCT 2nd	ADULT £13.50 CHILD £6.50
C.D.4	POWERSCOURT GARDENS	14.15	18.00	SUNDAYS ONLY	JUNE 5th - SEPT 18th	ADULT £10.00 CHILD £5.00
C.D.11	KAVANAGH COUNTRY & CARLINGFORD LOUGH	09.30	19.30	SATURDAYS	JULY 2nd & 16th & 30th AUG 13th & 27th Sept 10th	ADULT £17.00 CHILD £8.50
C.D.12	NAVAN & ARMAGH	09.00	19.30	SATURDAYS	JUNE 25th, JULY 9th & 23rd AUG 6th & 20th Sept 3rd	ADULT £17.00 CHILD £8.50
C.D.14	MOUNTAINS OF MOURNE (Including lunch and cruise)	10.00	22.00	MONDAY TO SATURDAY EXCL. FRI.29th & SAT.30th JULY & MON. AUG.1st	JULY 4th - AUG 27th	ADULT £16.00

ALL TOURS EXCEPT D.D.1 DEPART FROM CENTRAL BUS STATION (BUSARAS) AT TIMES STATED ABOVE.

Note: Check the answers on the tape but remember that they are model answers only.

Exercise 15

You are working for the organising committee of the 'National Catering Exhibition'. Spanish exhibitors enquire about this trade fair. Based on the document below, give them as much information as possible on the fair (location, dates, opening hours and admittance, etc.).

NATIONAL CATERING EXHIBITION

DUBLIN

R.D.S. SIMMONSCOURT

FEBRUARY 15 · 16 · 17 · 18

Presented by

THE CATERING EQUIPMENT ASSOCIATION

WITH BWG FOODS CATERSERVICE

EXHIBITION OPEN

• MON. 15th, TUES 16th, WED 17th, 11. a.m. - 8 p.m. •

• THURSDAY 18th, 11 a.m. - 5.30 p.m. •

• TRADE ONLY • ADMITTANCE £5 (WITHOUT TICKET) •

• VISITORS 16 YRS & OVER •

THE ORIGINAL & LARGEST SHOWCASE FOR THE CATERING & HOSPITALITY INDUSTRY SINCE 1965

Note: Check the answers on the tape, but remember that they are model answers only.

Exercise 16

Read the document below on the Exhibition Centre in Barcelona and answer the questions which follow:

Situacion y accesos / Situacio i accessos

Metro - Metro: Líneas I, III y V (Estación Pza. España)

Autobuses Urbanos - Autobusos Urbans
- Línea 1 (Pza. España - Pza. Dante)
- Línea 8 (Ramblas - Ramblas)
- Línea 9 (Pza. Catalunya - Zona Franca)
- Línea 13 (Mercado de San Antonio - El Polvorín)
- Línea 27 (Pza. España - Valle Hebrón)
- Línea 48 (Ramblas - Ramblas)
- Línea 50 (Pza. España - Roquetas)
- Línea 56 (Collblanc - Besós)
- Línea 57 (Barceloneta - Collblanc)
- Línea 91 (Ramblas - Bordeta)
- Línea 101 (Arco del Triunfo - Pza. España)
- Línea 109 (Calabria/Sepúlveda - Zona Franca)

Autobuses Suburbanos - Autobusos Suburbans
- Línea CO (Pza. España - Cornellá)
- Línea EB (Pza. España - Bellvitge)
- Línea EC (Pza. España - El Prat)
- Línea EJ (Pza. España - Sant Just Desvern)
- Línea PR (Pza. España - El Prat)
- Línea UC (Pza. Universidad - Castelldefels)

RENFE - RENFE
Servicio Aeropuerto. Trenes cada 15 m.
Salida Estación de Sants (Pza. Països Catalans)

Ferrocarriles Catalanes - Ferrocarrils Catalans
Línea Pza. España - Igualada - Manresa

RECINTO FERIAL. INFORMACION DE INTERES

Los Salones Monograficos de Fira de Barcelona atraen, año tras año, a un numero cada vez mayor de expositores y visitantes de todo el mundo. Saben que, en un espacio muy concreto y en breve plazo de tiempo, van a entrar en contacto con lo mas actual y lo mas importante de su especialidad.

166

1. Where is the Exhibition Centre situated?
    a. east of the city
    b. west of the city
    c. south of the city

2. Where is the Ferry Terminal situated?
    a. north of the Exhibition Centre
    b. west of the Exhibition Centre
    c. south of the Exhibition Centre

3. Where is the underground station nearest to the Exhibition Centre?

    ....

4. At which station do you have to get off to get to the airport by train?

    ....

5. How often are there trains to the airport?
    a. every hour
    b. every half-hour
    c. every fifteen minutes

6. What are the names of the two train companies which provide services to the
    Exhibition Centre?

    a. ....

    b. ....

7. Which two languages are used in the document?

    ....

    ....

(R.S.)

(A.L.M.)

(R.S.)

(A.L.M.)

(SEID)

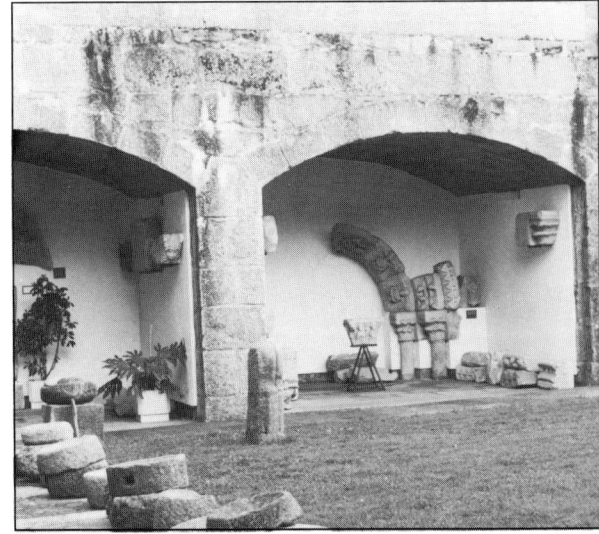

(A.L.M.)

Listening 1

a. **1.** Juan Romero
   2. Jorge González
   3. Carmen Otero
   4. Fernando López
   5. Pablo Pérez
   6. Concha Montes
   7. Mercedes Iglesias
   8. Alberto Blanco
   9. Antonio García
   10. Luisa Rama

b.   Hola/4   Buenos días/8   Bienvenido/2

   ¿Cómo se llama?/6   ¿Cuál es su nombre?/4   Por favor/10

Listening 3

a. **1.** P-E-S-S-O-A
   2. J-I-M-E-N-E-Z
   3. F-E-D-E-R-I-C-O
   4. S-H-A-W
   5. R-E-S-N-A-I-S

b. Countries: Portugal,   España,   Italia,   Irlanda,   Francia.

   Cities: Oporto,   Barcelona,   Milán,   Dublín,   Lyon.

Listening 5 — See tape script

Listening 6

1. D;   **2.** B;   **3.** E;   **4.** A;   **5.** C.

Listening 7

1. 6   **2.** 10   **3.** 44   **4.** 9   **5.** 7.

Listening 8

1. A;   **2.** C;   **3.** B;   **4.** E;   **5.** D.

Exercise 1

1. FERNÁNDEZ   **2.** PÉREZ   **3.** GARCÍA   **4.** ROMERO   **5.** GONZÁLEZ   **6.** LÓPEZ

Exercise 2

A Gracias....................................   **B**   De nada

  Adiós...   Adiós

  Buenos días.............................   Buenos días

  ¿Cuál es su dirección?...........   Calle Alameda, 54

  ¿Cómo se llama?....................   Mercedes López

  Buenas tardes.........................   Buenas tardes

  ¿Cómo se escribe?.................   M-E-R-C-E-D-E-S

  ¿Cuál es su nacionalidad?.....   Soy mejicana

  ¿Es usted azafata?.................   No, soy guía

  Aquí tiene su acreditación......   Muchas gracias

Exercise 3

b. 1. Me llamo Ana Pérez. P-E-R-E-Z
    Soy española. Vivo en Sevilla, en el Paseo de la Habana, 34. Mi número de teléfono es el
    452 3243. Soy guía turística.

   2. Mi nombre es Juana Otero.
    Soy argentina. Vivo en la calle de León, nº 16 de Buenos Aires, en Argentina. Mi número
    de teléfono es el 356 42 19. Soy azafata de congresos.

Exercise 4 — See tape script

Exercise 5 — See tape script

Listening 2

A.

B.

C.

D.

E.

F.

Listening 3

A. 11.00

B. 6.15

C. 12.45

D. 8.20

E. 6.10

F. midday

Listening 4

a. Excursión a Andalucía

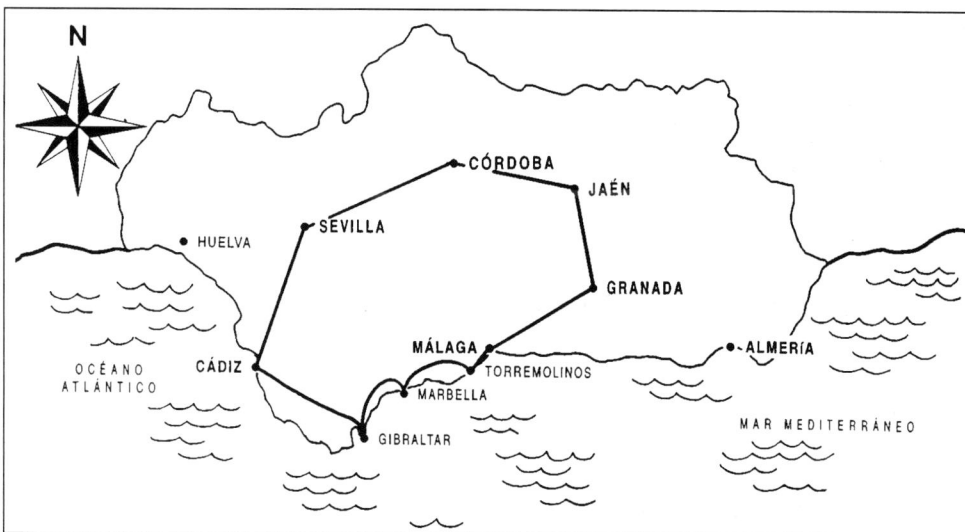

b.

	MAÑANA	TARDE	NOCHE
LUNES		Sevilla	Sevilla
MARTES	Sevilla	Córdoba	Córdoba
MIÉRCOLES	Granada	Granada	Granada
JUEVES	Granada	Málaga	Málaga
VIERNES	Torremolinos	Marbella	Marbella
SÁBADO	Cádiz	Cádiz	Cádiz
DOMINGO	Sevilla	Sevilla	

Listening 5

1. d;   **2.** f;   **3.** b;   **4.** a;   **5.** g;   **6.** k;

7. j;   **8.** l;   **9.** i;   **10.** h;   **11.** c;   **12.** e.

Listening 6

1.

> **BANCO**
>
> Abierto de 9.00 a 13.30
> y de 15.00 a 17.30
> Cerrado los domingos

2.

> **EXPOSICIÓN**
>
> Abierta de 10.00 a 12.00
> y de 17.00 a 20.30
> Cerrada los lunes

3.

> **PALACIO**
>
> Abierto de 10.00 a 17.00
> Cerrado en diciembre

4.

> **CATEDRAL**
>
> Abierta de 9.00 a 19.15

Listening 8

1. 5.000 ptas   **2.** US$ 680   **3.** IR£ 130

4. 8.500 pesos   **5.** 250 DM   **6.** 10.200 liras

Listening 9

a.   **1.** £ 55   **2.** £ 6   **3.** £ 15

    4. £ 13   **5.** £ 14   **6.** £ 3.50

b.

	perfume/ perfume	bombones/ chocolates	vino/ wine	salmón/ salmon	cigarrillos/ cigarettes	té/ tea
en efectivo/in cash		✓	✓			✓
con talón/by cheque	✓				✓	
con tarjeta de crédito/ by credit card				✓		

E x e r c i s e 1 - Crossword

ACROSS

1. After **martes**
5. The third month
6. Before **noviembre**
7. After **julio**
9. Between **jueves** and **sábado**
11. The eleventh month
13. Before **viernes**

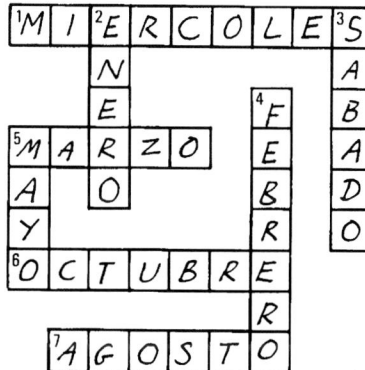

DOWN

2. The first month
3. Before **domingo**
4. The second month
5. **marzo, abril,** ...
7. Between **marzo** and **mayo**
8. Before **julio**
10. After **lunes**
12. After **domingo**

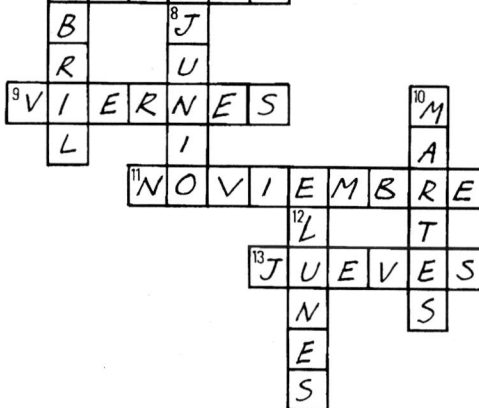

```
 ¹M  I  ²E  R  C  O  L  E  ³S
     N              A
     E        ⁴F    B
 ⁵M  A  R  Z  O     E    A
 A      O          B    D
 Y                 R    O
 ⁶O  C  T  U  B  R  E
                   R
    ⁷A  G  O  S  T  O
     B        ⁸J
     R        U
 ⁹V  I  E  R  N  E  S        ¹⁰M
     L        I              A
        ¹¹N  O  V  I  E  M  B  R  E
              ¹²L           T
           ¹³J  U  E  V  E  S
              N           S
              E
              S
```

Exercise 2

a. **1.** La Galería Nacional está abierta de 9,00 a 6,00. Cierra los lunes.

2. El castillo de Dublín está abierto de 10,00 a 12 y media y de 1 y media a 5,00. Los domingos está cerrado.

3. La piscina está abierta de 8 de la mañana a 10 de la noche.

4. Correos está abierto de 9 y media a 5 y cuarto. Cierra los sábados y los domingos.

b. **1.** La Galería Nacional cierra a las 6 de la tarde.

2. La Galería Nacional cierra los lunes.

3. No, Correos no abre los sábados.

4. El castillo abre a las 10 de la mañana.

5. No, la Galería Nacional cierra los lunes.

6. Sí, el castillo cierra los domingos.

7. Correos abre a las 9 y media.

8. Sí, la piscina está abierta todos los días.

9. No, Correos cierra los domingos.

10. El castillo cierra a las 5.

Exercise 3 — See tape script

Exercise 4 — See tape script

Listening 1

b.

4

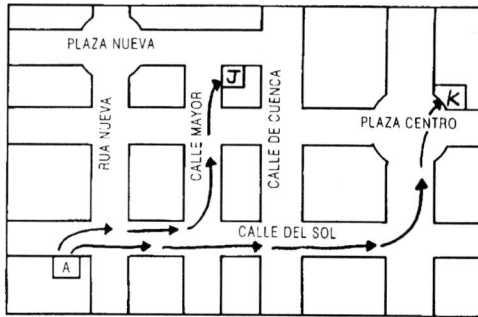

5

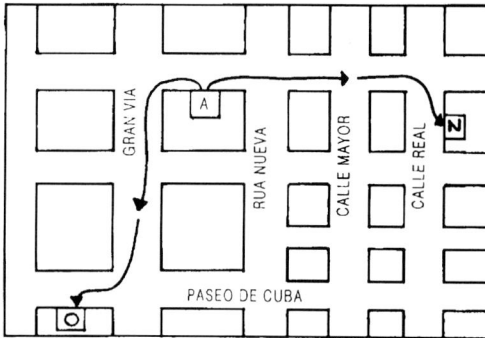

6

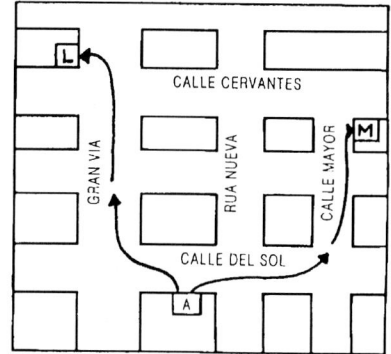

Listening 2

los aseos	7	los teléfonos	8
los ascensores	2	el autoservico	6
la librería	1	la cafetería	5
el guardarropa	3	las escaleras	4

Listening 3

	a pie/ andando	taxi	metro	autobús	coche	tren
Parque del Retiro ③	✓					
Ayuntamiento ①	✓		✓	✓		
Hipódromo ⑦		✓			✓	✓
Estación de Atocha ②	✓					
Ciudad Universitaria ⑥			✓			
Parque de Atracciones ⑤		✓		✓	✓	
Palacio Real ④			✓	✓		

1. Ayuntamiento
2. Estación de Atocha
3. Parque del Retiro
4. Palacio Real
5. Parque de Atracciones
6. Ciudad Universitaria
7. Hipódromo de la Zarzuela

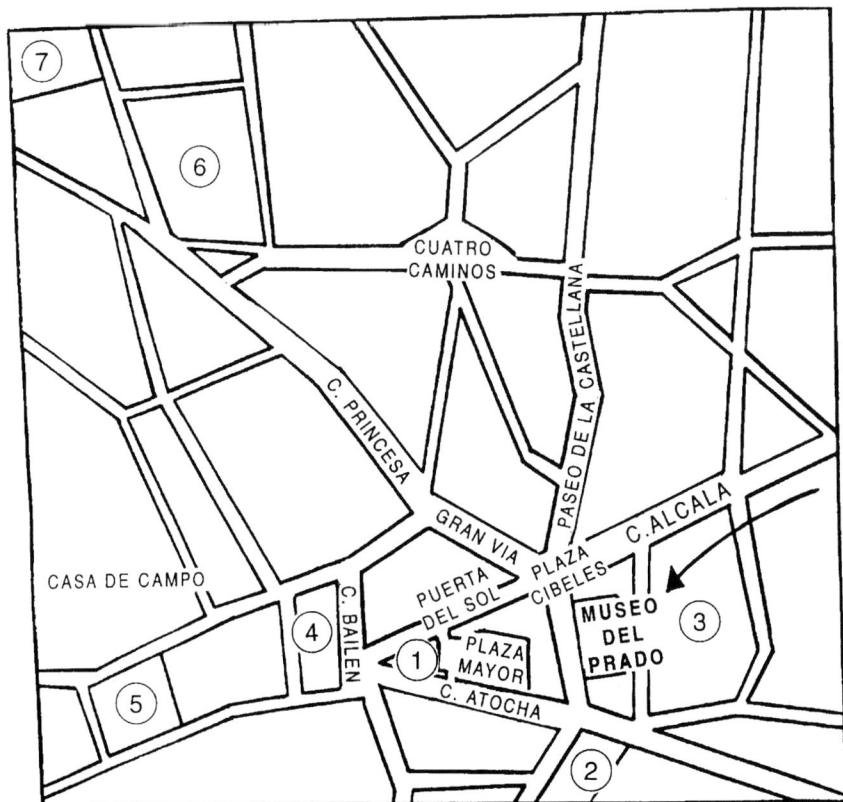

Listening 4

Playas (beaches)	Distancia km	Dirección	Pueblos (towns)	Distancia km	Dirección
San Juan	4	norte	Benidorm	45	nordeste
Los Arenales	12	sur	Santa Pola	17	sur
Castillos Castles)			Torrevieja	48	sur
La Mola	30	oeste	Elche	19	oeste
Biar	47	norte/ noroeste	Alcoy	53	norte

Listening 5

1. i   **2.** n   **3.** j   **4.** h   **5.** c   **6.** k   **7.** e

8. b   **9.** a   **10.** f   **11.** d   **12.** m   **13.** l   **14.** g

Listening 6

b.

1.   2.   3.

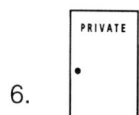

4.   5.   6.

Exercise 1 — See tape script

Exercise 2

a. 1. El hotel   **2.** La farmacia   **3.** El cine   **4.** El restaurante   **5.** La iglesia

b. 1. Correos está enfrente de la cafetería.

2. El museo está al lado de la farmacia.

3. La piscina está a la izquierda, en la calle Mayor.

4. El banco está entre la librería y el supermercado.

5. La cafetería está a la derecha, en la calle Real.

Exercise 3 — See tape script

Exercise 4

1. Zaragoza está a doscientos noventa y seis kilómetros.

2. Bilbao está a seiscientos viente kilómetros.

3. Santiago está a mil ciento vienticinco kilómetros.

4. Madrid está a seiscientos veintiún kilómetros.

5. Valencia está a trescientos cuarenta y nueve kilómetros.

6. Cáceres está a novecientos dieciocho kilómetros.

7. Lisboa está a mil doscientos sesenta y cuatro kilómetros.

8. Sevilla está a mil cuarenta y seis kilómetros.

Exercise 5

1. Quiere decir no fumar/prohibido fumar/no se puede fumar.

2. Significa aseos/servicios de señoras.

3. Quiere decir guardarropa.

4. Quiere decir (que) no funciona/no se puede usar.

Exercise 6 — See tape script

Listening 1

1. b, a, d, c.   **2.** a, c, b, d.   **3.** d, a, b, c.   **4.** c, b, a, d.

Listening 2

Hotel Manila	
Call for:	Julio Durán
Room number:	21

Hotel Continental	
Call for:	Sra. Castro Lamas
Room number:	78

Hotel Plaza	
Call for:	Mercedes Blanco
Room number:	289

Hotel Las Vegas	
Call for:	Sra. García Prado
Room number:	526

Listening 3

a.   **1.** c.   **2.** c.   **3.** b.   **4.** c.   **5.** Alejandro García.   **6.** His name.

b.

FICHA DE RECADOS TELEFÓNICOS
TELEPHONE MESSAGE

Para (To):   *Maite Blanco*

De parte de (From):   *Alejandro García*

Teléfono (Tel No):   *352 41 37*

    Volverá a llamar (will call again)   **a las** (at): _____

✔ **Desea que le llame** (please call back)   **a las** (at): ___*17,30*___

    Desea verle (wants to see you)   **a las** (at): _____

Listening 4

a. 1. c   **2.** b   **3.** a   **4.** d

b.

Salón/Feria Trade Fair	de from	para for	contacto establecido contact made	recado message
Deporte	/	representante de Adidas	sí	
Mueble	Cristina Reino	Sr. Bravo extensión 213	no	Llamará más tarde
Vehículo	/	extensión 863	no	Llamará más tarde
Informática	Rosa Castro	director	no	Desea verle a las seis

Exercise 1

-Hotel Central. Dígame.

-¿Podría ponerme con la habitación doce?

-Un momento, por favor, ahora le pongo.

-Muchas gracias.

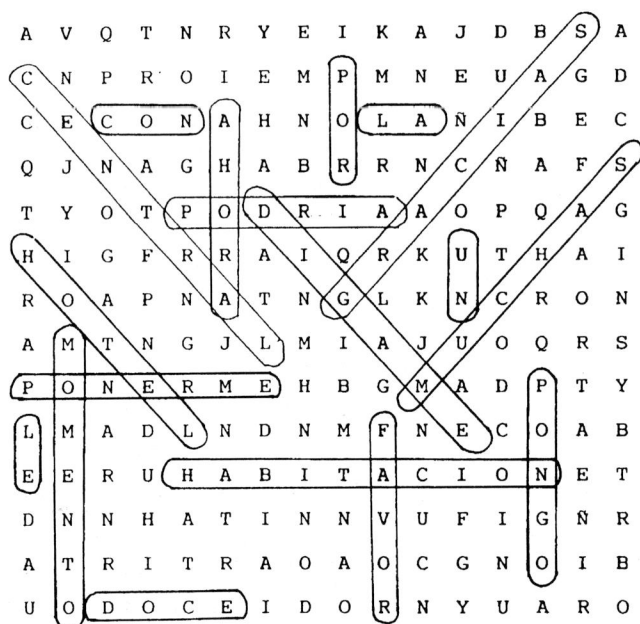

Exercise 2 — See tape script for model answer

Exercise 3 — See tape script for model answer

Exercise 4 — See tape script for model answer

Exercise 1

1. FLORES   **2.** GARCÍA   **3.** FUENTE   **4.** SAIZ   **2.** BLANCO

Exercise 2

1. 86   **2.** 54   **3.** 122   **4.** 315   **5.** 479   **6.** 567

Exercise 3

Guest	Room Number	Call Time
1	38	8.30
2	415	10.45
3	341	6.15
4	183	7.30

Exercise 4

1. 9.30 am - 12.00 pm (midday)   **2.** 3.00 pm   **3.** 12.30 pm - 7.30 pm

4. 8.00 pm - 12.00 am (midnight)   **5.** 1.30 am - 11.00 am   **6.** 4.30 am

Exercise 5

a. 1.   4.550 ptas   **2.**   5.200 ptas   **3.**   7.590 ptas
   4.   6.800 ptas   **5.**   9.150 ptas   **6.**   10.960 ptas

b. 1. El fin de semana en Roma cuesta sesenta y una mil cuatrocientas cincuenta (61.450) pesetas.
   2. El fin de semana en Venecia cuesta setenta y dos mil trescientas (72.300) pesetas.
   3. El fin de semana en Praga cuesta cincuenta y ocho mil ochocientas veinte (58.820) pesetas.
   4. El fin de semana en Túnez cuesta cuarenta y tres mil novecientas (43.900) pesetas.
   5. El fin de semana en Nueva York cuesta noventa y dos mil quinientas (92.500) pesetas.
   6. El fin de semana en Londres cuesta treinta y nueve mil setecientas ochenta (39.780) pesetas.

Exercise 6

1. The post office: G   **2.** The train station: B   **3.** The bureau de change: K

Exercise 7 — See tape script

Exercise 8

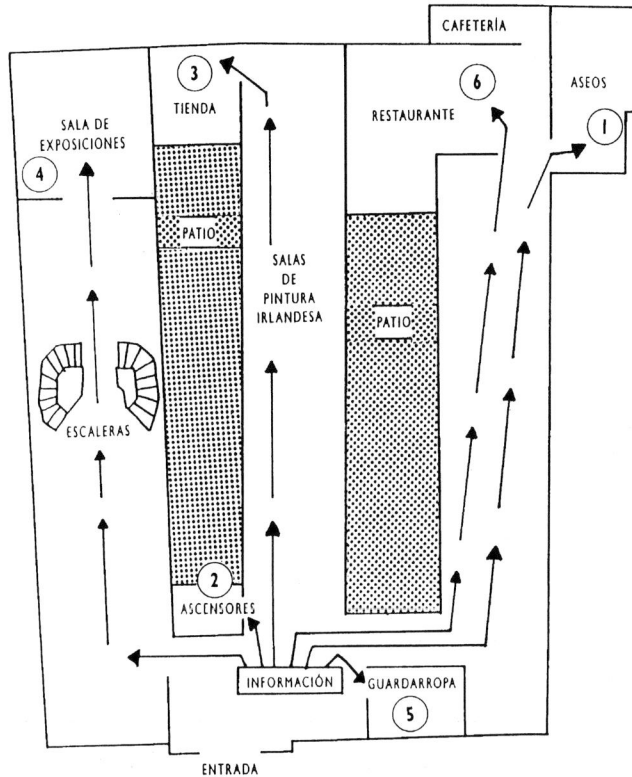

Exercise 9

1. B.   **2.** A.   **3.** F.   **4.** E.   **5.** D.   **6.** C.

Exercise 10

	Fecha	Salida	Llegada	Precio en pesetas (ida y vuelta)
1. Madrid-Londres	5 de mayo	6,15	7,35	26.800 ptas
2. Madrid-Ibiza	6 de noviembre	11,20	12,10	13.750 ptas
3. Madrid-Lisboa	13 de febrero	18,30	20,20	44.650 ptas
4. Madrid-La Habana	2 de diciembre	22,05	22,15	109.900 ptas

Listening 1

La basílica, el ayuntamiento, el castillo, el polideportivo, la Casa Ciurana, la Puerta del Rey.

Listening 2

1. Castellfort 30km   Herbés 20km
   Catí 30km   Peñíscola 80km

2. Hotel Rey D. Jaime
   Hostal Elías
   Vivienda Turismo Rural

3. a) A leaflet.

4. No.

Listening 3

a. 1. b.   **2.** c.   **3.** d.   **4.** a.

b.

	días de apertura opening days	**horario de apertura** opening hours
Basílica	**todos los días** every day	9.00am-8.00pm
Castillo	**todos los días salvo el domingo** every day except Sunday	3.00-9.30pm
Museo	**todos los días excepto el lunes** every day except Monday	10.00-12.00am 5.00-7.30pm
Palacio	**sólo sábados y domingos** Saturday and Sunday only	2.00-6.00pm

Listening 4

a. vinos,   mantas,   alfombras,   cerámica,   queso,   jerseis.

b. 1. False;   **2.** True;   **3.** True;   **4.** False;   **5.** False.

Listening 5

a.

> ## HOJA DE RESERVAS
> ### Hotel El Fuerte. Marbella.
>
> Número de personas: 2
> ....
>
> Número de noches: 6
> ....
>
> Tipo de habitación: Doble con baño
> ....
>
> Nombre del cliente: Manuel García Ramos
> ....

b.   **1.** a;   **2.** Yes;   **3.** * * * *;   **4.** dinner.

Listening 6

a.   **1.** False;   **2.** True;   **3.** True;   **4.** False;   **5.** True;   **6.** True.

b.

Name of customer:	Miguel Fernández
Booking for:	tonight
Amount paid:	10.520 ptas
Method of payment:	cheque

Exercise 1

a. 1. c;   **2.** a;   **3.** d;   **4.** e;   **5.** b.

b.

a map	**un mapa**	every day	**todos los días**
a show	**un espectáculo**	a street map	**un plano**
a brochure	**un folleto**	tonight	**esta noche**
a room	**una habitación**	with bath	**con baño**
free	**gratuito**	a dinner	**una cena**
a ticket	**una entrada**	a breakfast	**un desayuno**

Exercise 2 — See tape script

Exercise 3 — See tape script

Exercise 4 — See tape script

Exercise 5 — See tape script

Listening 1

a.

b.

Ruta/Route	**Duración de la travesía/** duration of crossing	**Precio/** price
Vía Gran Bretaña/via Great Britain		
1. de: Bilbao a: Portsmouth	30 horas 74.600 ptas	
2. de: Santander a: Plymouth	24 horas	60.400 ptas
3. de: Dublin a: Holyhead	3 horas	25.400 ptas
Vía Francia/via France		
1. de: Cherburgo a: Rosslare	18 horas	82.500 ptas
2. de: Le Harve a: Rosslare	21 horas	82.500 ptas

c.   **1.** c;   **2.** b;   **3.** b;   **4.** a.

Listening 2

a.   **A.** 2;   **B.** 3;   **C.** 1.

b. — See tape script

Listening 3

De Madrid a:	en autocar-en autobús/ by coach duración/duration	en tren/by train duración/duration	en avión/by plane duración/duration
1. París	14h	13h	1h 45m
2. Roma	31h	32h	2h 15m
3. Lisboa	9h	10h	1h

Listening 4

a.   **1.** ida 19,30 - 08,30;   vuelta 20,00 - 08,32.
          2. ida 15,50 - 18,05;   vuelta 19,05 - 21,25.
          3. ida 22,00 - 07,00;   vuelta 22,00 - 07,00.

b. 1.

RENFE		Billete + litera		Clase: 2
IDA	**Hora**	**VUELTA**	**Hora**	
Salida: Madrid - Chamartín	19.30	**Salida**: París - Austerlitz	20,00	
Llegada: París - Austerlitz	08,30	**Llegada**: Madrid - Chamartín	08,32	
Fecha: 25/4		**Fecha**: 30/4........		
Reserva de literas: No. 31 No. 32		**Pesetas**: 25.800		

2.

IBERIA			
Nombre: Cristina Morán			
	Fechas	**Horas**	
		Salida	Llegada
De: MADRID - Barajas	17/5	15,50	18,05
A: ROMA - Fiumicino			
A: MADRID - Barajas	4/6	19,05	21,25
Tarifa: 59.400 ptas.			

3.

AUTOBUSES PENÍNSULA

MADRID - LISBOA - MADRID

Ida	Fecha	Hora	**Vuelta**	Fecha	Hora
Salida de Madrid:	30/11	22,00	Salida de Lisboa:	6/12	07,00
Llegada a Lisboa:		07,00	Llegada a Madrid:		22,00

Precio: 6.240 ptas.

Listening 5

1. FALSE   **2.** b)   **3.** c)   **4.** c)
5. a)   **6.** c)   **7.** b)   **8.** a)

Listening 6

AGENCIA DE VIAJES AZUL

HOJA DE INSCRIPCIÓN

RELLÉNESE CON MAYÚSCULAS*

Destino: CUBA

Salida de: MADRID

Fecha de salida: 10 DE SEPTIEMBRE   **Fecha de vuelta:** 18 DE SEPTIEMBRE

Viaje: AL CORAZÓN DE CUBA

Participantes:

Apellidos	Nombre	Fecha de nacimiento	Nacionalidad	Profesión
LAGE BLANCO	CARMEN	16 ABRIL 1954	ESPAÑOLA	PROFESORA
OTERO IGLESIAS	ISABEL	/	ESPAÑOLA	PROFESORA
RIO FRAGA	MARINA	/	MEJICANA	PROFESORA

Dirección   CALLE REAL, 58-2º IZQUIERDA. 28050 MADRID.

Teléfono particular: 316 37 86   Teléfono del trabajo: 562 35 92

Cantidad a pagar: 351.900 ptas

☐ en efectivo   ☐ con tarjeta de crédito   ☑ con talón

*complete in block capitals

Exercise 1

a. 1. -Puede ir a Italia en tren o en avión.

-¿Se puede ir en barco?

-Sí, también es posible.

2. -¿Prefiere visitar la zona en autobús/autocar o a pie?

-Prefiero visitarla en coche.

-De acuerdo. ¡Buen viaje!

b. 1. El viaje en barco dura unas catorce horas. En avión sólo lleva dos horas.
2. El autocar sale de Barcelona a las 8,00 de la tarde y llega a Bruselas al día siguiente.
3. De Sevilla a Madrid es posible viajar en el Ave (tren de alta velocidad). Se puede ir de noche o de día.

Exercise 2 — See tape script

Exercise 3 — See tape script

Exercise 4

1. a) golf, tennis and squash
 b) the price per day for a double room + full board
 c) accommodation + breakfast
 d) yes
 e) a golf course
 f) Benalmádena

2. a) 68
 b) yes
 c) 50%
 d) opening 17/12, closing 9/4
 e) New Year's Eve dinner for adults
 f) for 6 nights

Exercise 5 — See tape script

Listening 1

a. vela   submarinismo   golf   senderismo   windsurf

equitación   escalada   pesca   baile   bicicleta todo terreno

b. 1. True;   **2.** True;   **3.** False;

4. False;   **5.** True;   **6.** False.

Listening 2

1. El gorro de baño es obligatorio.

2. Los animales no pueden entrar en la piscina.

3. Los niños pueden usar el gimnasio.

4. La entrada en la discoteca está prohibida a los menores de 16 años.

5. Solamente se puede fumar en la sala de juegos.

Listening 3

a. Mañana: vela.

Tarde: excursión en bicicleta todo terreno (BTT).

22,00: baile irlandés.

b. 1. vela   **2.** piragüismo en canoa

3. senderismo   **4.** paseo a caballo

5. excursión en BTT   **6.** baile irlandés

Listening 4

a. 1. f;   **2.** h;   **3.** c;   **4.** c;

5. b;   **6.** c;   **7.** d;   **8.** g.

b. 1. yes;   **2.** yes;   **3.** no;   **4.** no;

5. yes;   **6.** yes;   **7.** no;   **8.** yes.

Listening 5

1. c;   **2.** b;   **3.** b;   **4.** a;   **5.** b;   **6.** a.

Listening 6

a.   **A.** 4;   **B.** 5;   **C.** 2;   **D.** 1;   **E.** 6;   **F.** 3.

b.   **1.** c;   **2.** f;   **3.** b;   **4.** d;   **5.** a;   **6.** e.

Exercise 1 — See tape script

Exercise 2

1. Submarinismo
2. Lavandería
3. Parque infantil
4. Tiro con arco/Tiro al arco
5. Plancha a vela/Windsurf
6. Oficina de cambio/Cambio de monedas
7. Musculación
8. Pesca
9. Tenis
10. Parking/Aparcamiento

Exercise 3

1. 1 - 5 days.
2. Apartamentos "Galicia".
3. Any three of the following: tennis, basketball, skiing, jogging, hill walking, pony trekking.
4. Jogging and hill walking.
5. Indoor swimming pool.
6. Yes.
7. Breakfast and either lunch or dinner.
8. Skiing course.

Exercise 4 — See tape script

Exercise 5 — See tape script

Listening 1

a.   **1.** a;   **2.** c;   **3.** c;   **4.** c;   **5.** b.

b. — See tape script

Listening 2

a. iglesia: 4;   isla: 3;   palacio: 4;   torre: 1;   panorámica: 2;

　　 vino: 1;   playa: 2;   puente: 3;   pescado: 1;   balneario: 2.

b.

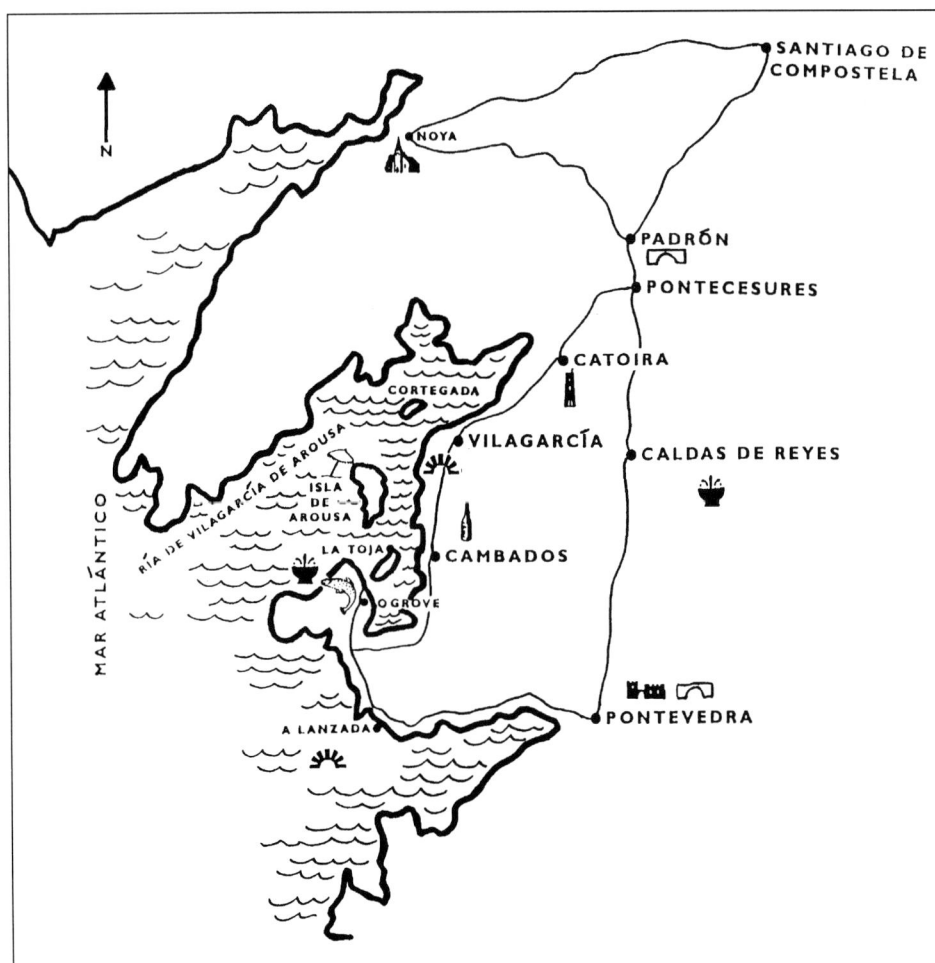

c. — See tape script

Listening 3

a.

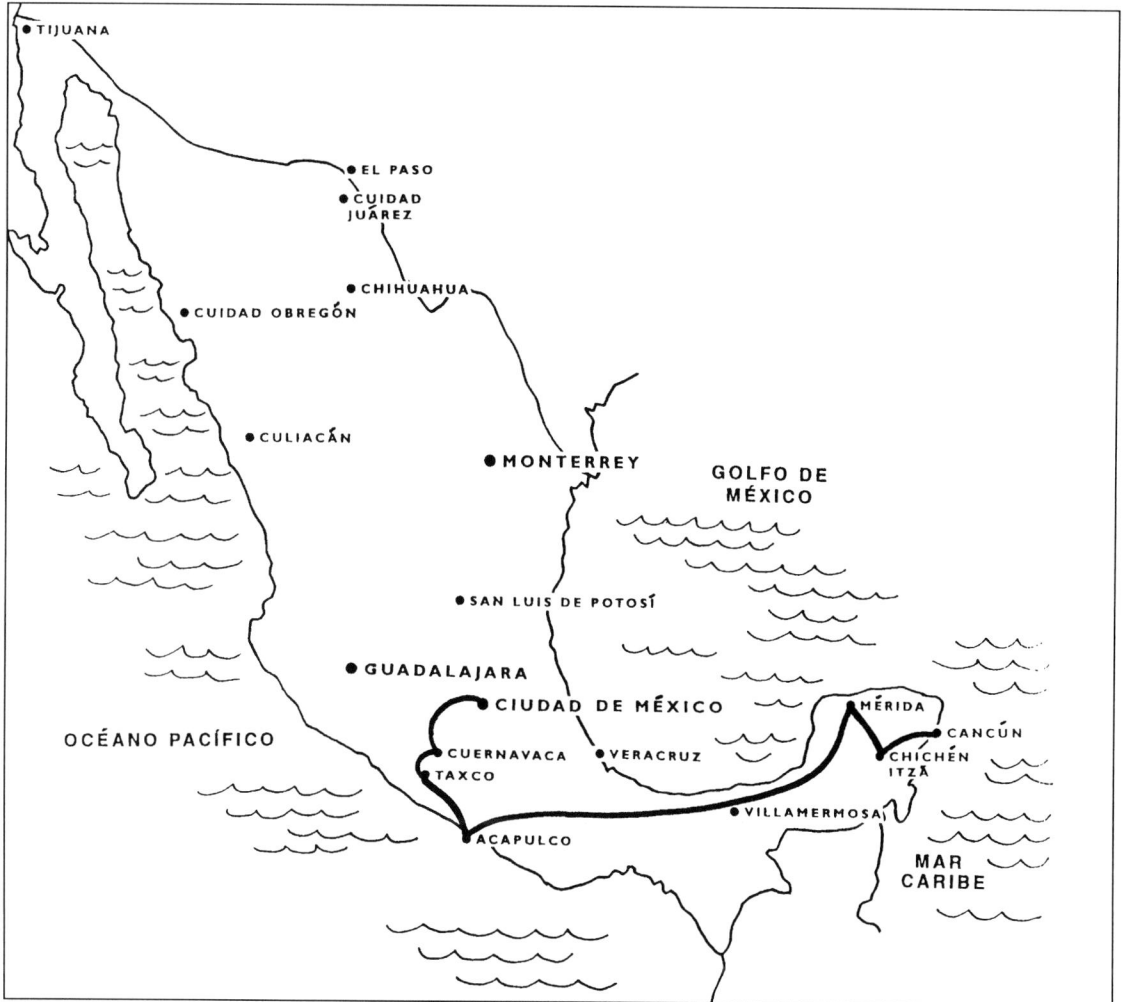

b. 1. a;   **2.** b;   **3.** b;   **4.** c;   **5.** a;   **6.** b;   **7.** c;
   8. c;   **9.** a;   **10.** c;   **11.** a;   **12.** a;   **13.** a;   **14.** b.

Listening 4

a.   **2.** un restaurante muy famoso;   **5.** una actuación de ballet;
     6. un recital de poesía;   **7.** una obra de teatro;   **8.** una discoteca.

b. A. (2) un restaurante muy famoso

B. (3) un concierto de música clásica

C. (1) un paseo tranquilo

D. (8) una discoteca

E. (4) un festival de música folclórica

c. **1.** 24.00; **2.** 23.00; **3.** 20.30; **4.** 23.30.

Listening 5

a. 1. La platería es famosa, la cerámica es muy original,

2. La tarta de almendra es exquisita, la tarta de manzana es deliciosa.

3. Los encajes son de excelente calidad, los trabajos en madera y los artículos de cristal son típicos.

4. Los platos son de diseño exclusivo, los cuencos son baratos y muy bonitos, los objetos de plata son un buen recuerdo.

b. En el mercado: 4

Al lado del hotel: 3, 4

En la Rúa del Villar: 2

En la Rúa Nueva: 1

Por toda la ciudad: 2, 1

Alrededor de la catedral: 1, 3

En el casco antiguo: 3, 4

Listening 6

a. Esta mañana hace	buen tiempo frío viento	Esta mañana hay	lluvias
b. Esta tarde hará	fresco sol	Esta tarde habrá	nieve tormentas
c. Mañana va a hacer	calor	Mañana va a haber	nubes nieblas heladas

d.

Listening 7

a.

Destino/ destination	Tiempo/weather				Temperaturas/temperatures		
	🌡	🌡	☀	☁🌧	⤵	Media/ average	Min	Max
1. Francia	✓			✓		22	12	34
2. Irlanda				✓	✓	16	10	25
3. Grecia			✓			31	-	-
4. Venezuela	✓		✓			27	23	36
5. Canadá			✓		✓	13	-	-
6. Filipinas	✓		✓			25	20	35
7. Islandia		✓		✓	✓	8	-	14
8. Egipto	✓		✓			32	-	-

b. 1. Irlanda: primavera y verano

   2. Venezuela: verano e invierno

   3. Canadá: verano

   4. Egipto: invierno y otoño

Exercise 1

1. vino de la comarca
2. edificios de estilo románico
3. recorrido un poco más largo
4. típicas tabernas
5. visitas interesantes
6. sitios atractivos
7. famoso balneario
8. puente medieval
9. playas preciosas
10. excursión muy cómoda
11. pequeña iglesia
12. pueblos pintorescos
13. viaje muy variado
14. torres prerromanas

Exercise 2

a. Example: En Zarauz hay un castillo

En Guetaria pueden visitar el puerto pesquero

En Zumaya tienen un museo

Exercise 3

a. En el norte hay nubes y lluvia.

En el centro hace frío y hay heladas.

En el este hay niebla y hace sol.

En el sur hace calor y hay tormentas.

En Baleares hace calor y viento.

En Canarias hace sol y calor.

Exercise 4

1. "Granjas de Irlanda"

2. **a.** double room with bath

   b. Irish breakfast

   c. tourist guidebook of the regions and map

   d. welcome tea

   e. farewell Irish coffee.

   f. free tickets (one in each region) for tourist attractions

   g. taxes

3. No

4. **a.** visit to a crystal factory

   b. visit to a museum

   d. visit to a castle

Exercise 5 — See tape script

Listening 1

A. **1.** b; **2.** b; **3.** c.

B. **1.** a; **2.** b.

C. **1.** e; **2.** c; **3.** b.

D. **1.** a; **2.** c.

E. **1.** a, d; **2.** a; **3.** c.

Listening 2

a.

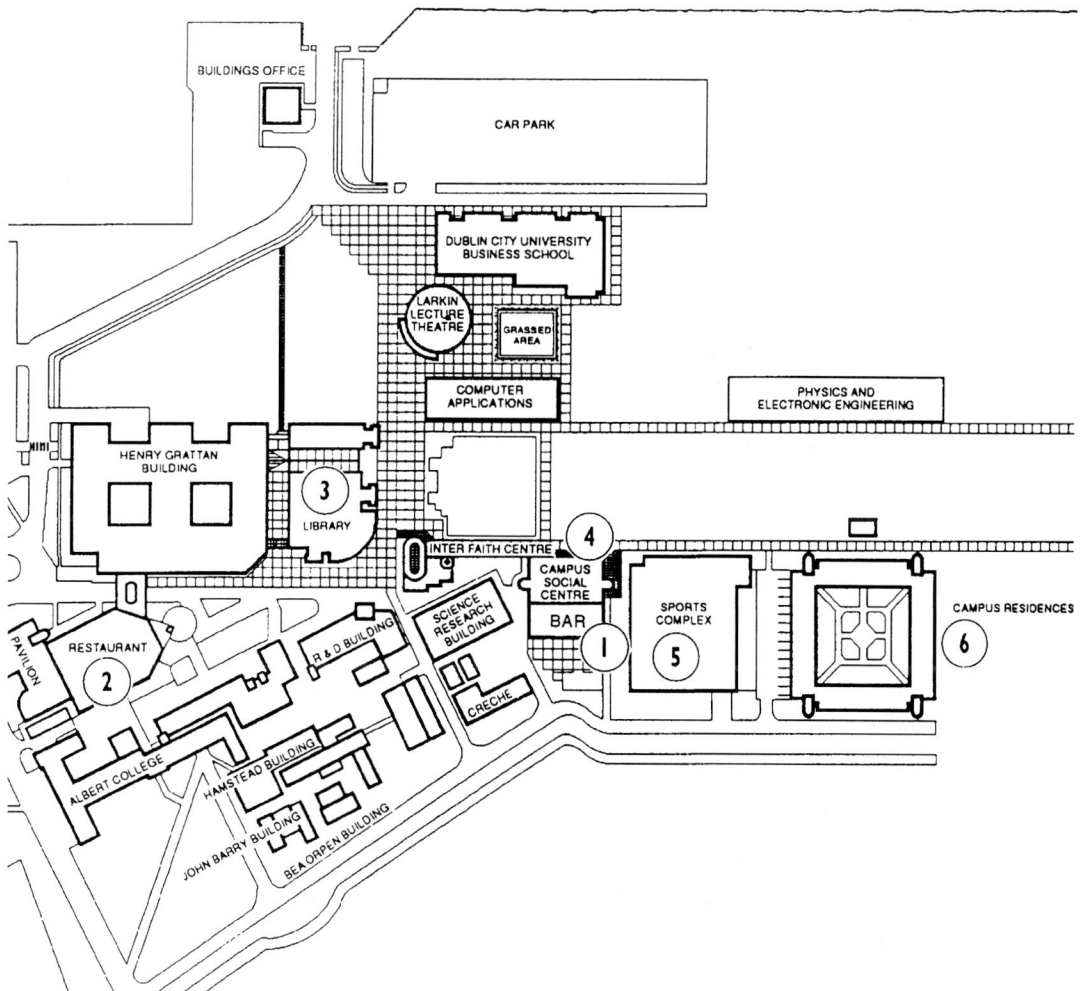

b.

BAR
Opening hours: 10.30am - 11.30pm
Closed (days): Sunday

RESTAURANT
Lunch served from: 12.00pm
to: 2.15pm

LIBRARY
Opening hours: Monday to Thursday 9.00am - 5.00pm
Closed (days): Saturday and Sunday
Location: Next to Henry Grattan building

STUDENTS SHOP
Opening hours: 9.00am-5.00pm
Closed (days): Saturday and Sunday
Location: The Social Centre

SPORTS COMPLEX
Opening hours: 8.00am-10.00pm
Location: Between the social centre and the campus residences
Fee for each visit: £1

RESIDENCE OFFICE
Opening hours: 7.30am-10.00pm
Telephone number: 704 5736
Fax number: 704 5777

Listening 3

INTERNATIONAL CONFERENCE FOR TOURISM STUDIES MAY 5-6-7						
Nombre	Temple Bar Hotel	Student Residences	Extra Nights	Accompanying Persons	Amount Paid	Amount Due
ALONSO Manuel	✔		~~1~~ 0	2	£708	/
DÍAZ Carmen	✔		0	0	£236	/
MORENO Alicia		✔	0	0	~~£185~~	£100
PÉREZ Alberto	✔		~~2~~ 0	1	£472	/
SOTO Ana	~~✔~~	✔	~~0~~ 1	0	£185	£19.50
VÁZQUEZ Fernando	✔		2	2	£708	£216

Listening 4

CONGRESO INTERNACIONAL DE TURISMO
5, 6 y 7 de MAYO

INTERNATIONAL CONFERENCE FOR TOURISM STUDIES
MAY 5-6-7
Viernes 5 de mayo/Friday, 5 May

Horario/Time	**Actividades**/Activity	**Lugar**/Location
9.00 - 9.30am	**Registro y entrega de documentación**/Registration and presentation of documentation	**Recepción**/Reception
9.30 - 11.00am	**Sesión plenaria**/Plenary session **Ceremonia de inauguración y Bienvenida**/Welcome and opening	**Auditorio Larkin**/ Larkin Lecture Theatre
11.00 - 11.30am	**Pausa-café**/Coffee-break	~~S210~~ 212
11.30 - 1.00pm	**Grupos de trabajo A - D**/ Workshops A - D	A: S230 C: ~~S232~~ 235 B: S231 D: S233
1.00 - 2.30pm	**Almuerzo**/Lunch	**Restaurante**/Canteen
2.30 - 3.30pm	**Debate general**/General discussion	**Auditorio Larkin**/ Larkin Lecture Theatre
3.30 - 4.00pm	**Pausa-café**/Coffee-break	S212
4.00 - 5.30pm	**Grupos de trabajo E - H**/ Workshops E - H	E: S210 G: ~~S212~~ 221 F: S211 H: ~~S213~~ 222
5.30 - 6.30pm	**Debate general**/General discussion	**Auditorio Larkin**/ Larkin Lecture Theatre
~~7.00~~ 6.45pm	**Autobús al centro**/Bus to town	**Aparcamiento**/Car park
~~7.30~~ 7.15pm	**Recepción ofrecida por el alcalde**/Reception hosted by Lord Mayor	Mansion House

Listening 5

10ª EDICIÓN DE LA FERIA INTERNACIONAL DE TURISMO

10TH WORLD FAIR FOR TOURISM

Lugar/Location: Barcelona, Palacio de Congresos.

Fechas/Dates: 24-31 de Mayo.

Jornadas técnicas para profesionales/Trade only: 24, 25, y 26.

Horario de apertura/Opening hours: 8,30am-9,00pm.

Días de apertura al público/Opening to the public: 27-31.

Horario de apertura/Opening hours: 10,00am-8,00pm.

Expositores/Exhibitors: 683.

Extranjeros/Foreign: 225.

Españoles/Spanish: 458.

Superficie ocupada/Total surface area: 10.380 metros cuadrados.

Número de visitantes esperados/Expected number of visitors: 65.000.

Número de teléfono de información/Information telephone number: 423 31 01, extensión 9000

Listening 6

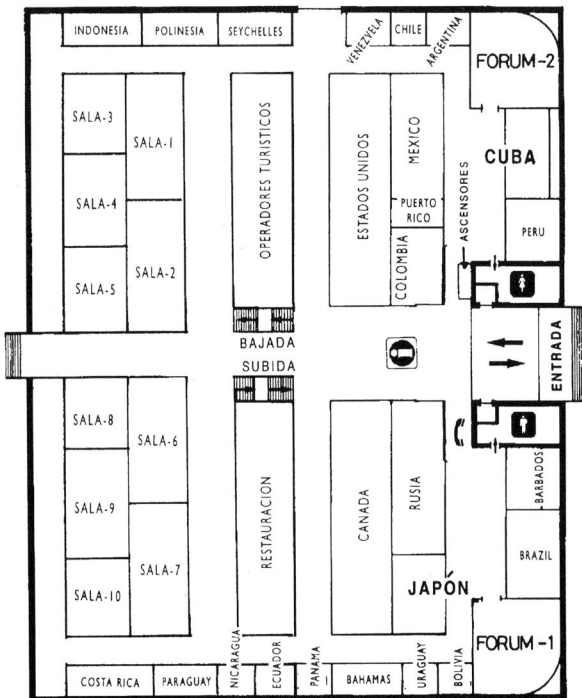

MAIN FLOOR

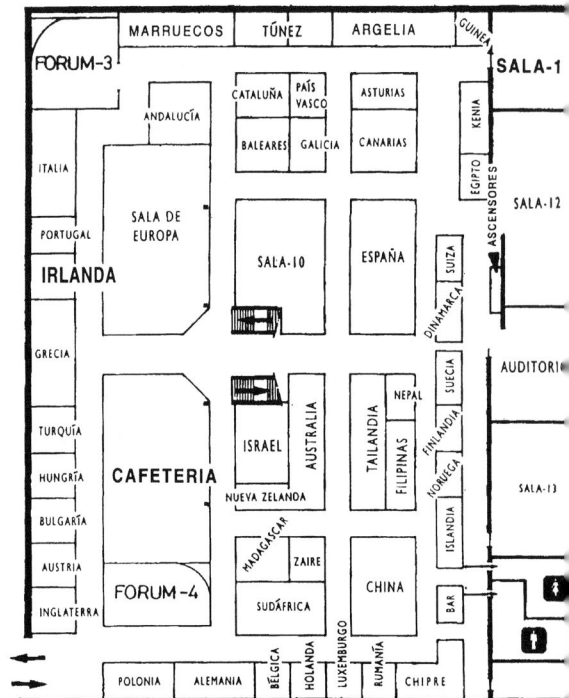

GROUND FLOOR

Listening 7

SALA DE EUROPA

Wednesday 10th May

16.00:	Presentation on	Tourism in the European Union.
18.30:	Presentation on	Tourism in France.

Thursday 11th May

11.30:	Presentation on	Tourism in the United States.
15.00:	Presentation on	Tour Operators in Great Britain
16.30:	Presentation on	Tourism in the Scandinavian Countries: Finland, Norway and Sweden
18.00:	Presentation on	Tourism in the Mediterranean Countries: Spain, Italy, Greece and Turkey.

Exercise 1 — See tape script

Exercise 2 — See tape script

Exercise 3

1. Está en la planta baja. Baje las escaleras, tome el pasillo de enfrente y luego el de la derecha. El stand de Italia está a la izquierda, entre el stand de Portugal y el Forum 3.

2. Los servicios de señoras están ahí mismo, a la izquierda, detrás de los ascensores.

3. Los ascensores están ahí al lado, a la izquierda.

4. Sí, hay un bar en la planta baja. Baje en el ascensor y al salir vaya a la izquierda. El bar está al final del pasillo, a la derecha, enfrente de los aseos.

5. Los teléfonos están ahí mismo, a la derecha, entre el stand de Rusia y los aseos de caballeros.

6. Tome ese pasillo de la izquierda y siga todo recto. El stand de Argentina está al final, al lado del Forum 2.

7. El Forum 3 está en la planta baja. Baje las escaleras, tome el pasillo de enfrente y luego gire a la derecha. El Forum 3 está al final del pasillo.

8. Tome ese pasillo de la derecha. El stand de Brasil está a la izquierda, entre el de Barbados y el Forum 1.

Exercise 4

CONGRESO INTERNACIONAL DE TURISMO
5, 6 y 7 de MAYO

INTERNATIONAL CONFERENCE FOR TOURISM STUDIES
MAY 5-6-7

Sábado 6 de mayo/Saturday, 6 May

Horario/Time	**Actividades/**Activities	**Lugar/**Locations
9,30 - 11,00am	**Sesión plenaria/**Plenary session	**Auditorio Larkin/** Larkin Lecture Theatre
11,00 - 11,30am	Pausa-café	S212
11,30 - 1,00pm	Grupos de trabajo I, J, K y L	I: S534
		J: S535
		K: S540
		L: S542
1,00 - 2,30pm	Almuerzo	Restaurante
2,30 - 3,30pm	Debate general	Auditorio Larkin
3,30 - 4,00pm	Pausa-café	S213
4,00 - 5,00pm	Grupos de trabajo M y N	M: S318
		N: S320
5,00 - 6,00pm	Debate general	Auditorio Larkin
6,30pm	**Autobuses para la recepción en el Castillo/**Buses to the reception in Dublin Castle	Aparcamiento

Exercise 5 — See tape script

Exercise 1

a. **1.** antigua;   **2.** original;   **3.** pintoresca;   **4.** interesante;   **5.** alemana.

b. **1.** preciosas;   **2.** grandes;   **3.** famosos;   **4.** locales;   **5.** irlandeses.

Exercise 2

1. cuarta planta
2. treinta y una mil pesetas
3. setecientas veinte libras
4. tercer día
5. quinientas pesetas
6. décima edición

7. un dólar
8. cuarto pasillo
9. veintiún museos
10. séptimo piso
11. doscientas cincuenta libras
12. ochocientos treinta y cuatro marcos

Exercise 3

a.
1. ¿Les interesa escuchar música?
2. ¿Le interesa viajar en tren?
3. ¿Les interesa reservar las entradas?
4. ¿Le interesa jugar al tenis?
5. ¿Le interesa hacer submarinismo?
6. ¿Les interesa comprar algo?

b.
1. ¿Le gustaría comer pescado?
2. ¿Les gustaría dar un paseo?
3. ¿Les gustaría visitar el museo?
4. ¿Le gustaría probar el vino?
5. ¿Les gustaría montar a caballo?
6. ¿Le gustaría hacer un crucero?

Exercise 4

1. Usted va a llegar por la mañana.
2. Va a haber niebla.
3. Los turistas van a visitar el palacio.

4. A la izquierda va a ver la iglesia.
5. Ustedes van a volver mañana.
6. Va a hacer frío.

Exercise 5

a.
1. Puede llamar más tarde.
2. Puede bajar en el ascensor.
3. Puede comprar algún recuerdo.
4. Puede girar a la izquierda.
5. Puede seguir todo recto.
6. Puede salir por la planta baja.

b.
1. Espere un momento.
2. Continúe todo recto.
3. Pase por León.
4. Escriba su dirección.
5. Diga su nombre.
6. Vaya por la carretera.

Exercise 6

1. ¿Cuál prefiere?   **2.** ¿Qué quiere beber?   **3.** ¿Cómo le gustaría ir?
4. ¿Cuántas botellas quiere? **5.** ¿A dónde va el visitante? **6.** ¿Cuánto cuesta el perfume?

Exercise 7

1. b   **2.** canoeing, mountaineering, fishing, skiing   **3.** yes   **4.** on the 25th of July
5. b, c, e   **6. a.** Corao; **b.** Labra; **c.** Cangas, río Dobra; **d.** Cangas, **e.** Cardes, Covadonga.

Exercise 8 — See tape script

Exercise 9 — See tape script

Exercise 10 — **1.** no;   **2.** b, c, d, f;   **3.** a;   **4.** c;   **5.** b;   **6.** a.

Exercise 11 — **1.** b, c;   **2.** b, d, f, g;   **3.** b;   **4.** b;   **5.** c;   **6.** no.

Exercise 12 — See tape script

Exercise 13

Map **A** : description 3 : Rutas de los Castillos de Andalucía
Map **B** : description 4 : Rutas de los Museos de Andalucía
Map **C** : description 2 : Rutas de ANDALUCÍA ISLÁMICA
Map **D** : description 1 : Rutas de ANDALUCÍA ANTIGUA

Exercise 14 — See tape script

Exercise 15 — See tape script

Exercise 16

1. b;   **5.** c;
2. c;   **6.** Renfe and Ferrocarriles Catalanes.
3. Plaza de España;   **7.** Spanish and Catalan.
4. Estación de Sants;

Spanish grammar has been kept to a minimum in the nine units, but for those who would like to know a bit more about how the Spanish language functions, this chapter provides a summary of the main points.

Grammatical terms are essential tools in understanding the way any language works; these are the basic terms used in this section:

1. **Nouns:**

   A noun is a word used for naming - people, places, objects, animals or concepts, **e.g. Nicola, Ireland, car, horse, tourism.**

2. **Articles:**

   An article is a word used meaning **the** or **a.** It is used before a noun or its accompanying adjective in English.

   The is called the *definite* article.

   A and **an** are called *indefinite* articles.

3. **Adjectives:**

   An adjective is a word which describes a noun and gives more information about it, e.g. an **old** castle, a **good** idea.

4. **Numeral adjectives:**

   Numbers function as adjectives when they are used before a noun, e.g. **ten** women, the **first** chapter.

5. **Possessive adjectives:**

   In English, possessive adjectives include **my, your, his, her** and so on. They refer to the possessor and in English their form never varies, so the possessive adjective remains the same whether the thing possessed is *singular* or *plural*.

6. **Demonstratives:**

   In English, demonstratives include **this, that, these** and **those.** They are used to point out which person or object you are talking about.

7. **Adverbs:**

   An adverb is a word used to give extra information about, or modify, verbs, adjectives or other adverbs, e.g. he speaks **slowly**, this is **very** interesting, they eat **too quickly.**

8. **Comparatives:**
This term refers to the way an adjective or adverb changes when two or more things are being compared; for example, **big** changing to **bigger** or **fast** to **faster.**

9. **Verbs:**
A verb is a word which expresses an action or a fact, e.g. **to turn, to be, to want.**
A *regular* verb will follow the same pattern or rule as a number of other verbs in its *tenses.* There are, of course, exceptions to these rules. These are called *irregular* verbs.

   a) **Present tense:** the present tense is used to describe:
      1. an action occurring in the present, e.g. **I am making a 'phone call.**
      2. a fact in the present, e.g. the line **is** engaged.
      3. what normally happens, e.g. the train **arrives** at 8 o'clock.

   b) **Present perfect:** the present perfect is used for past or recent actions when the time is not mentioned. It is formed with the present tense of *have* and the *past participle* of the main verb, e.g. you **have booked** a double room, you **have paid** two pounds.

   c) **Future tense:** the future tense is used to talk about things that will happen. It is formed with *will* and the verb, e.g. It **will be** cold, you **will see** it on the right. The *immediate future* (d) is commonly used as a colloquial alternative to the future tense.

   d) **Immediate future:** in English, this is the form **I am going to** ...
      or **it is going to** ...

   e) **Conditional tense:** the conditional tense is formed with *would* and the *past participle* of the main verb and is so called because there is often a condition involved, e.g. I **would do** something, if I could.
      It is also used for others purposes, e.g. being polite: I **would like** to call ...

   f) **Imperative:** the imperative is used to make a request, give advice, a direction or an order, e.g. **wait** a minute, **visit** the old town, **take** the first street, **go** to the station.

g)   **Infinitive:** the infinitive is a form of the verb which does not change for *tenses* or *persons* (**I, you, she, etc.**); in English it usually consists of **to** followed by the verb: e.g. **to go; to like.**

Note: It is helpful to know that three basic principles apply to Spanish grammar: **gender, number** and **agreement.**

Gender: Spanish nouns are either *masculine* or *feminine*.

Number: the *number* of a *noun* refers to whether it is *singular* or *plural.*

Agreement: in Spanish the agreement system is far more widespread than in English. So for example:

(a)   *articles* agree with *nouns* in *gender* and *number:*
      el banc**o**, **la** iglesia, **los** vin**os**, **las** ferias

(b)   *adjectives* agree with *nouns* in *gender* and *number:*
      la taberna típic**a**, **el** puente roman**o**
      las visitas atractiv**as**, **los** edificios históric**os**

(c)   *verbs* agree with *subjects:*
      usted llega, **ustedes** lleg**an**

10. **Interrogatives:**
     These are words or sentences which ask a *question.*

1. Nouns

(a) Gender

In Spanish all nouns are either *masculine* or *feminine.* The *gender* is indicated by the *article:*
masculine: **el** (the) or **un** (a/an)
feminine: **la** (the) or **una** (a/an)
e.g. **la** torre, **una** iglesia, **el** pescado, **un** río.

So remember to learn the *article* every time you learn a new noun.

Nouns referring to <u>people</u> have usually one form for *masculine* and another form for *feminine* in accordance with the following rules:

1. Most such nouns end with **-o** in the *masculine* form and with **-a** in the *feminine* form, e.g. **el** secretari**o**, **la** secretari**a**.

2. If the noun ends with a consonant, the *feminine* form is obtained by adding an **-a** to the *masculine,* e.g. **un** dané**s**, **una** danes**a**.

3. If the noun ends with **-e**, the *feminine* form remains the same, e.g. **el** agent**e**, **la** agent**e**.

However, there are exceptions to these rules:

— Some nouns ending either in **-o** or in **-a** have the same ending for both *masculine* and *feminine* forms, e.g. **el** guí**a**, **la** guí**a**; **el** soprano**o**, **la** soprano**o**.

— All nouns of professions ending in **-ista** have the same ending in the *masculine* and the *feminine* forms, e.g. **el** dent**ista**, **la** dent**ista**

— There is a tendency to use a *feminine* form ending in **-a** for nouns of professions that end in **-e**, e.g. **el** asistent**e**, **la** asistent**a**.

(b) **Number**

1. Nouns ending in **-e**, **-a** and **-o** take an **-s** in the *plural* form: e.g. **los** cliente**s**, **las** tarta**s**, **los** barco**s**.

2. Nouns ending in a consonant add **-es** in the plural form: e.g. **los** español**es**, **los** tren**es**, **las** direccion**es**.

2. Articles

(a) Definite article

	masculine	feminine
singular	**el**	**la**
plural	**los**	**las**

— **El** preceded by the *prepositions* **a** (to) or **de** (of/from) combines with them to give:

   a + el = **al**

   de + el = **del**

e.g. ir **al** castillo (to go to the castle)

   la duración **del** viaje (the length of the journey)

— In some cases Spanish uses definite article where English does not, e.g. ¿le gustan **los** deportes? (do you like sports?) or cerrado **los** martes (closed on Tuesdays)

(b) Indefinite article

	masculine	feminine
singular	**un**	**una**
plural	**unos**	**unas**

— After a negative, **un, una, unos** and **unas** are not used, e.g. **no hay** jardín (there is no garden), **no hay** bares (there are no pubs)

Sometimes **ningún** and **ninguna** (not any, none) are used with a negative e.g. no hay **ningún** castillo (there is no castle), no hay **ninguna** basílica (there is no basilica).

— The indefinite article is not used in Spanish to give someone's profession, e.g. soy recepcionista (I am **a** receptionist)

3. Adjectives

(a) Gender

In Spanish all adjectives agree in *gender* and *number* with the *noun* they describe.

1. Adjectives ending in **-o** in the *masculine* change their ending to **-a** in the *feminine* form, e.g. **un** puerto precios**o**, **una** panorámica precios**a**.

2. Adjectives ending in any other vowel or in a consonant generally have the same ending for both *masculine* and *feminine* forms, e.g. **un** regalo original, **una** tienda original; **un** pueblo grand**e**, **una** ciudad grand**e**.

   However, there are some exceptions to this rule:

   — Adjectives of nationality or regional origin ending in a consonant take an **-a** in the *feminine* form, e.g. **un** turista alemán, **una** turista aleman**a**; **un** pueblo andalu**z**, **una** ciudad andalu**za**.

(b) Number

1. Adjectives ending in a vowel add an **-s** to form the *plural,* e.g. **un** folleto gratuit**o**, **unos** folletos gratuit**os**; **el** campo verd**e**, **los** campos verd**es**; **una** muñeca **cara**, **unas** muñecas **caras**

2. Adjectives ending in a consonant add **-es** to form the *plural,* e.g. **una** comida especia**l**, **unas** comidas especial**es**

(c) Position

Adjectives are usually placed after the *noun,* e.g. un viaje atractivo.

Many of them can also be placed before the *noun,* but some of these lose their final **-o** when placed before a *singular masculine* noun, e.g. **ningún** museo, un **buen** hotel, el **mal** tiempo. **Grande** loses its final syllable before a *singular noun,* whether it is *masculine* or *feminine:* e.g. **una gran** ciudad, **un gran** puerto.

4. Numeral adjectives

There are two kinds of numbers:

a)　cardinals:
   uno, dos, tres, cuatro, etc.

b)　ordinals:

primero/primera/primer	(1º, 1ª, 1er)	segundo/segunda	(2º, 2ª)
tercero/tercera/tercer	(3º, 3ª, 3er)	cuarto/cuarta	(4º, 4ª)
quinto/quinta	(5º, 5ª)	sexto/sexta	(6º, 6ª)
séptimo/séptima	(7º, 7ª)	octavo/octava	(8º, 8ª)
noveno/novena	(9º, 9ª)	décimo/décima	(10º, 10ª)

The ordinal numbers above the tenth are normally replaced by the corresponding cardinal numbers (once, doce, etc.), e.g. el piso **doce** (the twelfth floor).

As *adjectives,* all numbers follow these rules:

1.　They are usually placed before the *noun,* e.g. **dos** horas, el **quinto** día.

2.　Ordinals always agree with the *noun* in *gender* and *number,*
   e.g. **el** segund**o** piso, **la** cuart**a** calle, **las** primer**as** horas.

3.　Cardinals do not agree with the *noun,* either in *gender* or in *number,*
   e.g. **siete** person**as**, **cincuenta** niñ**os**.

   Exceptions: **uno**, **veintiuno** and all numbers ending in **-tos** (from doscien**tos** to novecien**tos**) agree with the *noun* only in *gender,* e.g. veintiun**a** entrad**as**, doscien**tas** peset**as**.

4.　**Uno** and **veintiuno**, **primero** and **tercero** lose their final **-o** when placed before a *masculine noun*, e.g. treinta y **un** museos, **tercer** piso.

Note:　A point is used to separate thousands and a comma to separate decimals, e.g. 2.000 ptas; 10,50 metros cuadrados. For the time of the day either a point or a comma can be used, e.g. las 12,15; la 1.10.

5. Possessive adjectives

These come before the *noun* and, as *adjectives,* agree with it.

In Spanish, possessive adjectives are determined by the *number* and *gender* of the thing possessed.

	singular	plural
my	mi	mis
your	tu	tus
his/her/its/your(formal)	su	sus

	singular		plural	
	masculine	*feminine*	*masculine*	*feminine*
our	nuestro	nuestra	nuestros	nuestras
your	vuestro	vuestra	vuestros	vuestras
their/your (formal)	su	su	sus	sus

The forms **su** and **sus** are the polite forms for the *second person.* **Su** must be used when it refers to one thing, **sus** must be used when it refers to two or more things.

6. Demonstratives

	singular			plural		
	this	that (near)	that (far)	these	those (near)	those (far)
masculine	este	ese	aquel	estos	esos	aquellos
feminine	esta	esa	aquella	estas	esas	aquellas
neuter	esto	eso	aquello			

212

— *Masculine* and *feminine* demonstratives always agree with the *noun* they refer to in *gender* and *number,* e.g. **este** pasill**o** (this corridor), **esas** cas**as** (those houses).

— Neuter demonstratives refer to something indeterminate (either we do not know what it is or what its name is), e. g. ¿Qué es **eso**? (what is that?)

7. Adverbs

These are the most common adverbs:

mucho	very much	**poco**	very little
bien	well	**mal**	badly
bastante	enough	**demasiado**	too
siempre	always	**nunca**	never
a veces	sometimes	**a menudo**	often
despacio	slowly	**rápido**	quickly

8. Comparatives

Más in front of an *adjective* is equivalent to the English **more,**
e.g. es **más** caro (it is **more** expensive), es **más** grande (it is bigg**er**)

Menos is equivalent to the English **less,**
e.g. es **menos** caro (it is **less** expensive)

9. Verbs

A verb is usually referred to in its *infinitive* form and you have to change its ending depending on the *tense* it is in or the *person* it is used with.

Examples:	*infinitive*	**visitar** (to visit)
	present tense [first person]	yo visit**o** (I visit)

The *subject* of a verb can be a *noun* or *pronoun.*

Personal pronouns:

I	**yo**
you	**tú/usted** (formal)
he/she/it	**él/ella**
we	**nosotros/nosotras**
you	**vosotros/vosotras/ustedes** (formal)
they	**ellos/ellas**

The *subject pronoun* is not usually expressed in Spanish but it is indicated in the verb ending, e.g. est**án** cerca (they are near).

Se can also be used as the *subject pronoun* to mean that an action is attributed to people in general. In this case the verb can be either in the *third person singular,* when it is followed by a *singular noun,* or in *third person plural* if the verb is followed by a *noun* in the *plural.*

Examples: **se** pued**e** ver **la** is**la** (you can see the island),

se pued**en** visitar **las** bodeg**as** (you can visit the wine cellars)

Regular and **irregular** verbs:

Regular verbs are divided in three categories according to their endings in the *infinitive* form:

— infinitives ending in **-ar**: reserv**ar** (to book)
— infinitives ending in **-er**: com**er** (to eat)
— infinitives ending in **-ir**: viv**ir** (to live)

Irregular verbs are a minority, but many of them are used very frequently, for example:
* **ser** (to be), * **estar** (to be), **tener** (to have), **ir** (to go), **hacer** (to do/to make), **dar** (to give), **decir** (to say), **querer** (to want), **poder** (to be able to), **volver** (to return)

* **ser** is used mainly to indicate nationality, profession or the characteristics of a thing, e.g. **Soy** español (I am Spanish), **es** el guía (he is the guide), la iglesia **es** grande (the church is big).

* **estar** is mainly to indicate either position or state, e.g. **está** cerca (it is near), ¿**está** bien? (are you all right?)

(a) Present tense

In English there are two forms of the *present tense:* he speaks, she is speaking. In Spanish, the *present tense* is used for both these meanings.

The present tense is formed by adding certain personal endings to the *stem* (the *infinitive* minus **-ar, -er,** or **-ir**):

Infinitive ending in:	**-AR**	**-ER**	**-IR**
	RESERV-**AR**	COM-**ER**	VIV-**IR**
yo	reserv-**o**	com-**o**	viv-**o**
tú	reserv-**as**	com-**es**	viv-**es**
él/ella/usted	reserv-**a**	com-**e**	viv-**e**
nosotros/nosotras	reserv-**amos**	com-**emos**	viv-**imos**
vosotros/vosotras	reserv-**áis**	com-**éis**	viv-**ís**
ellos/ellas/ustedes	reserv-**an**	com-**en**	viv-**en**

Note: The most common verbal forms found in this book are the ones corresponding to **usted** and **ustedes,** the polite forms which are normally used in professional interactions with customers.

There are a few verbs that are normally used with an *indirect object pronoun* (**me, te, le, nos, os,** and **les**) instead of the *personal pronoun.* When these verbs, e.g. **GUSTAR, INTERESAR, PARECER,** are used with the *indirect object pronoun,* they are always either in the *third person singular* or in the *third person plural,* depending on the thing — *singular* or *plural* — to which they refer.

Examples:
¿**Le** gust**a el** té? (Do you like tea?)
¿**Les** interes**a la** música? (Are you interested in music?)
¿**Le** gust**an los** deportes? (Do you like sports?)
Me interes**an los** museos (I am interested in museums)
La habitación **nos** parec**e** cara (We think the room is expensive)

Note: These verbs may also be used with an *infinitive,* in which case the verb is in *third person singular.*

Examples: ¿**Le** gus**ta** esquiar? (Do you like skiing?) ¿**Les** interesa visitar la iglesia? (Are you interested in visiting the church?)

Present tense of some irregular verbs:

SER	ESTAR	IR	* HABER	TENER	QUERER	PODER	DECIR	VOLVER
soy	estoy	voy	he	tengo	quiero	puedo	digo	vuelvo
eres	estás	vas	has	tienes	quieres	puedes	dices	vuelves
es	está	va	ha	tiene	quiere	puede	dice	vuelve
somos	estamos	vamos	hemos	tenemos	queremos	podemos	decimos	volvemos
sois	estáis	vais	habéis	tenéis	queréis	podéis	decís	volvéis
son	están	van	han	tienen	quieren	pueden	dicen	vuelven

* HABER has two different uses:

1. To form the *perfect tenses* (see next section) of all *regular* and *irregular* verbs, e.g. **he** pagado, **has** pagado, **ha** pagado, etc.

2. As the main 'existential' verb to mean there is or there are. In this case it has a special form for the *third person singular* of the *present tense:* **hay.** This form must be used for both *singular* and *plural* forms, e.g. **hay** un puent**e** (there is a bridge), **hay** lag**os** (there are lakes).

(b) Present perfect

It is formed with the *present* of **HABER** and the *past participle* of the main verb.

The *past participle* has two different endings (the same for all the *persons*) according to the endings of the *infinitive:*

Infinitive ending in	**-AR**	**-ER** and **-IR**	
	RESERV-**AR**	COM-**ER**	VIV-**IR**
	reserv-**ado**	com-**ido**	viv-**ido**

Present perfect:

RESERV**AR**		COM**ER**		VIV**IR**	
he	reserv**ado**	**he**	com**ido**	**he**	viv**ido**
has	reserv**ado**	**has**	com**ido**	**has**	viv**ido**
ha	reserv**ado**	**ha**	com**ido**	**ha**	viv**ido**
hemos	reserv**ado**	**hemos**	com**ido**	**hemos**	viv**ido**
habéis	reserv**ado**	**habéis**	com**ido**	**habéis**	viv**ido**
han	reserv**ado**	**han**	com**ido**	**han**	viv**ido**

A few verbs are *irregular* in the present perfect because they have an *irregular past participle* (p.p.). Some of these are:

ABRIR, p.p.: **abierto** **VOLVER**, p.p.: **vuelto** **HACER**, p.p.: **hecho**

VER, p.p.: **visto** **DECIR**, p.p.: **dicho** **ROMPER**, p.p.: **roto**

PONER, p.p.: **puesto** **ESCRIBIR**, p.p.: **escrito** **CUBRIR**, p.p.: **cubierto**

(c) **Future tense**

The *future* is formed by adding to the *infinitive* the endings **-é, -ás, á, -emos, -éis, -án.**

RESERV**AR**	COM**ER**	VIV**IR**
reservar-**é**	comer-**é**	vivir-**é**
reservar-**ás**	comer-**ás**	vivir-**ás**
reservar-**á**	comer-**á**	vivir-**á**
reservar-**emos**	comer-**emos**	vivir-**emos**
reservar-**éis**	comer-**éis**	vivir-**éis**
reservar-**án**	comer-**án**	vivir-**án**

Some verbs are a little *irregular* in the future form, but their endings are the same as in *regular* verbs. Example:

HABER: habré, habrás, habrá, ... **HACER:** haré, harás, hará, ...

SALIR: saldré, saldrás, saldrá, ... **PODER:** podré, podrás, podrá, ...

TENER: tendré, tendrás, tendrá, ...

(d) Immediate future

The *immediate future* is formed with the present tense of **ir** (to go) + **a** + *infinitive*:
e.g. **vamos a** ver la iglesia (we are going to see the church).

(e) Conditional tense

The *conditional* is formed by adding to the *infinitive* the endings:
-ía, -ías, -ía, -íamos, -íais, -ían.

RESERVAR	COMER	VIVIR
reservar-**ía**	comer-**ía**	vivir-**ía**
reservar-**ías**	comer-**ías**	vivir-**ías**
reservar-**ía**	comer-**ía**	vivir-**ía**
reservar-**íamos**	comer-**íamos**	vivir-**íamos**
reservar-**íais**	comer-**íais**	vivir-**íais**
reservar-**ían**	comer-**ían**	vivir-**ían**

The verbs which are *irregular* in *future* have the same type of irregularity in the *conditional* form, but they have the same endings as *regular* verbs.

HABER: habría, habrías, habría, ...   **HACER**: haría, harías, haría, ...
SALIR: saldría, saldrías, saldría, ...   **PODER**: podría, podrías, podría, ...
TENER: tendría, tendrías, tendría, ...

(f) Imperative

There are two polite *imperative* forms in Spanish: *singular,* to address one person only, and *plural* to address two or more people. According to the ending in the *infinitive,* they have different endings:

Infinitive ending in	**-AR**	**-ER**	**-IR**
	VISIT**AR**	COM**ER**	ESCRIB**IR**
singular	visit**e**	com**a**	escrib**a**
plural	visit**en**	com**an**	escrib**an**

Some verbs are *irregular* in the imperative. Example:

IR: vaya, vayan   **SALIR: salga, salgan**   **DECIR: diga, digan**
SEGUIR: siga, sigan   **VOLVER: vuelva, vuelvan**   **TENER: tenga, tengan**

(g) **Infinitive**

The *infinitive* is used:

1.   directly after some verbs such as:
     querer: ¿quieren viajar en avión? (do you want to travel by plane?)
     poder: puede visitar el convento (you can visit the convent)
     gustar: ¿le gustaría comprar algo? (would you like to buy something?)
     deber: deben reservar las entradas (you must book the tickets)
     preferir: ¿prefiere ir en coche? (do you prefer to go by car?)
     interesar: me interesa visitar las bodegas (I am interested in visiting the wine cellars)

2.   after any *preposition*.
     e.g. después **de** cenar (after having dinner), **sin** decir nada (without saying anything).

10. Asking questions

There are different types of questions: questions which only require a yes or no answer, and questions which require more information and start with an interrogative word such as where, when, what, etc.

(a) **Yes** or **no** questions

1.   The most common way of asking a yes or no question in Spanish is to keep a sentence as it is, and indicate it is a question by changing the intonation, i.e. raising your voice at the end of the sentence.

     Example: va a Cork   (you are going to Cork)
                       ¿va a Cork? (are you going to Cork?)

2. You can also use the *subject pronoun* either before or after the *verb.*

Examples: ¿quiere **usted** ir en tren? (do you want to go by train?)
¿**usted** quiere ir en tren? (do you want to go by train?)

(b) **Where? When? How? Why? What? Which?** and **Who?** questions

1. To ask these questions in Spanish you must start the sentence with the *interrogative pronouns* — **dónde, cuándo, cómo, por qué, qué, cuál, quién** — followed by the verb.

Examples:
¿**Cuál** prefiere?   (Which one do you prefer?)
¿**Qué** le interesa ver?   (What are you interested in seeing?)

2. The *subject pronoun* may also be placed after the *verb.*

Examples:
¿**Cómo** van **ustedes** a París?   (How are you travelling to Paris?)
¿**Cuándo** sale **usted**?   (When do you leave?)

Note: When **dónde** is used with the *verb* **ir** (to go), the *preposition* **a** must be placed at the beginning of the question. Example: ¿**A dónde** quiere **ir**? (Where do you want to go to?)

(c) **How much?** and **How many?** questions

In Spanish *how much* is translated by **cuánto.**

Example: ¿**Cuánto** es todo? (How much is it in total?)

How many is translated by **cuántos** or **cuántas** depending on the *noun — masculine* or *feminine* — they are referring to.

Examples:
¿**Cuántos** folletos quiere?   (How many leaflets do you want?)
¿**Cuántas** noches va a quedarse? (How many nights are you going to stay?)

GLOSSARY

Key: f = feminine
      m = masculine
      pl = plural
      el = masculine singular noun
      la = feminine singular noun

A

a, to, at

  a la derecha, to/on the right

  a la izquierda, to/on the left

  a pie, on foot

  a las ocho, at eight o'clock

  a menudo, often

el **abanico,** fan

abierto/a (m/f), open

  abrir, to open

  abre de - a, open from - to

el **abrigo,** overcoat

abril, April

abrir, to open

  ¿A qué hora abre la tienda?

  What time does the shop open?

acabar, to finish, complete

el **aceite de oliva,** olive oil

acompañar, to accompany

aconsejar, to advise, recommend

la **acrediatación,** identification,

  badge

la **actividad,** activity

la **actuación de ballet,** ballet

acuático/a (m/f), aquatic, water

acudir, to come

adelante, forward, ahead

  más adelante, further on

adiós, good-bye

admitir, to admit

adulto/a (m/f), adult

el **aerobic,** aerobics

el **aeropuerto,** airport

afuera, out, outside

las **afueras,** outskirts

la **agencia de viajes,** travel agency

el **agente,** la **agente,** agent

agobiante (m+f), oppressive,

  burdensome, overwhelming

agosto, August

agradable (m+f), pleasant, enjoyable

el **agua** (f), water

ahí, there

ahora, now

  ahora mismo, right now,

  this very minute

el **aire climatizado,** air conditioning

el **alcalde,** la **alcalde,** Lord Mayor

el **alcohol,** antiseptic

Alemania, Germany

  alemán (m), **alemana** (f), German

la **alergia,** allergy

la **alfarería,** pottery

la **alfombra,** carpet

algo, something

el **algodón,** cotton (wool)

algún/alguno (m), **alguna** (f),

  some, any

algunos/as (m,pl/f,pl), some, any

allí, there

  allí mismo, right there

la **almendra,** almond

el **almuerzo,** lunch

el **alojamiento,** accommodation,

  lodging

alquilar, to rent, hire

alrededor, around

los **alrededores,** surrounding area,

  neighbourhood

alto/a (m/f), high, tall

amable (m+f), kind, nice

  muy amable, thank you,

  that's very kind

el **ambiente,** atmosphere

la **ambulancia,** ambulance

América, America

    americano (m), **americana** (f), American

andando, walking

    andar, to walk

animado/a (m/f), lively

el **animador cultural,** la **animadora cultural,** leisure assistant

el **animal,** animal

anunciar, to announce

    anunciado/a (m/f), announced

antes, before

antiguo/a (m/f), old, ancient

el **año,** year

el **aparcamiento,** car park

aparte de, apart from

el **apellido,** surname, family name

apoyar, to lean, rest

aproximadamente, approximately, roughly

aquel (m), **aquella** (f), that

aquellos (m,pl), **aquellas** (f,pl), those

aquí, here

    aquí mismo, right here, on this very spot

Argelia, Algeria

la **Argentina,** Argentina

    argentino (m), **argentina** (f), Argentinian

el **arquitecto,** la **arquitecta,** architect

arquitectónico/a (m/f), architectural

la **artesanía,** craft work

el **artículo,** article, item

artístico/a (m/f), artistic

el **ascensor,** lift, elevator

los **aseos,** toilets

    los **aseos de caballeros,** mens toilets

    los **aseos de señoras,** ladies toilets

así, so, in this way, thus

asistir, to attend

la **aspirina,** aspirin (tablet)

la **atención,** attention

    la **atención prestada,** attention given

la **atmósfera,** atmosphere

la **atracción,** attraction

atractivo/a (m/f), attractive, appealing

audiovisual, audio-visual

el **auditorio,** auditorium

el **aula** (f), classroom, hall

Austria, Austria

    austríaco (m), **austríaca** (f), Austrian

el **autobús,** bus, coach

    ir en autobús, to go by bus

el **autocar,** coach

el **autoservico,** self-service restaurant

la **avenida,** avenue

la **aventura,** adventure

el **avión,** aeroplane

avisar, to tell

¡ay!, ow!, ouch!, oh!

ayer, yesterday

ayudar, to help, assist

el **ayuntamiento,** town council, town hall, city hall

la **azafata de congresos,** conference assistant

azul (m+f), blue

B

la **bahía,** bay

bailar, to dance

el **baile,** dance, dancing

la **bajada,** way down

bajar, to go down

 baje las escaleras, go down the
 stairs

bajo/a (m/f), low

el **ballet,** ballet

el **balneario,** spa, health resort

el **baloncesto,** basketball

el **banco,** bank

el **bar,** pub

 los **bares,** bars, pubs

barato/a (m/f), cheap

Barbados, Barbados

el **barco,** boat, ship

el **barro,** pottery

la **basílica,** basilica

bastante (m+f), enough, sufficient,
 quite

beber, to drink

Bélgica, Belgium

 belga (m+f), Belgian

bello/a (m/f), beautiful, lovely

 un **bello conjunto**
 arquitectónico, an area with
 beautiful buildings

Berlín, Berlin

la **biblioteca,** library

la **bicicleta,** bicycle

 la **bicicleta todo terreno (BTT),**
 mountain bike

bien, well

¡bienvenido/a! (m/f), welcome

el **billete,** ticket

blanco/a (m/f), white

la **boca,** mouth

la **bodega,** wine cellar

los **bombones,** chocolates

bonito/a (m/f), pretty, nice

la **bota,** boot

la **botella,** bottle

el **Brasil,** Brazil

británico (m), **británica** (f), British

Bruselas, Brussels

bueno/a (m/f), good, nice, pretty

¡buenas noches! good night,
 good evening

¡buenas tardes! good afternoon

¡buenos días! good morning

buen tiempo, good weather

 hace buen tiempo,
 the weather is fine

¡buen viaje! have a good trip!

el **bufet,** buffet

Bulgaria, Bulgaria

buscar, to look for, search

C

el **caballero,** gentleman

 Caballeros, mens toilets

el **caballo,** horse

la **cabeza,** head

la **cabina,** cabin

cada (m+f), each

el **café,** coffee, café

la **cafetería,** café, coffee shop

la **caja,** box, cashdesk

la **calefacción,** heating

caliente (m+f), hot

la **calle,** street

el **calmante,** pain killer

el **calor,** heat

la **cámara,** camera

el **camarote,** cabin

cambiar, to change

el **cambio,** change

 en **cambio,** on the contrary

el **camping,** campsite

el **campo,** field

el **campo de golf,** golf course

el **Canadá,** Canada

caribeño/a (m/f), Caribbean

caro/a (m/f), expensive

la **carretera**, road, highway

el **cartel**, sign, notice

el **cartón,** box

la casa, house

el **casco**, helmet, quarter

   el **casco antiguo,** the old quarter
   (of a town)

el **castillo**, castle

la **catedral**, cathedral

catorce, fourteen

célebre (m+f), famous

la **cena**, dinner, evening meal

cenar, to dine, have dinner

centígrado (m), centigrade

la **centralita de hotel**, hotel
   switchboard

el **centro**, centre, middle

   el **centro de aventuras,**
   adventure centre

   el **centro comercial,**
   shopping centre

   el **centro de congresos,**
   conference centre

   el **centro de deportes,** sports
   centre

   el **centro recreativo,** leisure
   centre

la **cerámica**, ceramics, pottery

cerca, near, nearby

   cerca de, near to, close to

cercano/a (m/f), nearby, near

   la más cercana, the nearest one

la **ceremonia**, ceremony

cero, zero

cerrado/a (m/f), closed, shut

cerrar, to close, lock

   cierra de una a dos, it closes
   from one to two o'clock

la **cestería**, wickerwork,
   basketmaking

el **chaleco salvavidas**, life jacket

la **chaqueta**, jacket

el **cheque**, cheque

Cherburgo, Cherbourg

Chile, Chile

Chipre, Cyprus

China, China

   chino (m), **china** (f), Chinese

el **chocolate**, chocolate

cien, (one) hundred

los **cigarrillos**, cigarettes

cinco, five

cincuenta, fifty

   cincuenta y uno, fifty one

   cincuenta y dos, fifty two

el **cine**, cinema

la **ciudad**, city, town

   la **ciudad de vacaciones,**
   holiday village

   Ciudad Universitaria, a
   University Campus in Madrid

¡claro que sí! yes, of course!

la **clase preferente**, business class

la **clase turística**, tourist class

el **cliente**, la **cliente**, client, customer

el **clima**, climate

el **club**, club

   el **club de squash**, squash club

el **coche**, car

coger, to take, catch

el **Colegio de Arquitectos,**
   Association of Architects

colgar, to hang, hang up (telephone)

   no cuelgue, hold the line

Colombia, Colombia

la **comarca**, region

comarcal (m+f), regional, local

la **combinación,** connection
(transport)
comenzar, to begin, start
comer, to eat
la **comida,** food, meal, lunch
la **comisaría de policía,** police
station
como, as, like
como máximo, at most
¿cómo? how?, what?
¿cómo se escribe? How is it
written?
¿cómo se llama usted? What is
your name?
cómodo/a (m/f), comfortable
la **compañía,** company
comprar, to buy
las **compras,** shopping
ir de compras, to go shopping
comprender, to understand
comunicar, to communicate
la **comunidad,** community
con, with
con baño, with bathroom
con pensión completa, with full
board
el **concierto,** concert
el **condado,** county
la **conferencia sobre el turismo,**
conference on tourism
el **congreso internacional de**
turismo, international conference
for tourism studies
conseguir, to get, obtain, secure
el **conjunto,** group, whole
la **conservación,** conservation,
preservation
el **contacto,** contact, touch
contemplar, to look at, watch

contestar, to answer, reply
continuamente, continually
continuar, to go on, continue
contra, against
el **convento,** convent
la **copa,** glass, drink
el **corazón,** heart
Correos, post office
correr, to run
cortar, to cut
corto/a (m/f), short
la **cosa,** thing
la **costa,** coast
Costa Rica, Costa Rica
costar, to cost
cuesta 50 libras, it costs £50
el **crédito,** credit
creer, to believe, think
la **crema,** cream
el **cristal,** crystal
el **crucero,** cruiser, cruise
la **Cruz Roja,** the Red Cross
cuádruple (m+f), four berth
¿cuál? which? what?
¿Cuál es su dirección?
What is your address?
¿Cuál es la ruta más
interesante? Which is the most
interesting route?
¿cuáles? (m,pl+f,pl), which?
¿Cuáles son los pueblos más
típicos? Which are the most
typical towns?
cualquier (m+f), any
cuando, when
¿cuándo? when?
¿cuánto? how much?
¿cuánto es? How much is it?

¿cuántos/as? (m,pl/f,pl), how many?

  ¿Cuántas horas dura el viaje?
  How many hours does the journey
  take?

cuarenta, forty

  cuarenta y uno, forty one

  cuarenta y dos, forty two

cuarto, quarter

  son las cinco y cuarto, it is
  quarter past five

cuarto/a (m/f), fourth

cuatro, four

cuatrocientos/as (m,pl/f,pl),
  four hundred

Cuba, Cuba

el **cuenco,** bowl

la **cuenta,** see **por mi cuenta**

el **cuero,** leather

cuesta 225 libras, it costs £225

  costar, to cost

la **cueva,** cave

D

danés (m), **danesa** (f), Danish

dar, to give

  dar un paseo, to go for a walk

de, of, from

  de estilo gótico, in the Gothic
  style

  el centro de la ciudad, the city
  centre

  de lunes a viernes, from Monday
  to Friday

  de acuerdo, okay, fine

  ¡de nada! don't mention it, you're
  welcome

  de Andalucía, from Andalucia

el **debate general,** general
  discussion

deber, to owe

decidir, to decide

décimo/a (m/f), tenth

decir, to say

  digo, I say

dedicarse, to devote oneself,
  to go in for

el **dedo,** finger

degustar, to taste, sample

dejar, to leave

deletrear, to spell

delicioso/a (m/f), delicious

demasiado/a (m/f), too

déme, give me, may I have...?

el **dentista,** la **dentista,** dentist

dentro, inside

depender de, to depend on

el **deporte,** sport, game

la **derecha,** right hand, right side

  a la derecha, to/on the right

desarrollarse, to take place

el **desayuno,** breakfast

describir, to describe

desde, from, since

  ¡desde luego! of couse!

desear, to want, desire, wish for

  ¿que desea? may I help you?

desinfectar, to disinfect

despacio, slowly, gradually

despertar, to wake up

después, after, then

el **detalle,** detail

  en detalle, in detail

detrás, behind, at the back of

el **día,** day

  ¡buenos días!, good morning

  días de apertura, opening days

el **día festivo,** bank holiday

diario, daily

diciembre, December

diecinueve, nineteen

dieciocho, eighteen

dieciséis, sixteen

diecisiete, seventeen

diez, ten

diferente (m+f), different

difícil (m+f), difficult

¡diga! hello! (telephone)

¿dígame? hello (telephone)

Dinamarca, Denmark

    danés (m), **danesa** (f), Danish

la **dirección,** direction, way, address

directamente, directly

directo/a (m/f), direct, non-stop

el **director,** la **directora,** manager

la **discoteca,** disco

el **diseño,** design

la **distancia,** distance

diversos/as (m,pl/f,pl), several

divertido/a (m/f), enjoyable

doble (m+f), double

doce, twelve

la **documentación,** documents, papers

el **dólar,** dollar (United States unit of currency)

doler, to ache, hurt

    me duele la cabeza, I have a headache

el **dolor,** pain, ache

    el **dolor de cabeza,** headache

    el **dolor de muelas,** toothache

el **domingo,** Sunday

donde, where

¿dónde? where?

    ¿de dónde es usted, por favor? Where are you from, please?

dormir, to sleep

    duermen la primera noche, you sleep the first night

dos, two, second (of the month)

doscientos/as (m,pl/f,pl), two hundred

Dublín, Dublin

la **ducha,** shower

ducharse, to have a shower

la **duración,** duration, length of time

durante, during

durar, to last, continue

E

la **edición,** event, occasion

el **edificio,** building

Egipto, Eygpt

el **ejemplo,** example

el (m), the

él, he

ella, she

ellas (f, pl), **ellos** (m, pl), they

el **embutido,** sausage, cold meat

empezar, to start, begin

    empieza a las nueve, it starts at nine o'clock

en, in, on, at

    en el aula S212, in room S212

    en efectivo, in cash

    en total, in total, altogether

los **encajes,** pieces of lace

encantado/a (m/f), it's a pleasure

encontrar, to find

    encontrará lo que busca, you will find what you are looking for

encontrarse, to find oneself to be..., to be situated

    me encuentro mal, I feel ill

    a 20km se encuentra Padrón, Padrón is situated 20km away

enero, January

la **enfermedad,** sickness

enfermo/a (m/f), sick, ill

enfrente, opposite, in front

enseguida, immediately

entonces, then

la **entrada,** entrance, ticket

entrar, to enter

entre, between

la **entrega,** presentation, handing over

la **época,** time, period, season of the year

el **equipo,** equipment

la **equitación,** horse riding

es, it is, you are (polite)

ser, to be

esa (f), that

esas (f, pl), those

la **escalada,** rock climbing

la **escalera,** stairs

Escandinavia, Scandinavia

escandinavo (m),

escandinava (f), Scandinavian

escoger, to choose

depende de la ruta que escoja, it depends on the route you choose

escribir, to write

escuchar, to listen, hear

ese (m), that

eso es, this/that is, that's it!

esos (m, pl), those

la **espalda,** back

España, Spain

español (m), española (f), Spaniard, Spanish

especial, special

la **especialidad,** speciality

especialmente, especially

específico/a (m/f), specific

el **espectáculo,** show, performance

el **espectáculo de luz y sonido,** son et lumière, light and sound show

esperado/a (m/f), expected

esperar, to wait, expect

el **esquí,** ski

el **esquí náutico/acuático,** water skiing

esquiar, to ski

la **esquina,** corner

esta (f), **este** (m), this

la **estación,** station

la **estación de autobuses,** bus station

la **estación de ferrocarril/del tren,** railway station

la **estación marítima,** ferry terminal

estaciones del año, seasons of the year

el **estadio,** stadium

el **estado,** state

los **Estados Unidos,** United States of America

estar, to be

está abierta todos los días, it is open every day

como estaba anunciado, as announced

estas (f, pl), **estos** (m, pl), these

este (m), **esta** (f), this

el **estilo,** style

el **estómago,** stomach

estos (m,pl), **estas** (f, pl), these

la **estrella,** star

el **estudiante,** la **estudiante,** student

Europa, Europe

europeo (m) **europea** (f), European

exactamente, exactly

la **excursión,** trip

excelente (m+f), excellent

excepto, except

exclusivo/a (m/f), exclusive
explicar, to explain
la **exposición,** show, exhibition
el **expositor,** la **expositora,**
  exhibitor
exquisito/a (m/f), exquisite, delicious
la extensión, extension
extenso/a (m/f), extensive, vast
exterior (m+f), outdoor
extra (m+f), additional, extra
extranjero/a (m/f), foreign

F

la **fábrica,** factory
famoso/a (m/f), famous
la **farmacia,** pharmacy
fatal (m+f), terrible
febrero, February
la **fecha,** date
la **feria,** fair
  la **feria de muestras,** trade fair
el **festival,** festival
el **festivo,** bank holiday
la **ficha,** card
la **fiebre,** fever
  la **fiebre tifoidea,** typhoid
las **Filipinas,** the Philippines
  filipino, Philippine
el **fin,** end
  el **fin de semana,** weekend
el **final,** end
  al final, at the end
Finlandia, Finland
  finlandés (m), **finlandesa** (f),
  Finnish
la **flor,** flower, blossom
  las **flores secas,** dried flowers
fluvial, freshwater
el **folleto,** leaflet, brochure

el **fondo,** bottom
  al **fondo,** at the bottom, end
el **footing,** jogging
el **foro,** big room, meeting
la **fotografía,** photograph
Francia, France
  francés (m), **francesa** (f), French
la **fresa,** strawberry
fresco/a (m/f), fresh
frío/a (m/f), cold, chilly
fumar, to smoke
funcionar, to function, work
  no funciona, out of order, does
  not work
el **fútbol,** soccer

G

la **galería,** art gallery
la **garganta,** throat
la **gasa,** gauze
la **gasolina,** petrol
la **gasolinera,** petrol station
gastronómico/a (m/f), gastronomic
general (m+f), general, common
  en general, in general
el **gimnasio,** gymnasium
Ginebra, Geneva
la **gira,** tour, trip
girar, to turn
  gire a la izquierda, turn to the left
el **golf,** golf, golf course
el **gorro de baño,** swimming cap
gótico/a (m/f), Gothic
¡gracias! thanks!
el **grado,** degree
Gran Bretaña, Great Britain
  británico (m), **británica** (f), British
grande, big, large
la **granja,** farm
gratuito/a (m/f), free

Grecia, Greece

>**griego** (m), **griega** (f), Greek

el **grupo,** group

>el **grupo de trabajo,** workshop

el **guardarropa,** cloakroom

la **guía,** guidebook

el **guía,** la **guía,** guide

>el **guía turístico,** la **guía turística,** tour guide

Guinea, Guinea

gustar, to like

>¿**le gustan los deportes?** do you like sports?

H

haber, to have (in compound tenses), there is/are (impersonal)

>**ha reservado una habitación,** you have booked a room

>**hay bares,** there are pubs

>**no hay de qué,** you are welcome

la **habitación,** room, bedroom

hablar, to speak, talk

hacer, to make, to do, to be

>¿**qué quiere hacer?** what do you want to do?

>**hace frío,** it is cold

hacia, towards, to

hasta, as far as, until

>¡**hasta luego!** until later, see you later

hay, there is/are

la **helada,** frost

helado/a(m/f), frozen

la **hepatitis,** hepatitis

el **hipódromo,** racetrack, racecourse

la **hoja de inscripición,** registration form

la **hoja de reservas,** reservation form

¡**hola!** Hello!

Holanda, Holland

>**holandés** (m), **holandesa** (f), Dutch

la **hora,** time, hour

el **horario,** timetable

>el **horario de actividades,** timetable of events

>el **horario de apertura,** opening hours

horrible (m+f), horrible, dreadful

el **hospital,** hospital

>el **hospital provincial,** provincial hospital

la **hostelería,** hotel business

el **hotel,** hotel

>el **hotel club,** hotel leisure club

>un **hotel de cuatro estrellas,** four star hotel

hoy, today

húmedo/a (m/f), humid, moist, wet

Hungaría, Hungary

I

la **ida,** departure

>**ida y vuelta,** round trip, return ticket

la **iglesia,** church

igualmente, equally

importar, to matter

>**no importa,** it doesn't matter

imprescindible (m+f), essential, necessary

impresionante (m+f), impressive, striking

el **impuesto,** tax, duty

la **inauguración,** inauguration, opening

incluir, to include

>**incluido/a** (m/f), including

individual (m+f), individual

Indonesia, Indonesia

la información, information

el informador, la informadora de
turismo, tourist information officer

informar, to provide information,
to inform

la informática, information
technology

Inglaterra, England
inglés (m), inglesa (f), English

inscrito/a (m/f), enrolled, entered
inscribir, to enrol, enter

interesante, interesting

interesar, to be interested in
me interesa visitar la iglesia,
I am interested in visiting the
church

el interés, interest, concern

la interferencia, interference

interior (m+f), inside, interior

el interior, inland

internacional (m+f), international

el invierno, winter

ir, to go, travel
ir de compras, to go shopping

Irlanda, Ireland
irlandés (m), irlandesa (f), Irish

la irritación, irritation

la isla, island

Islandia, Iceland

islámico/a (m/f), Islamic

Italia, Italy
italiano (m), italiana (f), Italian

el itinerario, itinerary

izquierda, left hand, left side
a la izquierda, to/on the left

J

el jacuzzi, jacuzzi

el jamón, ham

el Japón, Japan

el jardín, garden

el jersei, jumper
los jerseis de Arán, Aran
jumpers

la jornada, congress, conference

el juego, game

el jueves, Thursday

jugar, to play

julio, July

junio, June

K

el kilómetro, kilometre

Kenia, Kenya

L

la (f), the, it
prefiero visitarla en coche,
I prefer to visit it by car

el lado, side
al lado de, beside

la lana, wool

largo/a (m/f), long
a lo largo, throughout

las (f,pl), the, them

la lata, tin, can

Latinoamérica, Latin America

la lavandería, laundry

le, him, you (polite)
le aconsejo el hotel,
I recommend the hotel (to you)

la lectura, reading

leer, to read

lejos, far, far away, far off
lejos de aquí, far from here

les, them, you (polite, plural)
les voy a informar, I am going to
tell you

el **letrero,** sign, notice

la **libra,** pound (Irish and British unit
of currency)

la **librería,** bookshop

el **libro,** book

la **línea,** line

el **lino,** linen

Lisboa, Lisbon

la **lista,** list

la **litera,** couchette

llamar, to call

llamarse, to be called, be named

    Me llamo Juan, My name is John

la **llegada,** arrival

llegar, to arrive, come

lleno/a (m/f), full

llevar, to wear, take

    tiene que llevar gorro, you have
to wear a cap

    quiero llevar el coche, I want to
take my car

llover, to rain

    llueve, it is raining

la **lluvia,** rain

lo, him, it

    a lo largo, throughout

local (m+f), local

la **localización,** location

Londres, London

los (m, pl), the, them

luego, then, after

el **lugar,** place, spot

    en lugar de, instead of

el **lunes,** Monday

Luxemburgo, Luxembourg

    luxemburgués (m),
luxemburguesa (f), native of
Luxembourg

la **luz,** light, daylight

M

la **madera,** wood

magnífico/a (m/f), magnificent,
splendid

mal, badly, poorly, bad

la **malaria,** malaria

la **mano,** hand

la **manta,** blanket

la **manzana,** apple

mañana, tomorrow

la **mañana,** the morning

el **mapa,** map

el **mar,** sea, ocean

marcar, to dial

el **marco,** mark (German unit of
currency)

los **mariscos,** shellfish, seafood

Marruecos, Morocco

el **martes,** Tuesday

marzo, March

más, more, most

    más difícil, more difficult

máxima/o (m/f), maximum

maya (m+f), Mayan, pertaining to the
Maya, a native people of Central
America and Southern Mexico
who developed a remarkable
civilisation

mayo, May

las **mayúsculas,** block capitals

la **media,** the average

la **medianoche,** midnight

la **medicación,** medication,
treatment

el **médico,** la **médica,** doctor

medieval (m+f), medieval

medio/a (m/f), half, mid, middle

  son las dos y media,

  half past two

  en el medio de la plaza,

  in the middle of the square

el **mediodía,** midday

el **Mediterráneo,** Mediterranean Sea

  mediterráneo/a (m/f),

  Meditrerranean

mejicano (m), **mejicana** (f), Mexican

mejor (m+f), best, better

  lo **mejor,** the best

los **menores,** juveniles, under age

menos, less, least

  las siete menos veinte,

  twenty minutes to seven

el **mercado,** market

la **mermelada,** jam

el **metro,** metre, underground train

  system

México (also **Méjico**), Mexico

  mejicano (m), **mejicana** (f),

  Mexican

el **miércoles,** Wednesday

mi (m+f), my

mil, thousand

  dos mil, two thousand

Milán, Milan

la **milla,** mile

el **millón,** million

el **minibar,** mini bar (hotel rooms)

mínimo/a (m/f), minimum

el **ministerio,** Ministry

el **minuto,** minute

mirar, to look at, gaze at

mismo/a (m/f), same, right

  aquí mismo, right here

  la **misma carretera,**

  the same road

el **momento,** moment

  ¡un momentito! just a moment!

el **monasterio,** monastery, convent

la **montaña,** mountain

el **montañismo,** mountaineering,

  climbing

el **monumento,** monument,

  memorial

la **mosca,** fly

el **mosquito,** mosquito

el **mostrador,** desk

muchas gracias, thank you very

  much

  ¡muchísimas gracias!

  very many thanks!

mucho/a (m/f), a lot of, much

el **mueble,** a piece of furniture

la **muela,** tooth

la **muestra,** sample

  la **feria de muestras,** trade fair

el **mundo,** world

  todo el mundo, everybody

la **muñeca,** doll

la **musculación,** weight training

el **museo,** museum, gallery

la **música,** music

  la música clásica, classical

  music

  la música folclórica, folk music

muy, very, greatly, highly

  muy bueno, very good

N

el **nacimiento,** birth

  la fecha de nacimiento, date of

  birth

nacional (m+f), national

la **nacionalidad,** nationality

nada, nothing

la **natación,** swimming

la **naturaleza,** nature
necesario/a (m/f), necessary
la **niebla,** fog, mist
la **nieve,** snow
ningún/ninguno (m), **ninguna** (f),
    no, none
la **niña,** girl, little girl, child
el **niño,** boy, little boy, child
los **niños,** children
la **noche,** night, evening
    ¡buenas noches! good evening!
el **nombre,** name
la **norma,** regulation, rule
el **norte,** north,
Noruega, Norway
    noruego (m), **noruega** (f),
    Norwegian
nosotros (m), **nosotras** (f), we
novecientos/as (m,pl/f,pl),
    nine hundred
noveno/a (m/f), ninth
noventa, ninety
    noventa y uno, ninety one
    noventa y dos, ninety two
noviembre, November
la **nube,** cloud
Nueva York, New York
Nueva Zelanda/Zelandia,
    New Zealand
nueve, nine
nuevo/a (m/f), new
el **número,** number
    el **número de teléfono,**
    telephone number

O

o, or
el **objeto,** object
obligatorio, compulsory, obligatory

la **obra,** play, work
    una **obra de teatro,** play
ochenta, eighty
    ochenta y uno, eighty one
    ochenta y dos, eighty two
ocho, eight
ochocientos/as (m/f), eight hundred
octavo/a (m/f), eighth
octubre, October
ocupado/a (m/f), busy, engaged
el **oeste,** west
la **oficina,** office
    la **oficina de cambio,**
    bureau de change
    la **oficina de turismo/turística,**
    tourist information office
ofrecer, to offer, present
¡oiga! excuse me!
los **ojos,** eyes
olvidar, to forget
la **opción,** option
el **operador turístico,** la **operadora**
    turística, tour operator
Oporto, Porto
organizar, to organise
la **orientación,** orienteering
original (m+f), original
el **otoño,** autumn
otro/a (m/f), other, another

P

pagar, to pay
el **país,** country, land, region
    los **países mediterráneos,**
    Mediterranean countries
el **palacio,** palace, mansion
la **panorámica,** viewing point
el **paquete,** parcel

para, for, intended for

    ¿Para cuántas personas?
    For how many people?

la **parada de autobús,** bus stop

parar, to stop

parecer, to seem

    me parece un poco caro,
    it seems to be a little expensive

París, Paris

el **parque,** park

    el **parque de atracciones,**
    amusement park

    el **parque infantil,** playground

la **parte,** part

    ¿de parte de quién? who's
    speaking? (telephone)

la **participación,** the participation

el **participante,** la **participante,**
    participant

participar, to participate

el **participio,** participle

particular (m+f), particular, private

    en particular, in particular

particularmente, particularly

partir, to leave, depart

    parten en autobús, you leave
    by bus

pasar, to pass, transfer

    le paso con él, I will transfer you
    to him

el **paseo,** stroll, walk, avenue

    dar un paseo, to go for a walk

    los **paseos en bicicleta,**
    cycling trips

    los **paseos a caballo,** pony
    trekking

el **pasillo,** passage, corridor

el **paso,** step

    paso a paso, step by step

la **pastelería,** cake shop

la **pastilla,** tablet

el **patio,** courtyard, patio

la **pausa,** pause, break

la **pausa-café,** coffee-break

la **península,** peninsula

el **penique,** penny

pensar, to think

la **pensión,** board and lodging

    la **pensión completa,** full board
    and lodging

el **pensionista,** la **pensionista,**
    pensioner

pequeño/a (m/f), small

perdone, excuse me

el **perfume,** scent, perfume

la **perfumería,** perfume shop

permitir, to allow, permit

pero, but, yet

el **perro,** dog

la **persona,** person

el **Perú,** Peru

la **pesca,** fishing

el **pescado,** fish

pescar, to fish, catch

la **peseta,** peseta (Spanish unit of
    currency)

peso, peso (Mexican unit of currency)

pesquero/a (m/f), fishing

la **picadura,** bite

el **pie,** foot

pintoresco/a (m/f), picturesque

la **pintura,** painting

el **piragüismo en canoa,** canoeing

el **piragüismo en kayak,** kayaking

la **piscina,** swimming pool

    la **piscina cubierta,** indoor
    swimming pool

    la **piscina exterior,** outdoor
    swimming pool

el **piso,** floor, storey

la pista de tenis, tennis court

el **placer,** pleasure

la **plancha a vela,** sail board

el **plano,** plan, map

la **planta,** floor

    la **planta baja,** ground floor

    la **planta principal,** main floor

la **plata,** silver

la **platería,** silverware

el **plato,** plate, dish

la **playa,** beach

la **plaza,** square, public square

    la **plaza de toros,** bullring

    la **Plaza Mayor,** main square

la **población,** town

poco/a (m/f), little, small

poder + infinitive, can, be able to

    ¿podría deletrearlo? Could you
    spell it?

    ¿puede hablar más alto?
    Can you speak louder?

la **poesía,** poetry

el **polen,** pollen

la **policía,** police force

el **polideportivo,** sports centre,
    sports complex

Polonesia, Polonesia

Polonia, Poland

poner, to put

    le pongo con él, I will transfer
    you to him

por, for, through, along

    por aquí, around here

    por la carretera, along the road

    por ejemplo, for example

    por favor, please

    por mi cuenta, at my own
    expense

    por persona, per person

¿por qué?, why?

    por supuesto, of course

la **porcelana,** porcelain

Portugal, Portugal

    portugués (m), **portuguesa** (f),
    Portuguese

la **postal,** postcard

el **postre,** dessert

practicar, to do, practise

Praga, Prague

el **precio,** price, cost

    el **precio en pesetas,** price in
    pesetas

precioso/a (m/f), beautiful

preferir, to prefer

    prefiero ir en avión, I prefer to go
    by 'plane

el **prefijo telefónico,** dialling code

la **pregunta,** question

la **prenda de lino,** linen garment

la **prenda de lana,** woollen garment

preocupar, to worry

prerromano/a (m/f), pre-Roman

previo/a (m/f), previous

la **primavera,** spring, springtime

primer/primero (m), **primera** (f),
    first

principal (m+f), main, principal

privado/a (m/f), private

probar, to try, taste

el **problema,** problem

producirse, to take place, be made

    cambios que se van a producir,
    changes that are going to be
    made

el **producto,** product

la **profesión,** profession, career

profesional (m+f), professional

el **programa,** programme, plan

prohibido/a (m/f), banned, prohibited

el **promontorio,** headland

el **pronóstico,** forecast

propio/a (m/f), own, itself

protector/a (m/f), protective

la **provincia,** province

la **peseta/pta,** peseta (Spanish unit
of currency)

el **público,** public

el **pueblo,** village, town

el **puente,** bridge

la **puerta,** door, gate

el **puerto,** port, harbour

Puerto Rico, Puerto Rico

el **puesto,** stall

Q

que, who, that

que lo pase bien, have a good
time

es que no se oye, I can't hear
properly

¿qué? what?

¿qué hora es, por favor?
what time is it, please?

¿qué desea? may I help you?

quedar, to arrange to meet

quedarse, to stay

querer, to want, wish

quiero comer en el hotel, I want
to eat in the hotel

quería hablar con ... I would like
to speak to ...

quería hacer una reserva...
I wish to make a reservation

el **queso,** cheese

quince, fifteen

quinientos/as (m,pl/f,pl),
five hundred

quinto/a (m/f), fifth

R

rápido/a (m/f), quickly

la **raqueta,** racket

real (m+f), real, royal

realmente, really

el **recado teléfonico,** telephone
message

la **recepción de hotel,** hotel
reception

el **recepcionista,** la **receptionista**
receptionist, desk clerk

el **recinto ferial,** exhibition centre

un **recital de poesía,** poetry reading

recomendar, to recommend

le recomiendo el bar,
I recommend the bar

recorrer, to cross, travel, go through

el **recorrido,** tour

el **recuerdo,** souvenir, momento

el **regalo,** present

el **régimen,** terms

en régimen de media pensión,
with half board

registrar, to register, record

el **registro,** registration

regresar, to come back, return

el **regreso,** return

relacionado/a (m/f), related

rellenar, to fill in

**RENFE, Red Nacional de los
Ferrocarriles Españoles**
Spanish National Rail System

repetir, to repeat

el **representante,** la **representante,**
representative

representar, to represent, mean

la **reserva,** reservation

reservar, to reserve, book

la **residencia universitaria**,
   university residence

respecto a, with regard to

responder, to answer, reply

el **restaurante**, restaurant

Retiro (Parque del Buen Retiro),
   a large urban park in Madrid

reunido/a (m/f), at a meeting

la **reunión**, meeting, gathering,
   la reunión informativa,
   information session

reunirse, to meet

la **ría**, a drowned valley typical of the
   coastline of Galicia

el **río**, river, stream

Roma, Rome

romano/a (m/f), Roman

romper, to break
   me he roto el tobillo, I have
   broken my ankle

rosado, pink, rosé (wine)

la **rúa**, street

la **ruina**, ruin

Rumanía, Romania

Rusia, Russia

la **ruta**, route
   las **Rutas de Andalucía**, routes
   around Andalusia

S

el **sábado**, Saturday

saber, to know

sacar fotografías, to take
   photographs

la **sala**, room, hall
   la **sala de exposiciones**,
   exhibition room
   la **sala de fiestas**, night club
   la **sala de juegos**, games room

la **salida**, exit, way out, departure

salir, to come out, go out, leave
   salga hacia la derecha, go out to
   the right

el **salmón**, salmon

el **salón**, lounge, trade fair

la **salud**, health

salvo, except

la **sauna**, sauna

sea in **o sea**, in other words

seco/a (m/f), dry

el **secretario**, la **secretaria**,
   secretary

el **sector**, sector

seguir, to follow
   siga todo recto, go straight on

según, according to,
   in accordance with

segundo/a (m/f), second

el **segundo**, second

seis, six

seiscientos/as, (m,pl/f,pl),
   six hundred

el **semáforo**, traffic lights

la **semana**, week

el **seminario**, seminar

el **senderismo**, hill walking

sentir, to feel, to be sorry
   lo siento, I am sorry

el **señor**, man, gentleman
   el **Sr**, Mr

la **señora**, lady
   la **Sra**, Mrs, Miss

separar, to separate

septiembre, September

séptimo/a (m/f), seventh

ser, to be

    soy de Sevilla, I am from Seville

    es la una, it is 1 o'clock

    son las 5, it is 5 o'clock

los **servicios,** toilets, facilities

    los **servicios de caballeros,** men's toilets

    los **servicios de señoras,** ladies' toilets

sesenta, sixty

    sesenta y uno, sixty one

    sesenta y dos, sixty two

la **sesión,** session

    la **sesión plenaria,** plenary session

setecientos/as (m,pl/f,pl), seven hundred

setenta, seventy

    setenta y uno, seventy one

    setenta y dos, seventy two

Sevilla, Seville

sexto/a (m/f), sixth

Seychelles, Seychelles

si, if

sí, yes, indeed, certainly

siempre, always

siete, seven, seventh

significar, to mean

siguiente (m+f), following, next

sin, without

    sin embargo, however, still

el **sitio,** place

sobre, on, about

    sobre las doce, about twelve o'clock

    sobre todo, above all

el **sol,** sun, sunshine, sunlight

solamente, only, solely, just

solo/a (m/f), alone

sólo, only, solely, merely

el **sonido,** sound

el **Sr/Señor,** mister, sir

la **Sra/Señora,** lady, madam

el **stand,** stand

su (m+f), his/her, your (polite), its, their

    su apellido, your surname

la **subida,** way up

subir, to raise, lift, get up

el **submarinismo,** scuba diving

Suecia, Sweden

    sueco (m), **sueca** (f), Swedish

la **sugerencia,** suggestion

la **suite,** suite (hotel)

Suiza, Switzerland

el **suplemento,** additional charge

la **superficie ocupada,** total surface area occupied

el **supermercado,** supermarket

suponer, to suppose, assume

    supongo, I assume

el **sur,** south

sus, its, their, your (polite), his/her

    sus alrededores, its surroundings

T

el **tábano,** wasp

la **taberna,** pub, bar

la **tabla de windsurf,** windsurfing board

un **tablao de flamenco,** a flamenco display

el **talón,** cheque

    pagar con talón, pay by cheque

tal vez, perhaps

también, also, as well, too

tampoco, neither, not.....either

tanto, as much, as well

    tanto ... como, both

la **taquilla,** ticket office

tardar, to take time

    tarda dos horas, it takes two hours

tarde, late

la **tarde,** afternoon, evening

    ¡buenas tardes!, good afternoon

la **tarjeta,** ticket, card

    la **tarjeta de crédito,** credit card

la **tarta,** cake, tart, flan

    la **tarta de almendra,** almond cake

    la **tarta de chocolate,** chocolate cake

    la **tarta de fresa,** strawberry flan

    la **tarta de helada,** ice cream tart

    la **tarta de manzana,** apple tart

    la **tarta de queso,** cheese cake

la **tasa,** rate, charge, fees

el **taxi,** taxi

la **taza,** cup

el **té,** tea

el **teatro,** theatre

el **teléfono,** telephone

    los **teléfonos públicos,** public telephones

la **televisión,** television

la **temperatura,** temperature

temprano, early

tener, to have, possess

    ¿tiene hora? do you have the right time?

    tiene lugar en la catedral, it takes place in the cathedral

el **tenis,** tennis

tercer/tercero (m), **tercera** (f), third

terminar, to finish, complete

el **terreno,** soil, ground, earth, land

el **tétanos,** tetanus

el **tiempo,** weather, time

la **tienda,** shop

    la **tienda de recuerdos,** souvenir shop

    la **tienda libre de impuestos,** duty free shop

el **tinto,** red wine

típico/a (m/f), typical

el **tipo,** type

la **tirita,** bandage, plaster

el **tiro con arco,** archery

el **tobillo,** ankle

todo (m), **toda** (f), **todos** (m, pl), **todas** (f,pl), all, every

    todo recto, straight on

    todos los días, every day

tolteca, Toltec

tomar, to take, get, accept

    tome un folleto, take a brochure

la **tormenta,** storm

la **torre,** tower

trabajar, to work

el **trabajo,** work

tranquilo/a (m/f), quiet, peaceful

el **transbordador de coches,** car ferry

el **transporte,** transport

la **travesía,** voyage, crossing

trece, thirteen

treinta, thirty

    treinta y uno, thirty one

    treinta y dos, thirty two

el **tren,** train

tres, three

trescientos/as (m,pl/f,pl), three hundred

Túnez, Tunisia

el **turismo,** tourism

el **turista,** la **turista,** tourist

turístico/a (m/f), tourist

Turquía, Turkey

U

último/a (m/f), last

un/uno (m), **una** (f), a

unas (f,pl), **unos** (m,pl) some

la **unión**, union

> la **Unión Europea**,
> European Union

la **universidad**, university

universitario/a (m/f), universitary

> **residencia universitaria**,
> university residence

unos (m,pl), **unas** (f,pl), some

urbano/a (m/f), urban, city

usar, to use

usted, you (polite)

> **¿Es usted el Sr. López?**
> Are you Mr. López?
> **¿Es usted la Sra. Blanco?**
> Are you Mrs. Blanco?

ustedes, you/plural (polite form)

> **ustedes han reservado dos**
> **plazas**, you have reserved
> two places

utilizar, to use

V

las **vacaciones**, holidays

vacunar, to vaccinate

valer, to cost, be worth

> **¿cuánto vale este perfume?**
> how much does this perfume cost?

el **valle**, valley

variado/a (m/f), varied

la **variedad**, variety

varios/as (m,pl/f,pl), several

el **vaso**, glass

vaya, go

> **ir**, to go

el **vehículo**, vehicle

veinte, twenty

> **veintiuno**, twenty two
> **veintidós**, twenty two

la **vela**, sail, sailing

la **velada**, evening

Venecia, Venice

Venezuela, Venezuela

venir, to come, arrive

ver, to see

el **verano**, summer

la **verdad**, the truth, truly

> **¿verdad?** is that right?

verde (m+f), green

la **vez**, time, occasion, instance

> **tal vez**, perhaps
> **a veces**, sometimes

vía, by way of, via

> **vía Francia**, via France

viajar, to travel

el **viaje**, journey, trip

viejo/a (m/f), old

el **viento**, wind

el **viernes**, Friday

el **vino**, wine

la **visita**, visit

el **visitante**, la **visitante**, visitor

visitar, to visit

vivir, to live

volar, to fly

> el **vuelo**, flight

volver, to return, come back

> **vuelve el día 5**, you come back
> on the 5th

volver a llamar, to call again

el **vuelo**, flight

> **volar**, to fly

la **vuelta**, return

> **billete de ida y vuelta**,
> return ticket

W

el **windsurf,** windsurfing

Y

y, and

ya, now, already

yendo, going, travelling

yo, I

Z

los **zapatos,** shoes

Zaragoza, Zaragoza

la **zona,** area, zone